A New
Approach
to
Ear Training

Second Edition

Leo Kraft

NORTON PROGRAMMED TEXTS IN MUSIC THEORY

A New Approach to Ear Training   SECOND EDITION
Leo Kraft

Scales, Intervals, Keys, Triads, Rhythm and Meter   THIRD EDITION
John Clough, Joyce Conley, and Claire Boge

Basic Harmonic Progressions
John Clough and Joyce Conley

ASSOCIATED SOFTWARE

Computer-Assisted Software Project for Aural Skills Reinforcement (CASPAR)
CASPAR Development Team, Erik Lund, coordinator

ALSO BY LEO KRAFT

Gradus: The First Year   SECOND EDITION

Gradus: The Second Year and After   SECOND EDITION

With Sol Berkowitz and Gabriel Fontrier:
A New Approach to Sight Singing   FOURTH EDITION

With Allen Brings et al.:
A New Approach to Keyboard Harmony

A New Approach to Ear Training

A PROGRAMMED COURSE IN MELODIC AND HARMONIC DICTATION

Second Edition

LEO KRAFT

Professor Emeritus, Aaron Copland School of Music
Queens College of the City University of New York

W · W · NORTON & COMPANY   New York · London

The text of this book is set in Stone Serif with the display
set in Bodega and Futura
Composition by David Budmen, Willow Graphics, Woodstown, New Jersey
Manufacturing by Courier
Book Design by Jack Meserole

PRINTED IN THE UNITED STATES OF AMERICA

Second Edition

Library of Congress Cataloging-in-Publication Data

Kraft, Leo.
A new approach to ear training : a programmed course in melodic and harmonic dictation / Leo Kraft.—2nd ed.
p.   cm.—(Norton programmed texts in music theory)
ISBN 0-393-97217-8 (pbk.)
1.   Ear training—Programmed instruction.   I. Series: Norton programmed texts in music theory.
MT35.K818N5   1999
781.4′24—dc21   99-11655
                                                          CIP

W. W. Norton & Company, Inc., 500 Fifth Avenue, New York, N.Y. 10110
www.wwnorton.com

W. W. Norton & Company Ltd., 10 Coptic Street, London WC1A 1PU

1 2 3 4 5 6 7 8 9 0

CONTENTS

To the Student   1

CHAPTER **One**   MELODIC DICTATION   3

CHAPTER TWO HARMONIC DICTATION 205

To the Student

ABOUT THIS PROGRAM

The purpose of this program is to teach you to recognize and write down tonal music. It is generally agreed that the ability to recognize music as it is played or sung is an essential skill for any musician. This skill is taught here by means of programmed instruction. Programmed instruction means that you work through a series of exercises, organized into Lessons, which move gradually and progressively from the beginner's level to a fairly complex degree of difficulty.

The book is in two large chapters, which are to be used concurrently. Chapter One consists of exercises in melodic dictation, Chapter Two comprises exercises in harmonic dictation. Each chapter includes four sections, corresponding to four semesters of study. Thus, Section I of Chapter One is to be studied at the same time as Section I of Chapter Two, and so forth.

The exercises in this program are recorded on CDs. Some are performed on various acoustic instruments or electronic piano, and some are sung. The changes from one performing medium to another give you the opportunity to hear different tonal colors. You are not required to identify the instruments.

Your rate of progress through the program is determined by your speed and accuracy in doing the exercises. You proceed at your own pace, with ample opportunity for drill. You score each Lesson according to the procedure that is explained in each chapter Introduction. If you have achieved a level of 90 percent correct in any single-letter Lesson, you are directed to the next single-letter Lesson. If you do not achieve a level of 90 percent in any single-letter Lesson, you are directed to a double-letter Lesson, which affords you the opportunity for further drill on the same level. The first two sections of Chapter One: Melodic Dictation also include a rapid-advance feature in the single-letter Lessons. This feature enables you to move through the material more quickly if you find that you are making no errors.

In each of the sections of Chapter One, the Lessons are lettered A through HH. Lessons H and HH are Summary Lessons, which give you a chance to solidify what you have learned and prepare you for the Review and Test. The Reviews are done in class, under your instructor's supervision. The Tests conclude the sections. Chapter Two, Section I offers an additional single- and double-letter Lesson that appear just before the Review and Test for that section.

THE LESSONS IN *CASPAR*

If you have purchased the combined package of this book and *Computer-Assisted Software Project for Aural Skills Reinforcement* (*CASPAR*), you will be able to develop further your skill in melodic and harmonic dictation through an additional set of exercises for the computer. The Lessons in *CASPAR* are organized similarly to those in this program, enabling you to locate easily the appropriate melodic or harmonic exercises for whatever level you are mastering.

STARTING OUT

To start this program you need:

1. this workbook, which includes instructions, your Worksheets, and the answers;

2. the CDs that accompany the program and a CD player;
3. a pencil.*

It is important that you be seated comfortably, with good light, and have ample space in order to write on the pages of the workbook. Allow enough time to do one Lesson at a session. Try to work quickly, but don't rush yourself. Lessons can take anywhere from twenty minutes to an hour, depending on your own speed. We recommend that you do not try to do more than one Lesson per session, even if you are moving quickly.

Before you proceed to the exercises in each Lesson, be sure that you study the illustrative material for that Lesson; these consist of the demonstration melodies in Chapter One and the introductory chord progressions in Chapter Two. After you have finished the exercises, follow the scoring instructions carefully to gain an accurate assessment of your progress.

At the conclusion of the session, remove the worksheet from this book and either retain it for future reference, or give it to your instructor as required.

You are now ready to begin!

*If you are also using *CASPAR* you need:
4. CASPAR;
5. a Macintosh or Windows-based computer with at least 8 megabytes of RAM and a CD-ROM drive;
6. music manuscript paper and a pencil.

CHAPTER One

MELODIC DICTATION

ABOUT THIS CHAPTER

Chapter One consists of a series of Lessons in melodic dictation, organized into four large sections. Each section includes eight single-letter Lessons, eight double-letter Lessons, several Short Drills, a Review, and a Test. You do all the Lessons and Short Drills on your own; the Reviews and Tests are done in class.

Most single-letter Lessons start with a demonstration melody that introduces the essential melodic features of that Lesson. All single-letter Lessons in Sections I and II offer a rapid-advance feature. Double-letter Lessons follow the same procedure as single-letter Lessons but do not include introductory material or the rapid-advance feature.

THE BIG PICTURE: REMEMBER THE MELODY!

Your aim is to hear the notes of each melody in coherent groups, not a few at a time. Listening to the high and low notes of a melody gives you a framework within which all the notes move. Beyond that, imagining the harmonic background to a melody helps you hear notes in groups related to familiar chords; by doing so you can grasp all the notes, even when the melody moves quickly. Some melodies include repeated patterns; listening for these patterns will enable you to perceive a group of notes as one entity.

It helps, too, if you can see the melody in your mind's eye while you hear it in your mind's ear. The demonstration melodies that begin each Lesson will aid you in developing both auditory and visual memory.

HOW TO STUDY THE LESSONS IN CHAPTER ONE

Each Lesson begins with a new CD track number, listed at the top of the page in the following notation: CD 1/TRACK 1. Each exercise within a Lesson starts at the time indicated in the box to the left of that exercise or at the new index number listed below the time.*

You proceed through the program in the following way:

1. Read the introductory material on each Worksheet and play the demonstration melody on the compact disc, then press the Pause button on your CD player. Cover the demonstration melody or close your eyes and sing it back. Try to see the melody in your mind's eye as you sing. If you need to hear the melody again, enter the appropriate track number for the Lesson on your CD player. When you can sing back the melody correctly, proceed to Exercise 1.
2. Each exercise is preceded by the sounding of a preparatory (prep) note, which is always the tonic. The tonic is also the first note in the exercises of Sections I and II. As soon as you hear this note, press the Pause button and sing the scale that is built on that tonic. This will orient you in

*Not all CD players accommodate index numbers. If yours does not, use the timings that are indicated to the left of the exercise.

the key. Then listen to the first exercise. Memorize it as quickly as you can. Imagine how the melody would look on the page. The best way to learn is to write the melody only after you can sing it back in its entirety; it is not very useful to write down a few notes at a time.

3. To play the melody again, press and hold the Rewind button on your CD player until the counter indicates the starting time of the melody, or press the appropriate index number on your CD player. Try to listen to each melody no more than three times. Since you will hear each melody only three times on the Review and Test, it is best to get into the habit of listening only three times—or even fewer!—from the very beginning.

4. When you have finished Exercise 1, follow the same procedure for the next exercise.

5. The single-letter Lessons in Sections I and II have eight exercises each; those in Sections III and IV have fewer. For the single-letter Lessons in the first two sections you will be directed to check your work after Exercise 5; for double-letter Lessons and all Lessons in the last two sections you will score your answers only after you have finished the entire Lesson.

6. To check your answers against the correct answers given on the reverse of the Worksheet, tear the Worksheet *up* from the bottom along the perforation and fold along the dotted line. You will do this for Exercises 1–5 in Sections I and II, Exercises 1–4 in Section III, and Exercises 1–3 in Section IV.

   In Sections I and II, if you have made no errors in Exercises 1–5, you have completed the Lesson

and can go directly to the next single-letter Lesson. (Remember that this rapid-advance feature is not found in Sections III and IV.) Mark your Student Record Sheet accordingly, sign the Worksheet, remove it, and hand it in if your instructor requests it. If you made any errors in Exercises 1–5, complete Exercises 6–8. (Do not score at this point.)

7. To mark the rest of your answers, tear *down* from the top and fold along the dashed line. Score your answers according to the instructions given below and mark your score on the reverse of the Worksheet.

8. Then follow the next instruction. Mark your Student Record Sheet accordingly, sign the Worksheet, remove it, and hand it in if your instructor requests it.

SCORING THE MELODIC DICTATION

When you have completed a Lesson (or the first part of a Lesson in Sections I and II), fold your Worksheet according to the instructions given above, so that you can see both your answers and the correct answers. You are now ready to score. Compare your answers with the printed ones. Score your answer to the first exercise for pitch: mark an x *over* any incorrect, added, or omitted pitch. Then score the same exercise for rhythm: mark an x *under* any beat that isn't correctly notated. All of the notes within one beat must be correct for the beat to be considered correct. Follow the same procedure for each exercise.

Here are three illustrations of the scoring procedure:

1. All the pitches are correct, but the rhythms are not. All incorrect beats are marked *under* the answer. In the first bar, the last beat is a quarter note, not two eighths. Only one x is marked because the mistake involves only one beat. In the second bar, both the first and second beats have the wrong rhythm. In the third bar, the third and fourth beats are incorrect.

2. The rhythms are correct, but there are errors in pitch. Each is marked with an x *over* the incorrect pitch. Notice that in the third bar the sharps required to spell 6̂–7̂ in this minor key are omitted, counting as two errors.

Printed answer

Worksheet

3. Three pitches are incorrect; an x is marked *over* each one. In the third bar, both the third and fourth beats are considered incorrect rhythmically, even though the correct answer consists of only one note. An incorrect rhythm of the last note in any exercise is to be marked with only one x, even if more than one beat is involved. Thus, on the Worksheet the duration of the last note is two beats too long, but only one x is marked.

When you have completed marking all the exercises, you are ready to determine your score. Count up the total number of pitch x's and write this number on the reverse of the Worksheet in the space marked "Px." Count up the total number of rhythm x's and write it in the space marked "Rx." Subtract your Px and Rx from the given figures to get your P-score and your R-score. These are the figures you should compare with those in the instructions that immediately follow to see which Lesson you should do next.

What is the basis for the scoring? The figures given represent the total number of pitches and beats in a Lesson. You are required to write 90 percent or more of both pitches and rhythms correctly before proceeding to the next level; if you do not achieve 90 percent, the instruction on the reverse of the Worksheet directs you to a double-letter Lesson on the same level for further drill.

WHEN TO USE THE SHORT DRILLS

The Short Drills, which are given at the end of the section, will help you gain more facility in particular areas. Directives to turn to these drills have been placed at points in the program where the drills can be particularly useful, but you may do them at any point, depending on your need for additional practice. Look at the Short Drills in each section before you start that section so that you know what they focus on.

Like the single- and double-letter Lessons, each Short Drill begins with a new CD track number listed at the top of the page. Simply press the appropriate track number given at the top of the Short Drill and proceed as you did for the Lessons. Feel free to repeat or restudy the drills at any time.

WHEN TO USE *CASPAR*

CASPAR offers four complete exercises within each Lesson of Chapter One, as well as many different types of on-line help. You may choose to do these exercises to improve your listening skills at any time in your work on a particular level. Although the melodies in *CASPAR* are similar to those in this program, the different approach of the computer-based program may prove beneficial.

Remember that this program is a course of study, not a test. The purpose of scoring is to regulate your progress, to indicate the need for additional work, and to pinpoint your difficulties. The purpose of turning in your worksheets is to give your instructor an opportunity to diagnose your work. Your scores in the Lessons do not determine your grades. Your grades are determined by the tests that conclude each section and are given in class. The program prepares you for these tests and, beyond that, for music listening both in the classroom and outside of it.

SECTION I

STUDENT RECORD SHEET

- Circle the Lesson you are to do next: (A)
- After completing that Lesson, draw a line through the circle ~~(A)~~ and circle the Lesson the instructions tell you to do next: (B)
- Keep this sheet up to date. It is intended solely for your guidance.

A	AA
B	BB
C	CC
D	DD
E	EE
F	FF
G	GG
H	HH

Starting date ____________________

Completion date _________________

Keep this page in this book.

HOW TO STUDY SECTION I

Before starting Section I, be sure you have read carefully the introductory materials on pages 1–5.

Listening and Remembering

The first Lessons of Section I are short and quite simple. These Lessons give you a chance to familiarize yourself with the workings of the program. Just as important, in the first Lessons you will start to develop the habit of memorizing the melody and singing it back before writing it down. You want to develop the ability to retain melodies in your mind, and you can do so through this program as the melodies gradually become longer and more complex.

Be sure to study the demonstration melody and its explanation before proceeding to the exercises. When you can sing back this example without looking at it, you are ready to start the exercises.

The pitch and rhythm of the first note in each exercise is given on the Worksheet. Play each exercise on the CD as few times as possible, remembering as much as you can and writing from memory before playing it again. By starting this habit with the first exercise, you will learn to retain more and more as you proceed.

The Focus of the Melodies in Section I

The melodies in the first two Lessons are entirely stepwise; those in Lesson C introduce skips, which are all within the tonic triad. You will learn about triads in your study of harmony, but the triad has an important role in melody, too.

The remaining Lessons in Section I elaborate the triad with passing and neighbor motion. You can learn to hear groups of notes as single entities by relating those notes to the triad.

Many of these melodies end with a rest, which appears on the Worksheet. Do not score the rest, but pay attention to the duration of the last note. Being alert to its duration and that of the concluding rest will prepare you to recognize exact durations when the rest is no longer given. Remember that the last note can be marked with only one x, no matter what its duration.

Scoring

Score carefully, following the directions given below. It is in your interest to get an accurate assessment of your progress. You must score 90 percent on rhythm and 90 percent on pitch in order to proceed to the next single-letter Lesson.

1. Mark an x *over* any incorrect pitch.
2. Mark an x *under* any incorrect beat. (Do not score rests.)
3. Add up the number of pitch x's (*over* the notes) in the Lesson and enter in the space marked "Px" on the reverse of the Worksheet.
4. Add up the number of rhythm x's (*under* the notes) in the Lesson and enter in the space marked "Rx."
5. Subtract from the given figures to obtain your pitch score (P-score) and your rhythm score (R-score).

Remember that the double-letter Lessons are there to help you master each level of difficulty. Even if you score 90 percent or more on the single-letter Lessons, you may still wish to do the double-letter Lessons.

Section I includes a rapid-advance feature. If you have made no errors in the first five exercises of a single-letter Lesson, you have completed the Lesson and may proceed to the next one. You are also free to do the remaining exercises to reinforce your grasp of the material.

The Short Drills

The Short Drills focus on specific topics; your answers do not affect your progress through the program. It is a good idea to do the Short Drills even if you feel that you are doing well. They present the material from a slightly different point of view, and are useful for that reason.

NOTE: If there are any Lessons that you do not have to do, tear them out so that this instruction page will always conveniently face the Worksheet you are using.

The melodies in Lesson A all move stepwise. All start from the tonic note, 1̂, which you'll find at the beginning of each exercise. Now listen to the demonstration melody.

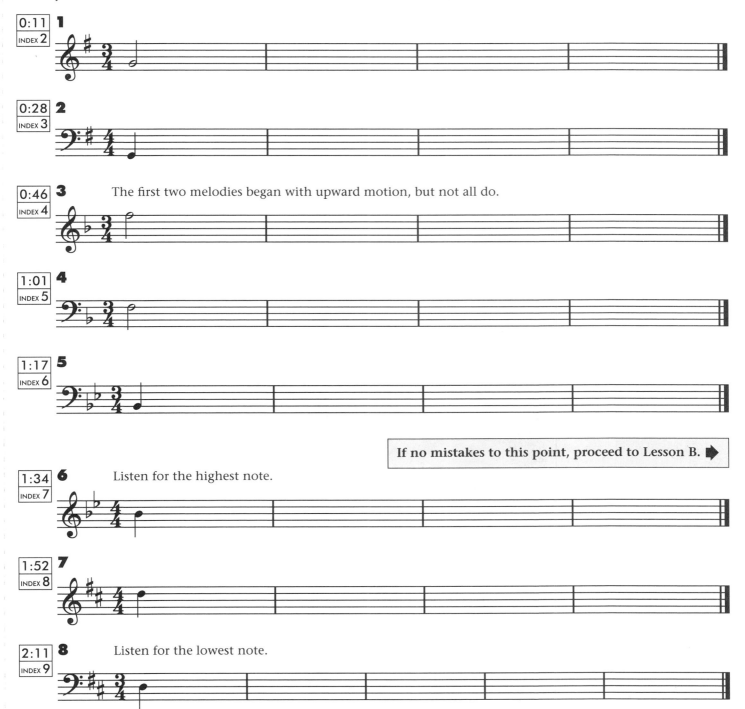

Sing the melody and notice its shape. It starts on 1̂, rises to 4̂, and descends to 1̂.

    Observe the overall shape of each melody as you hear it. That will help you remember the melody, and then you can write it down.

3 The first two melodies began with upward motion, but not all do.

If no mistakes to this point, proceed to Lesson B. ➤

6 Listen for the highest note.

8 Listen for the lowest note.

Scoring on Reverse ➤

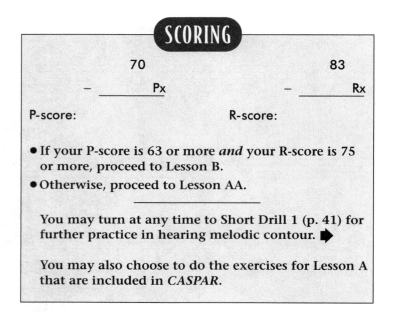

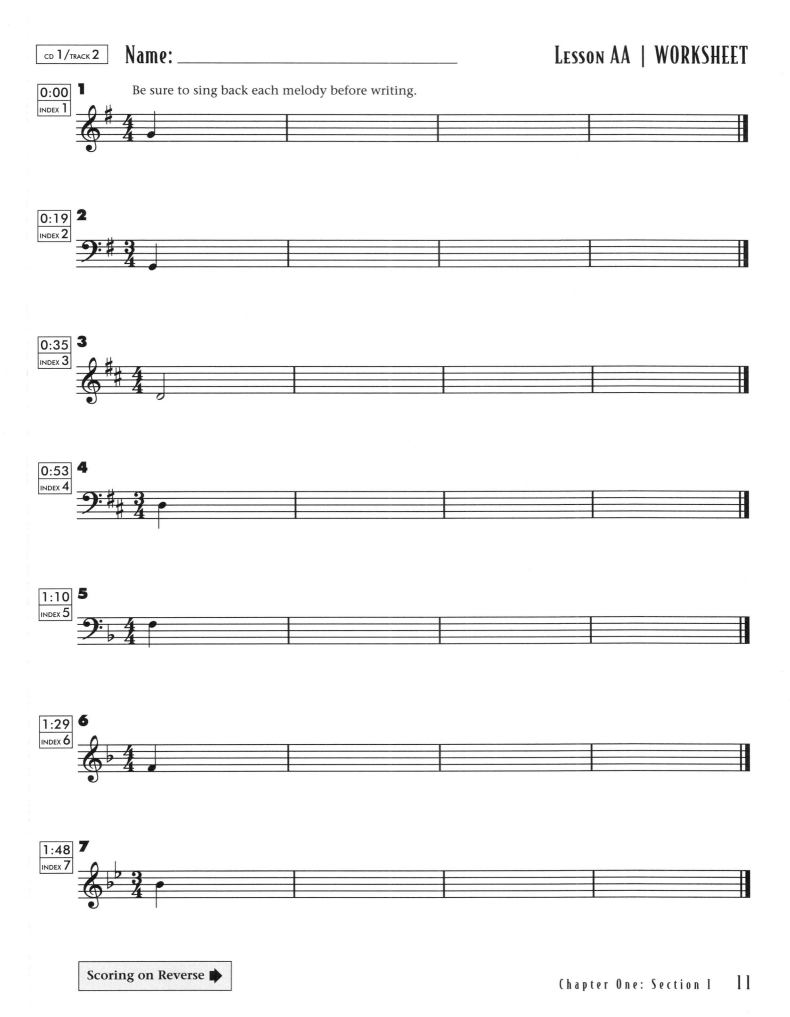

0:00 INDEX 1
1   Be sure to sing back each melody before writing.

0:19 INDEX 2
2

0:35 INDEX 3
3

0:53 INDEX 4
4

1:10 INDEX 5
5

1:29 INDEX 6
6

1:48 INDEX 7
7

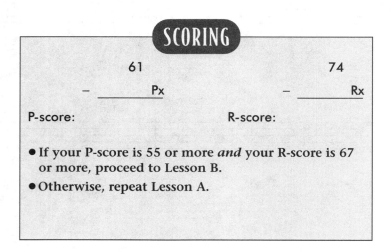

SCORING

	61			74	
–		Px	–		Rx

P-score: **R-score:**

- If your P-score is 55 or more *and* your R-score is 67 or more, proceed to Lesson B.
- Otherwise, repeat Lesson A.

This Lesson includes melodies in both the major and minor modes. You can tell from the given note whether an exercise is in the major or minor mode. In the minor mode, when $\hat{7}$ rises to $\hat{8}$ (remember that $\hat{8}$ is a higher version of $\hat{1}$), use a ♯ or ♮ sign before the leading note; if $\hat{6}$ precedes $\hat{7}$, another accidental is needed. Sing back the demonstration melody from memory.

1   Listen for both the highest and the lowest notes.

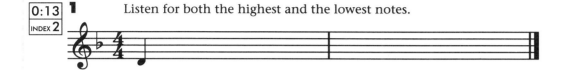

2   There are two versions of $\hat{6}$ in this melody.

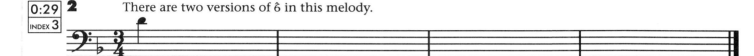

3   The meter sign 𝄵 is equivalent to $\frac{4}{4}$.

4

5

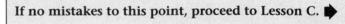

If no mistakes to this point, proceed to Lesson C. ▶

6

7

8

Scoring on Reverse ▶

8

7

6

SCORING

72   71

  – _____ Px   – _____ Rx

P-score: _____   R-score: _____

- If your P-score is 65 or more *and* your R-score is 64 or more, proceed to Lesson C.
- Otherwise, proceed to Lesson BB.

———————————

You may turn at any time to Short Drill 2 (p. 43) for further practice in hearing the highest and lowest notes of a melody. ➡

5

4

3

2

1

Name: _____ LESSON BB | WORKSHEET

1 Listen for high and low notes as you memorize the melodies.
0:00 INDEX 1

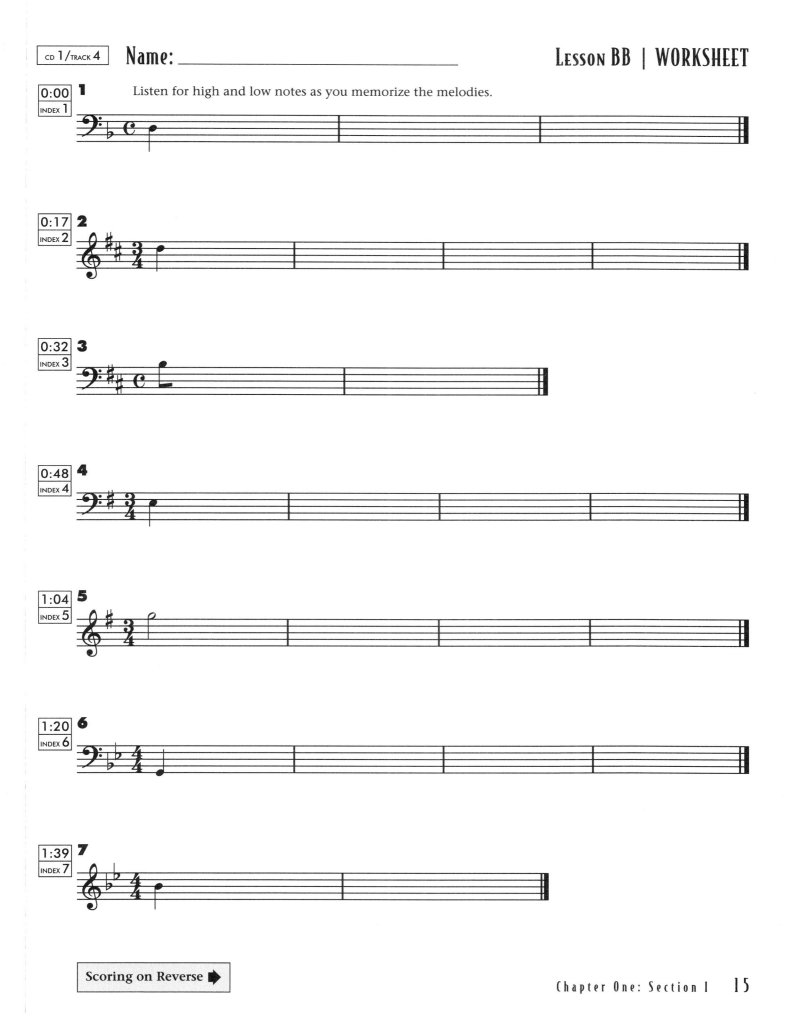

0:17 **2**
INDEX 2

0:32 **3**
INDEX 3

0:48 **4**
INDEX 4

1:04 **5**
INDEX 5

1:20 **6**
INDEX 6

1:39 **7**
INDEX 7

Scoring on Reverse ➡

SCORING

71   59

− _____ Px   − _____ Rx

P-score: R-score:

- If your P-score is 64 or more *and* your R-score is 53 or more, proceed to Lesson C.
- Otherwise, repeat Lesson B.

The exercises in Lesson C are built on the tonic triad in both major and minor. As soon as the prep note starts, sing î–ŝ–ŝ–ŝ–î quickly. That will help you to relate the melody's notes to the triad. Notice that the last measure of the demonstration melody ends with a rest.

0:00 INDEX 1

0:11 INDEX 2   **1**   Concluding rests are indicated on the worksheet.

0:24 INDEX 3   **2**   2/4 meter is introduced in this Lesson.

0:37 INDEX 4   **3**   The melody's range is not limited to an octave.

0:52 INDEX 5   **4**

1:10 INDEX 6   **5**

> **If no mistakes to this point, proceed to Lesson D.** ➡

1:29 INDEX 7   **6**

1:44 INDEX 8   **7**

1:58 INDEX 9   **8**

Scoring on Reverse ➡

8

7

9

SCORING

76   67

− _____ Px   − _____ Rx

P-score: R-score:

● If your P-score is 68 or more *and* your R-score is 60 or more, proceed to Lesson D.
● Otherwise, proceed to Lesson CC.

_____

You may turn at any time to Short Drill 3 (p. 45) for further practice in hearing the difference between steps and skips. ▶

5

4

3

2

1

0:00 | INDEX 1 | **1** Remember to sing the tonic triad as soon as the prep note starts.

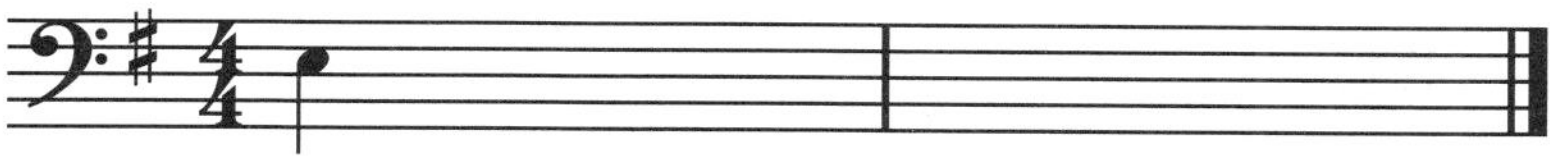

0:13 | INDEX 2 | **2**

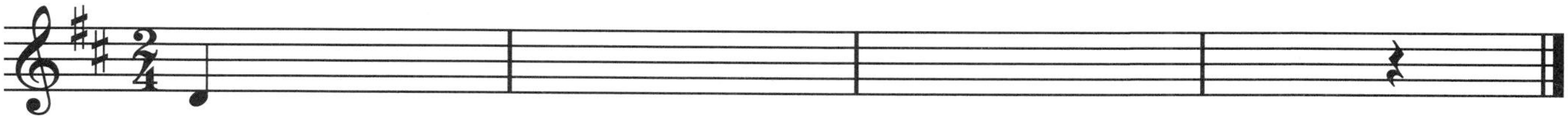

0:26 | INDEX 3 | **3**

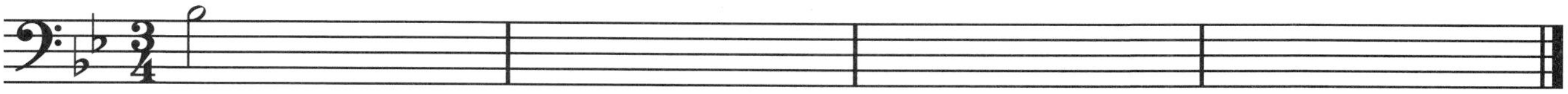

0:39 | INDEX 4 | **4**

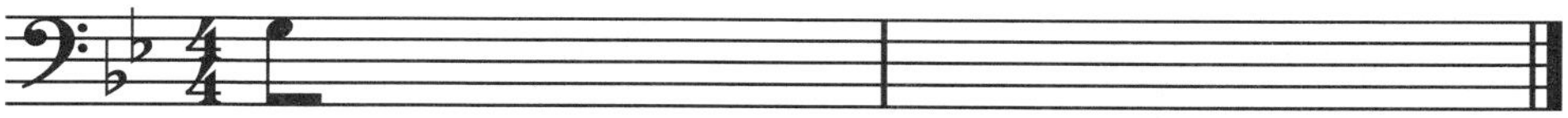

0:54 | INDEX 5 | **5**

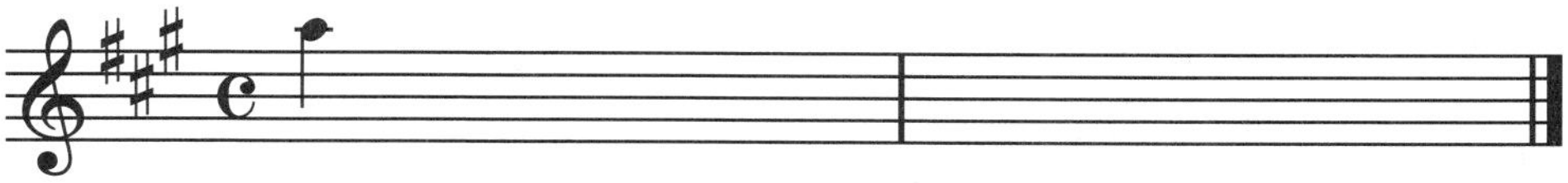

1:09 | INDEX 6 | **6**

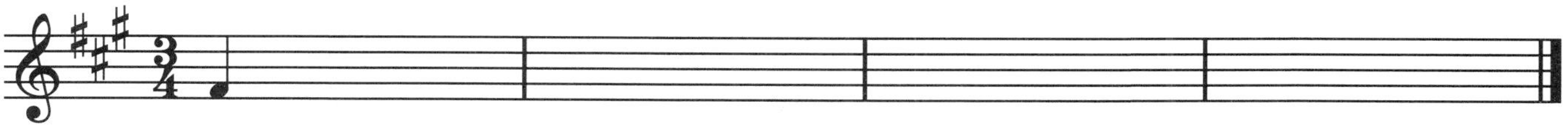

1:24 | INDEX 7 | **7**

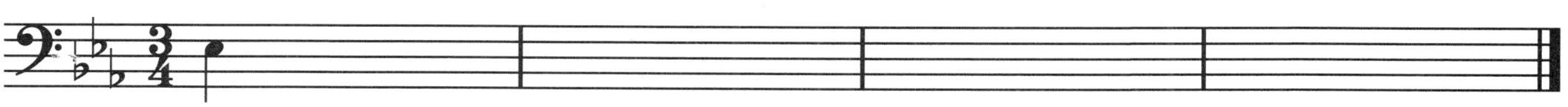

Scoring on Reverse ➡

SCORING

66   52

– _____ Px   – _____ Rx

P-score: R-score:

- If your **P-score** is **59 or more** *and* your **R-score** is **47 or more**, proceed to Lesson D.
- Otherwise, repeat Lesson C.

In Lesson D, the skips in the tonic triad are filled with passing notes, labeled P in the demonstration melody. Keep the triad in mind as you listen to the melody and as you sing it back.

0:00
INDEX 1

Notice that the melody ends an octave higher than where it began—still on î, to be sure.

0:15
INDEX 2
1   Keeping the triad in mind will help you to remember these longer melodies.
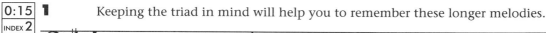

0:32
INDEX 3
2   Listen for a repeated measure.
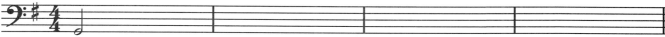

0:47
INDEX 4
3

1:02
INDEX 5
4
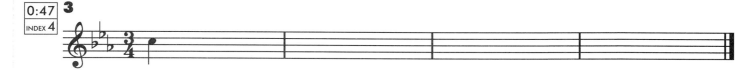

1:17
INDEX 6
5

If no mistakes to this point, proceed to Lesson E. ➡

1:37
INDEX 7
6
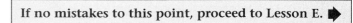

1:52
INDEX 8
7

2:07
INDEX 9
8

Scoring on Reverse ➡

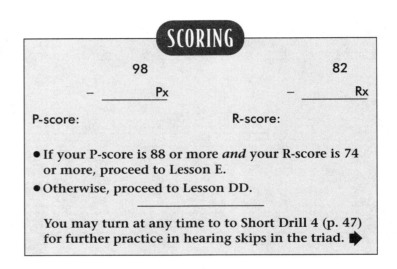

SCORING

98   82

− _____ Px   − _____ Rx

P-score: R-score:

- If your P-score is 88 or more *and* your R-score is 74 or more, proceed to Lesson E.
- Otherwise, proceed to Lesson DD.

You may turn at any time to to Short Drill 4 (p. 47) for further practice in hearing skips in the triad. ▶

Name: _____

1   0:00   INDEX 1   As you sing back the melody, keep the triad in mind.

2   0:13   INDEX 2

3   0:31   INDEX 3

4   0:47   INDEX 4

5   1:03   INDEX 5

6   1:18   INDEX 6

7   1:35   INDEX 7

Scoring on Reverse ➡

7

6

5

SCORING

89   77

− _____ Px   − _____ Rx

P-score: R-score:

- If your P-score is 80 or more *and* your R-score is 69 or more, proceed to Lesson E.
- Otherwise, repeat Lesson D.

4

3

2

1

The notes of the triad may be elaborated with neighbor (auxiliary) notes, labeled N. The demonstration melody includes upper and lower N's, as well as the four-note double neighbor, labeled DN. P's are included as well, but are not labeled.

0:00
INDEX 1

0:12 **1**
INDEX 2

0:28 **2**
INDEX 3

0:45 **3**
INDEX 4

1:00 **4**
INDEX 5

1:15 **5**   The first three bars of this opening melody from Brahms's Symphony No. 2 elaborate the triad.
INDEX 6
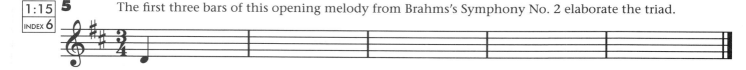

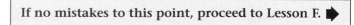
If no mistakes to this point, proceed to Lesson F.

1:31 **6**
INDEX 7

1:47 **7**
INDEX 8

2:06 **8**   This melody is almost entirely stepwise, but the triad is in the background.
INDEX 9
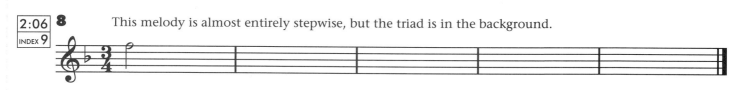

Scoring on Reverse ➡

SCORING

89   83

– _____ Px   – _____ Rx

P-score: _____   R-score: _____

- If your P-score is 80 or more *and* your R-score is 75 or more, proceed to Lesson F.
- Otherwise, proceed to Lesson EE.

_____

You may turn at any time to Short Drill 5 (p. 49) for further practice in distinguishing between P's, N's, and DN's. ➡

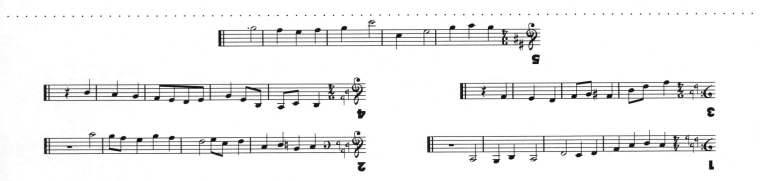

SCORING

85   70

‒ _____ Px   ‒ _____ Rx

P-score: R-score:

- If your P-score is 77 or more *and* your R-score is 63 or more, proceed to Lesson F.
- Otherwise, repeat Lesson E.

_____

Two beats to the measure, each beat pictured as a ♩: that's the meter known as "alla breve" (¢). Count and score each ♩ as one beat.

0:00 INDEX 1

0:14 INDEX 2
1   Listen for familiar scale and triad patterns.

0:30 INDEX 3
2

0:45 INDEX 4
3

0:59 INDEX 5
4

1:17 INDEX 6
5   In ¢, a beat may include ♫♫ or ♩ ♫.

If no mistakes to this point, proceed to Lesson G. ➡

1:36 INDEX 7
6   Focus on the first note in each measure.

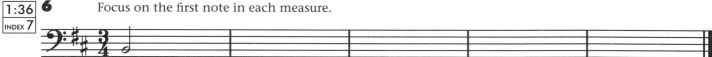

1:53 INDEX 8
7

2:15 INDEX 9
8
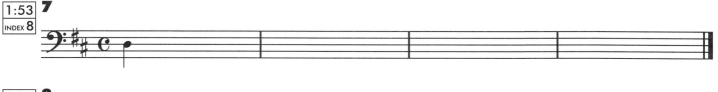

Scoring on Reverse ➡

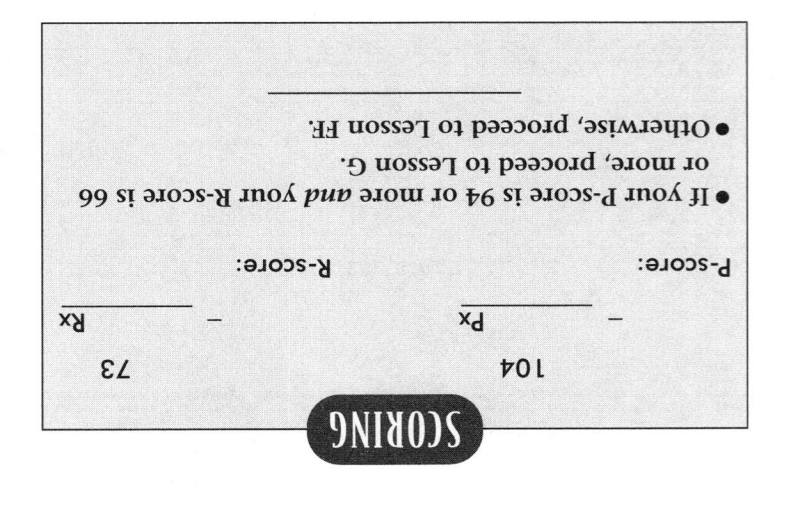

CD 1/TRACK 12   Name: _____

1
0:00
INDEX 1

2
0:17
INDEX 2

3
0:34
INDEX 3

4
0:48
INDEX 4

5
1:05
INDEX 5

6
1:23
INDEX 6

7
1:39
INDEX 7

Scoring on Reverse ➡

SCORING

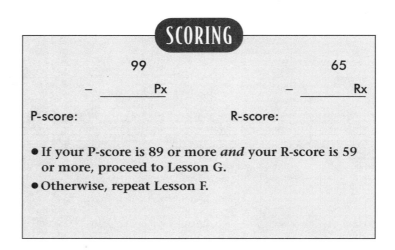

P-score: R-score:

- If your P-score is 89 or more *and* your R-score is 59 or more, proceed to Lesson G.
- Otherwise, repeat Lesson F.

Name: _____

This Lesson introduces $\frac{6}{8}$ meter. It is a duple meter. Each beat is represented by a ♩. and contains three ♪'s or the equivalent. Score each beat (♩., ♫♪, ♩♪) as a unit—all correct or incorrect. Thus, the following demonstration melody has eight beats; seven would be scored, since the last rest is given.

0:00
INDEX 1

1   0:16   The tonic triad is elaborated with N's and filled with P's.
INDEX 2

2   0:33
INDEX 3

3   0:53
INDEX 4

4   1:13
INDEX 5

5   1:30
INDEX 6

If no mistakes to this point, proceed to Lesson H. ▶

6   1:46
INDEX 7

7   2:03
INDEX 8

8   2:22
INDEX 9

Scoring on Reverse ▶

SCORING

125   65

− _____ Px   − _____ Rx

P-score: R-score:

- If your P-score is 113 or more *and* your R-score is 59 or more, proceed to Lesson H.
- Otherwise, proceed to Lesson GG.

  _____

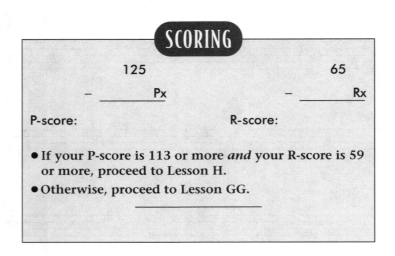

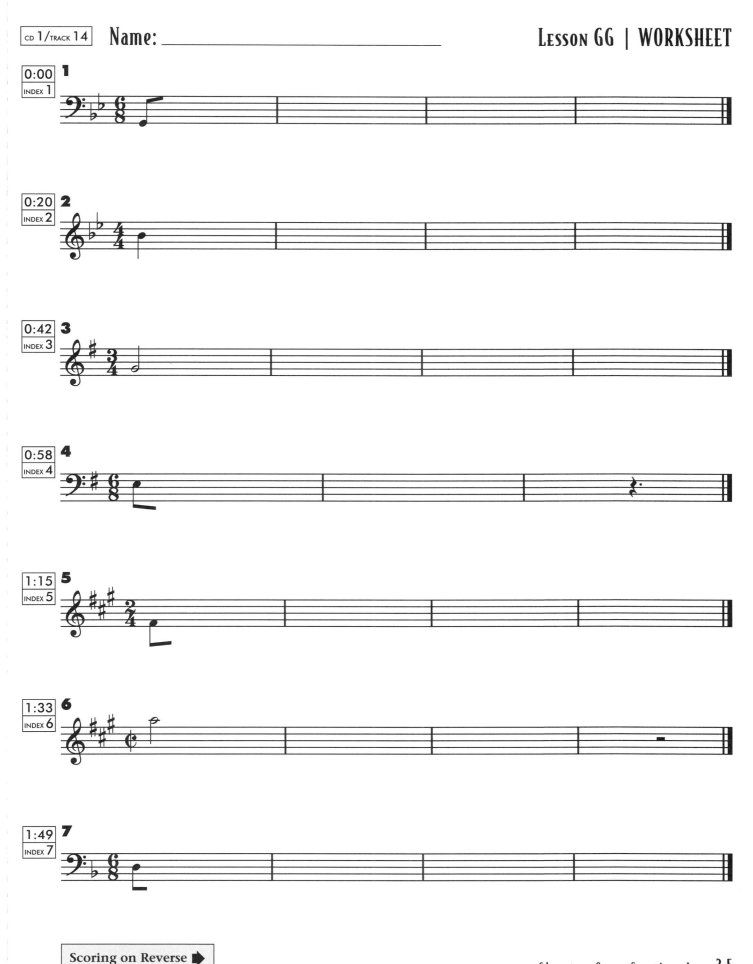

SCORING

96   59

－ _____ Px   － _____ Rx

P-score: _____   R-score: _____

- If your P-score is 86 or more *and* your R-score is 53 or more, proceed to Lesson H.
- Otherwise, repeat Lesson G.

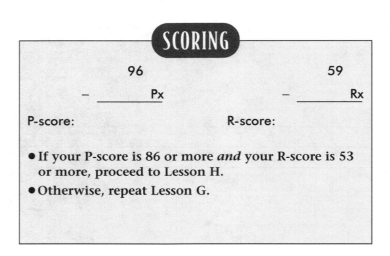

As the melodies become longer, it's important for you to listen for patterns. In this Lesson, concentrate on grouping the notes around the tonic triad. Although the demonstration melody is mostly stepwise, the tonic triad is in the background.

0:00 INDEX 1

Listen for the patterns: a descending triad, which is filled in, plus an N; a skip up of an octave that's filled with a descending scale, and an N.

0:16 INDEX 2   **1**

0:35 INDEX 3   **2**

0:52 INDEX 4   **3**   Although the skips in the first two bars are within the tonic triad, the skip in the third bar is part of a DN.

1:07 INDEX 5   **4**

1:26 INDEX 6   **5**   The melody rises through the triad and then falls through the scale.

> **If no mistakes to this point, you have completed Section I.**

1:43 INDEX 7   **6**

1:59 INDEX 8   **7**

2:13 INDEX 9   **8**

Scoring on Reverse ➡

SCORING

122   79

− _____ Px   − _____ Rx

P-score: R-score:

- If your P-score is 110 or more *and* your R-score is 71 or more, you have completed Section I.
- Otherwise, proceed to Lesson HH.

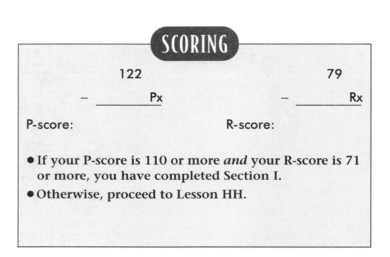

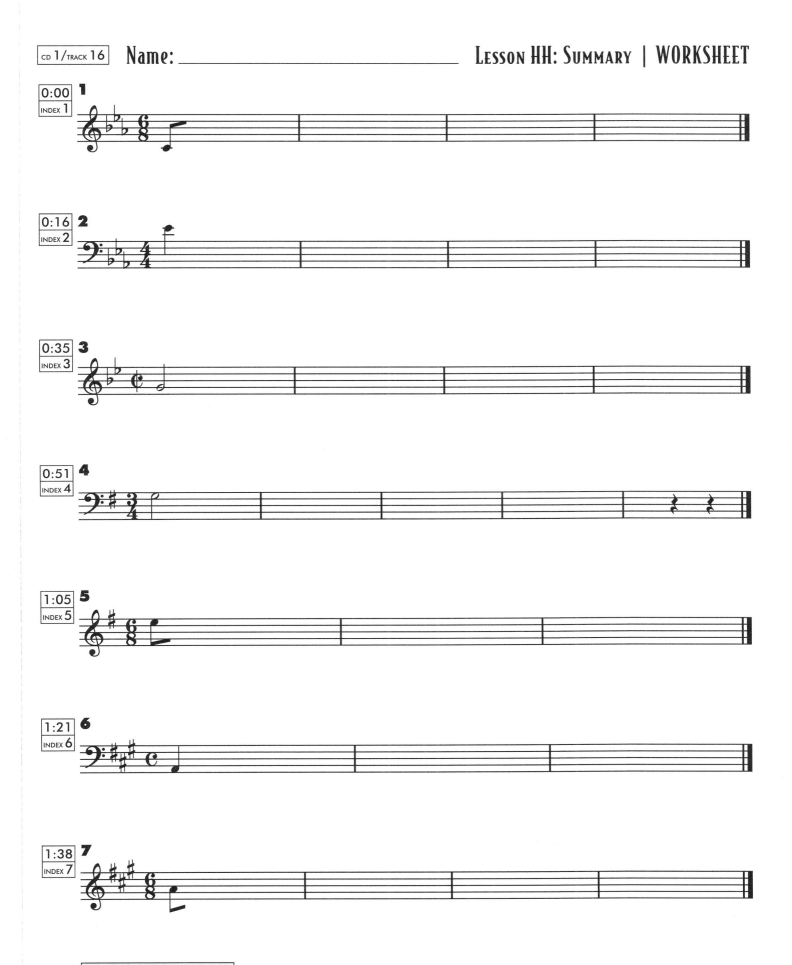

Scoring on Reverse ➡

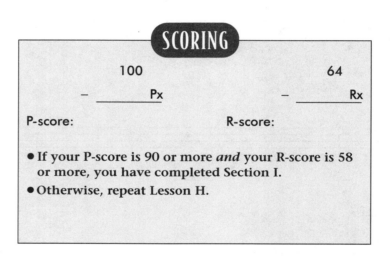

SCORING

100		64
– _____ Px		– _____ Rx
P-score:		R-score:

- If your P-score is 90 or more *and* your R-score is 58 or more, you have completed Section I.
- Otherwise, repeat Lesson H.

Melodic Contour

Here are visual representations of six different melodic contours. For each of the ten melodies that you hear, identify the contour by letter only. Try to do this in one hearing, without stopping the CD. In this and all other Short Drills, you will not hear a voice announcing each melody.

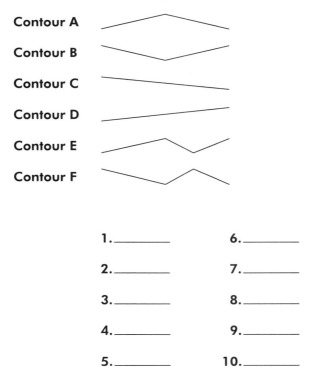

Contour A

Contour B

Contour C

Contour D

Contour E

Contour F

1._____   6._____

2._____   7._____

3._____   8._____

4._____   9._____

5._____   10._____

> **Find the answers on the reverse of this page by
> tearing the bottom of the page up.** ♠ **Do not score your answers.**

1.	A	**6.**	B
2.	E	**7.**	A
3.	D	**8.**	F
4.	E	**9.**	C
5.	F	**10.**	B

It's useful to be aware of the highest and lowest notes of a melody, and to think of those notes as the boundaries of the melody. In this Short Drill, concentrate on hearing the highest and lowest notes only. Write the numbers of the scale degrees (1̂–7̂) that form the boundaries of the melody. Write 1̂ for the tonic note, no matter where it appears.

Here is an example, which is not recorded.

Answer: highest note is 5̂, lowest is 1̂. These drills are played quickly.

Highest note	**Lowest note**
1. _____	_____
2. _____	_____
3. _____	_____
4. _____	_____
5. _____	_____
6. _____	_____
7. _____	_____
8. _____	_____

Find the answers on the reverse of this page by tearing the bottom of the page up. ⬆ **Do not score your answers.**

Highest note

1. 2.

Highest note **Lowest note**

	Highest note	Lowest note
1.	4 ↑	7 ↓
2.	5 ↑	1 ↑
3.	6 ↓	1 ↑
4.	1 ↑	1 ↑
5.	3 ↑	7 ↓
6.	5 ↑	7 ↓
7.	6 ↑	1 ↑
8.	1 ↑	7 ↓

This drill concentrates on recognition of two basic patterns, triads (skips) and scales (stepwise motion). There are no notes to write. Your answer is:

    T   if you hear only triadic skips.

    S   if you hear only scale motion.

    TS if you hear triadic skips followed by stepwise motion.

    ST if you hear stepwise motion followed by triadic skips.

These short melodies are played quickly, so you must focus your attention on the patterns only. Try to grasp the pattern in one hearing.

1._____   6._____

2._____   7._____

3._____   8._____

4._____   9._____

5._____

**Find the answers on the reverse of this page by
tearing the bottom of the page up.** ⬆ **Do not score your answers.**

---

1. TS

2. ST

3. T

4. ST

5. S

6. TS

7. TS

8. T

9. ST

Outlining Triads

Each exercise consist of four notes, played in rapid succession. The notes will be $\hat{1}$, $\hat{3}$, $\hat{5}$, or $\hat{8}$. The triads may be major or minor. Sing back what you hear and then write the answers below.

Each answer has two parts. Write M for major and m for minor; write the scale degrees of each pattern using scale degree numbers. Try to complete this Short Drill in one hearing.

M / m	Scale degrees
1. _____	_____
2. _____	_____
3. _____	_____
4. _____	_____
5. _____	_____
6. _____	_____
7. _____	_____
8. _____	_____
9. _____	_____
10. _____	_____

Find the answers on the reverse of this page by tearing the bottom of the page up. ⬆ **Do not score your answers.**

1.	m	$\hat{1}\,\hat{3}\,\hat{5}\,\hat{8}$	**6.**	m	$\hat{5}\,\hat{3}\,\hat{1}\,\hat{5}$
2.	M	$\hat{5}\,\hat{1}\,\hat{3}\,\hat{5}$	**7.**	m	$\hat{3}\,\hat{5}\,\hat{1}\,\hat{3}$
3.	M	$\hat{8}\,\hat{3}\,\hat{5}\,\hat{1}$	**8.**	m	$\hat{8}\,\hat{3}\,\hat{5}\,\hat{1}$
4.	m	$\hat{3}\,\hat{5}\,\hat{8}\,\hat{1}$	**9.**	M	$\hat{3}\,\hat{5}\,\hat{3}\,\hat{1}$
5.	M	$\hat{1}\,\hat{8}\,\hat{5}\,\hat{3}$	**10.**	M	$\hat{5}\,\hat{3}\,\hat{1}\,\hat{8}$

P's, N's, and DN's

In these short melodies a triad is elaborated with P's, N's, or DN's. Only one kind of elaboration is heard in each melody. Your answer: P, N, or DN.

1.＿＿＿＿＿＿   6.＿＿＿＿＿＿

2.＿＿＿＿＿＿   7.＿＿＿＿＿＿

3.＿＿＿＿＿＿   8.＿＿＿＿＿＿

4.＿＿＿＿＿＿   9.＿＿＿＿＿＿

5.＿＿＿＿＿＿   10.＿＿＿＿＿＿

**Find the answers on the reverse of this page by
tearing the bottom of the page up. ↑ Do not score your answers.**

1. N		**6.** P	
2. P		**7.** N	
3. DN		**8.** DN	
4. N		**9.** DN	
5. DN		**10.** P	

Name: ______________________________

REVIEW WORKSHEET

1

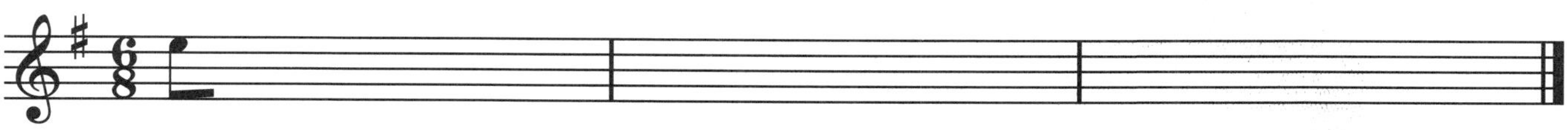

2

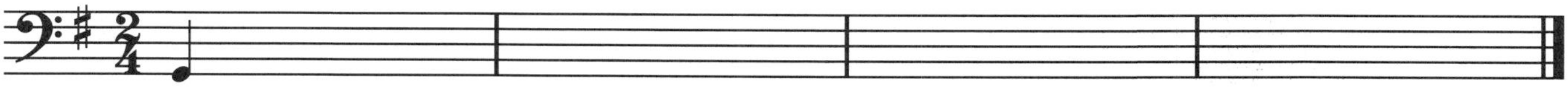

3

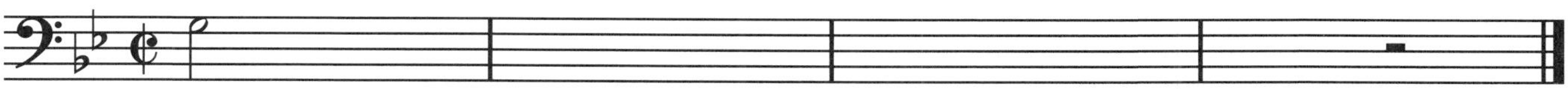

4

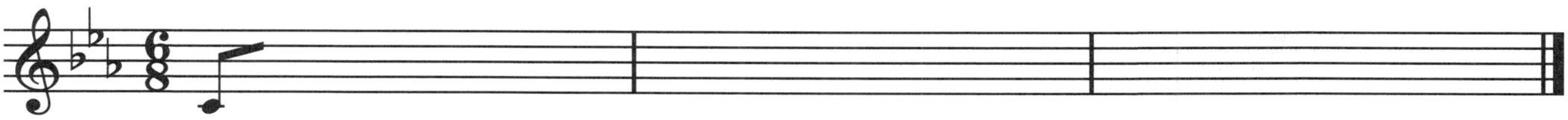

5

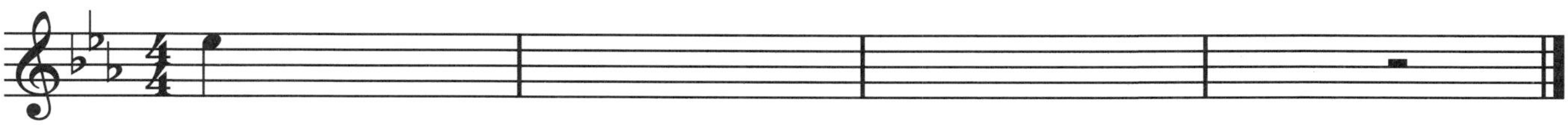

6

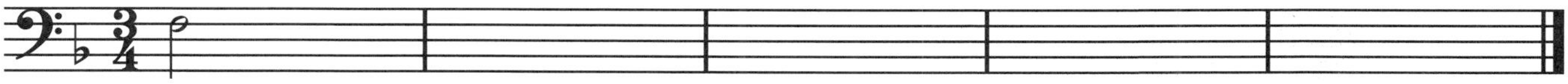

7

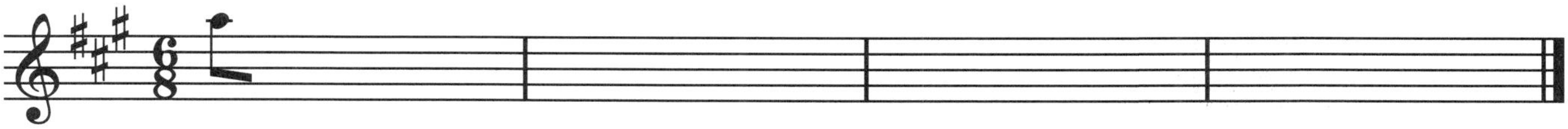

8

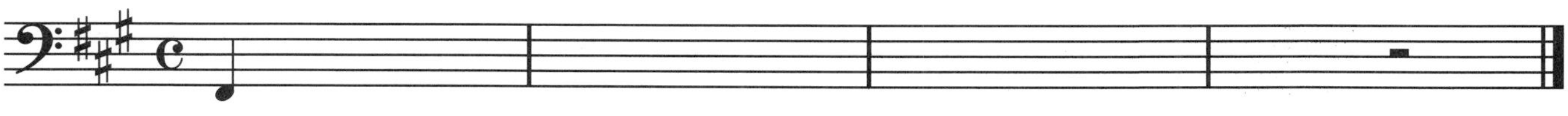

Scoring on Reverse

SCORING

110   68

— _____ Px   — _____ Rx

P-score: R-score:

For this review you will combine your P-score and
your R-score to get a total score.

P-score   _____

R-score   + _____

Total Score   _____

Now convert your score to a letter grade:

A: 178–160   B: 159–142   C: 141–125   D: 124–107

Your Grade:

Name: _____

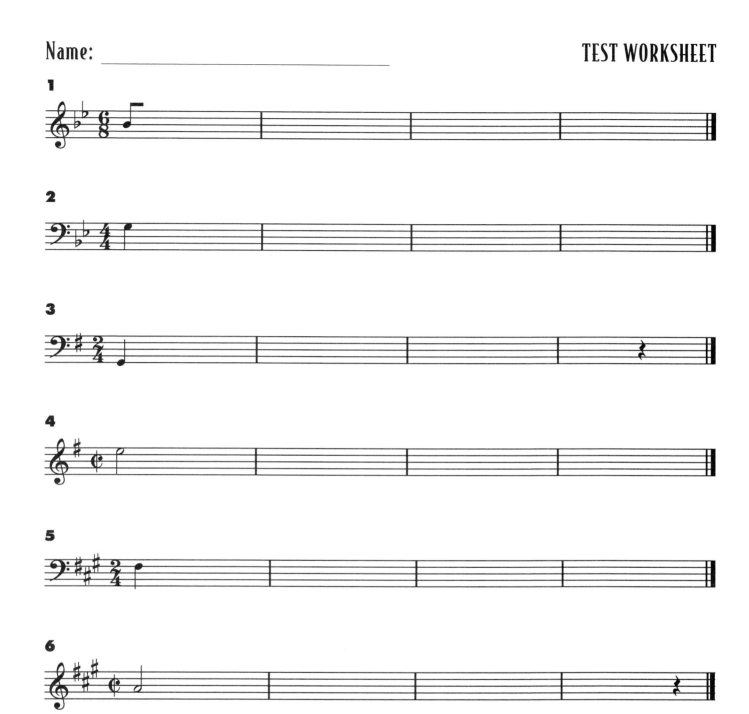

SCORING

139
−　_____ (Total x)

Final Score: _____　　　　Final Grade:

SECTION II

STUDENT RECORD SHEET

- Circle the Lesson you are to do next: (A)
- After completing that Lesson, draw a line through the circle (~~A~~) and circle the Lesson the instructions tell you to do next: (B)
- Keep this sheet up to date. It is intended solely for your guidance.

A	AA
B	BB
C	CC
D	DD
E	EE
F	FF
G	GG
H	HH

Starting date ____________________

Completion date ________________

Keep this page in this book.

HOW TO STUDY SECTION II

Section II introduces more rhythmic activity: dotted rhythms—dotted half, dotted quarter, and dotted eighth notes—and sixteenth notes. Skips in basic chords other than the tonic are also introduced.

Beginning in this section you will find the first pitch, the tonic, in parentheses and without rhythm. Be sure to include this note in your answer, in the correct rhythm. Score the rhythm, but not the pitch. Remember also that you do not score the concluding rests that are printed in some of the melodies.

The rapid-advance feature continues for the single-letter Lessons in this section.

The rhythm ♩. ♪ is introduced. This rhythm is found in the opening melody to Schubert's Great C-Major Symphony:

0:00 INDEX 1

0:24 INDEX 2
1 Keep the triad in mind as you listen to this melody.

0:43 INDEX 3
2 The ♩. may be the second note in ¾.

1:02 INDEX 4
3

1:20 INDEX 5
4 ♩. and ♩. in ¢.

1:40 INDEX 6
5

If no mistakes to this point, proceed to Lesson B. ➡

1:57 INDEX 7
6

2:12 INDEX 8
7 Scale plus triad? Triad plus scale?

2:28 INDEX 9
8

Scoring on Reverse ➡

SCORING

Reminder: in this section you score the rhythm of the first note but not the pitch.

113			96		
−	_____	Px	−	_____	Rx

P-score: _____   R-score: _____

- If your P-score is 102 or more *and* your R-score is 86 or more, proceed to Lesson B.
- Otherwise, proceed to Lesson AA.

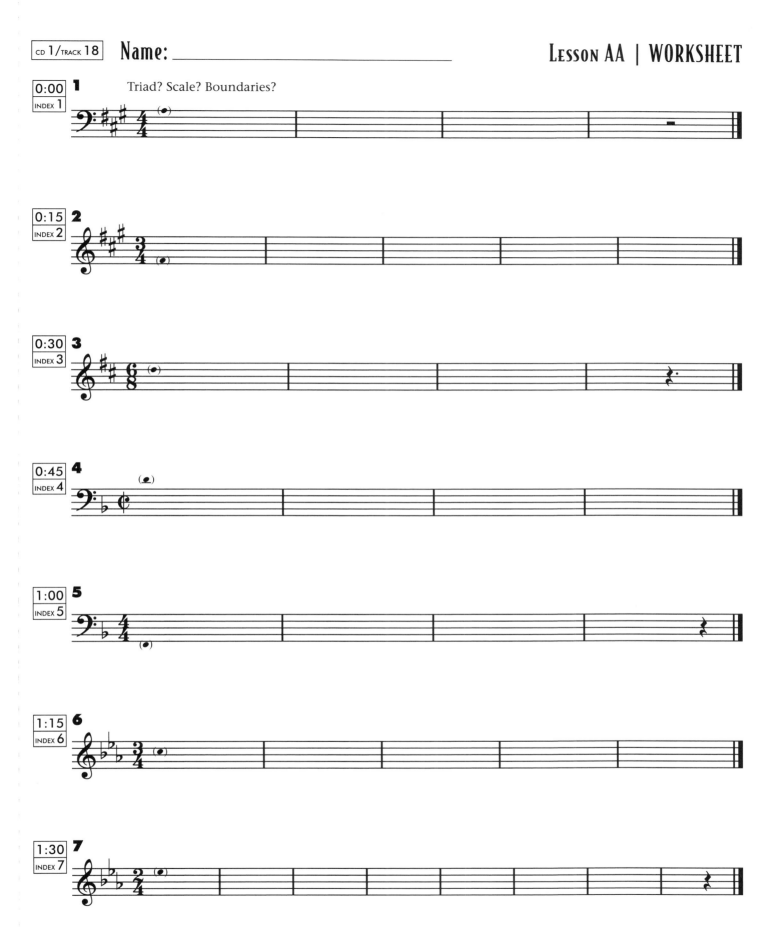

CD 1/TRACK 18   Name: _____

0:00 **1**   INDEX 1   Triad? Scale? Boundaries?

0:15 **2**   INDEX 2

0:30 **3**   INDEX 3

0:45 **4**   INDEX 4

1:00 **5**   INDEX 5

1:15 **6**   INDEX 6

1:30 **7**   INDEX 7

Scoring on Reverse ➡

101   84

$-$ _____ Px $-$ _____ Rx

P-score: R-score:

- If your P-score is 91 or more *and* your R-score is 76 or more, proceed to Lesson B.
- Otherwise, repeat Lesson A.

The V^7 chord is outlined in this melody. Notice the two versions of $\hat{7}$: an accidental is needed to spell V^7 in the minor.

0:00 / INDEX 1

 1

0:16 / INDEX 2

2

0:36 / INDEX 3

3 V is outlined in this melody.

0:54 / INDEX 4

4 Both V and V^7 are outlined in this melody.

1:11 / INDEX 5

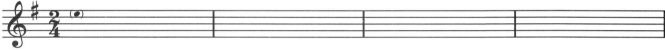

5

1:27 / INDEX 6

If no mistakes to this point, proceed to Lesson C. ➡

6

1:48 / INDEX 7

7 Listen to repetition in this melody.

2:08 / INDEX 8

8 A DN emphasizes the intermediate goal.

2:26 / INDEX 9

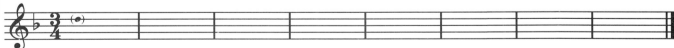
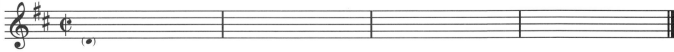

Scoring on Reverse ➡

8

7

9

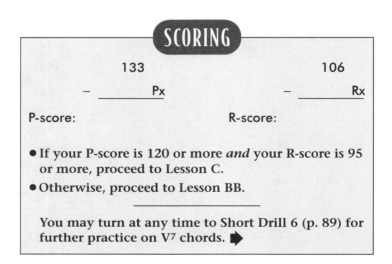

SCORING

133   106

– _____ Px   – _____ Rx

P-score: R-score:

- If your P-score is 120 or more *and* your R-score is 95
  or more, proceed to Lesson C.
- Otherwise, proceed to Lesson BB.

  _____

  You may turn at any time to Short Drill 6 (p. 89) for
  further practice on V⁷ chords. ➤

5

4

3

2

1

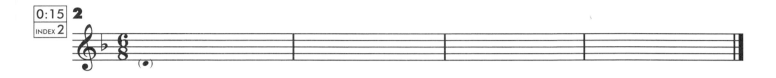

CD 1/TRACK 20 **Name:** ______________________________

0:00
INDEX 1
1

0:15
INDEX 2
2

0:31
INDEX 3
3

0:48
INDEX 4
4

1:04
INDEX 5
5

1:21
INDEX 6
6

1:38
INDEX 7
7

Scoring on Reverse ➡

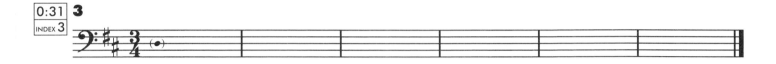

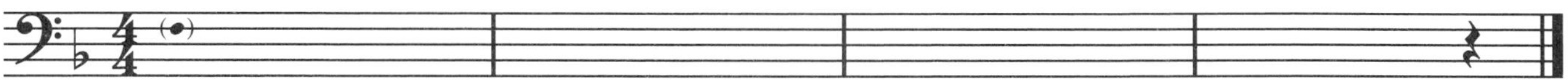

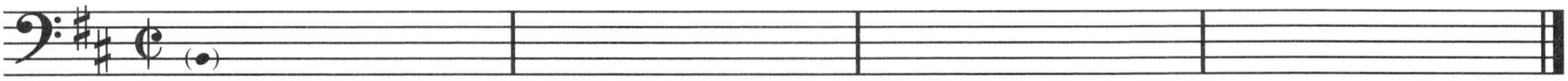

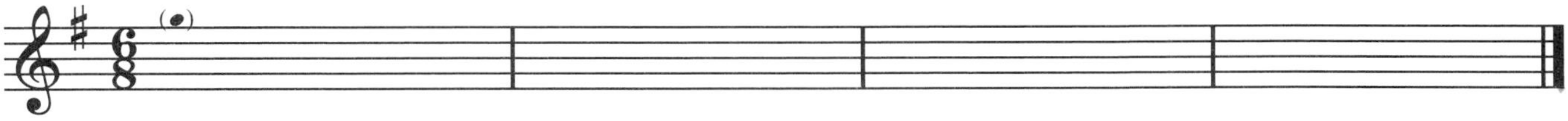

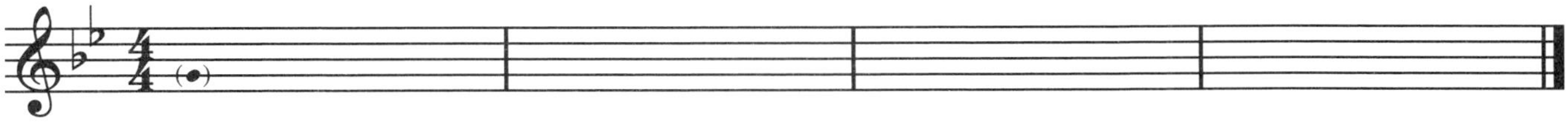

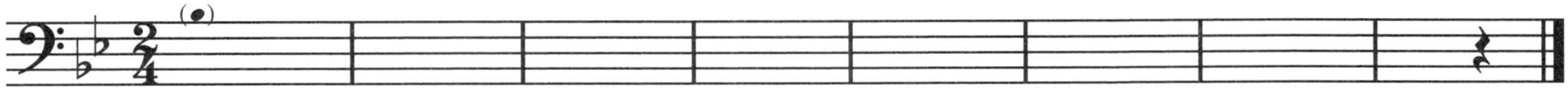

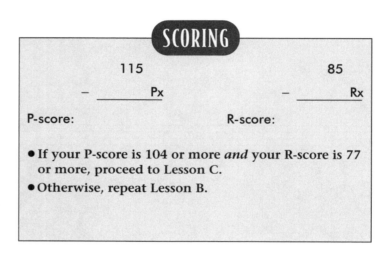

Name: _____

The rhythm ♩♪ is introduced.

0:00 | INDEX 1

1   Triad and scale patterns both occur in this melody.

0:13 | INDEX 2

2

0:32 | INDEX 3

3   Distinguish between ♩.♫ and ♫♩.

0:50 | INDEX 4

4

1:08 | INDEX 5

5

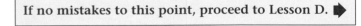

1:26 | INDEX 6

If no mistakes to this point, proceed to Lesson D. ➡

6

1:47 | INDEX 7

7

2:05 | INDEX 8

8

2:23 | INDEX 9

Scoring on Reverse ➡

SCORING

141   97

− _____ Px   − _____ Rx

P-score: R-score:

- If your P-score is 127 or more *and* your R-score is 87 or more, proceed to Lesson D.
- Otherwise, proceed to Lesson CC.

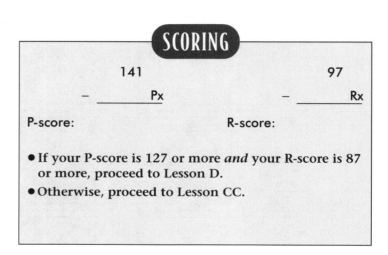

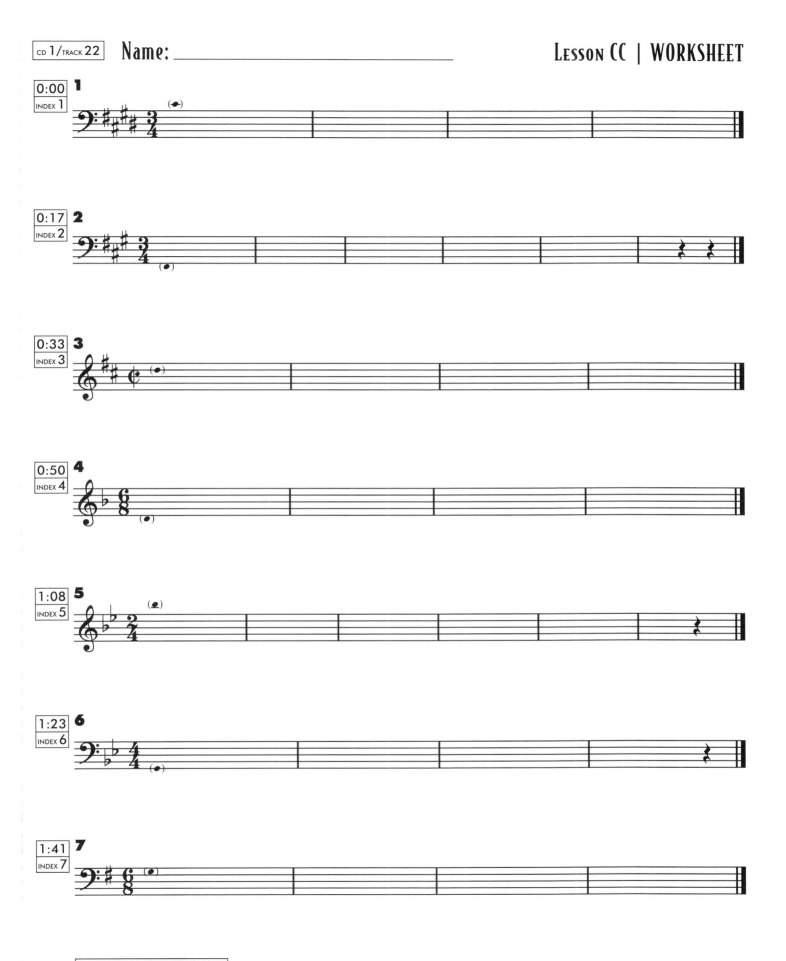

SCORING

122   76

− _____ Px   − _____ Rx

P-score: R-score:

- If your P-score is 110 or more *and* your R-score is 68 or more, proceed to Lesson D.
- Otherwise, repeat Lesson C.

The iv chord is outlined in this melody.

1   Listen for the IV chord in this major-mode melody.

2

3

4

5

If no mistakes to this point, proceed to Lesson E. ➡

6

7

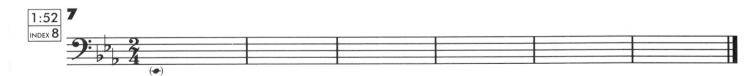

8

8

7

9

SCORING

109   72

−_____ Px   −_____ Rx

P-score: R-score:

- If your P-score is 98 or more *and* your R-score is 65 or more, proceed to Lesson E.
- Otherwise, proceed to Lesson DD.

_____

You may turn at any time to Short Drill 7 (p. 91) for further practice in IV, iv, and V chords. ➡

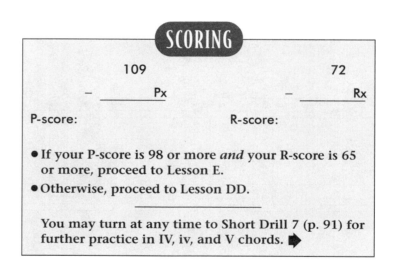

5

4

3

2

1

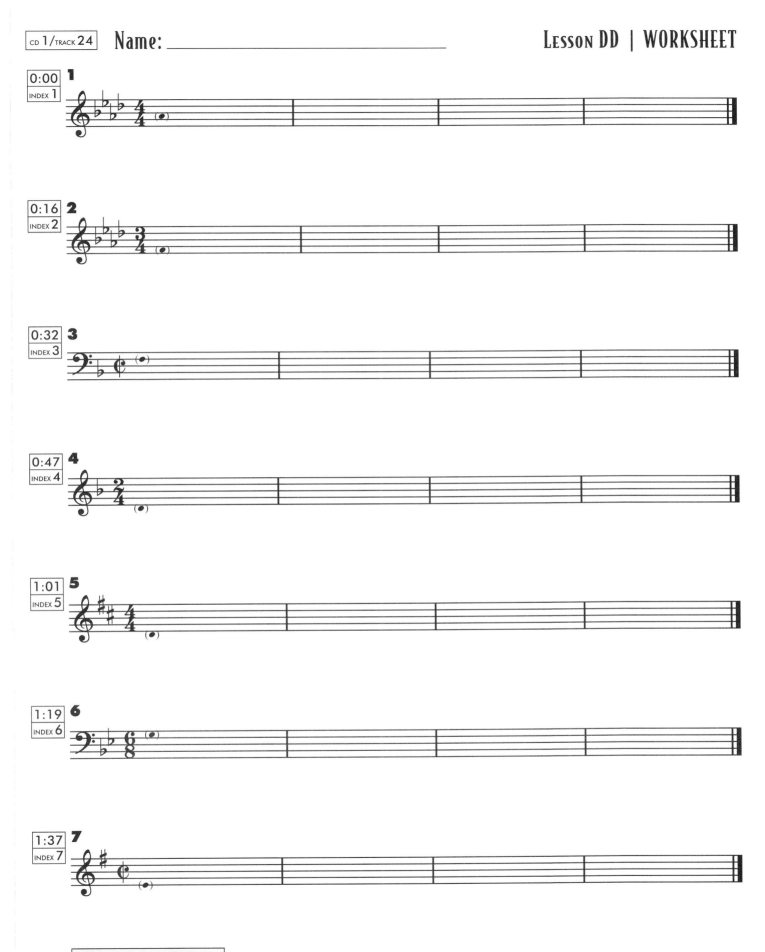

SCORING

103		74
− _____ Px		− _____ Rx
P-score:		R-score:

- If your P-score is 93 or more *and* your R-score is 67 or more, proceed to Lesson E.
- Otherwise, repeat Lesson D.

In the demonstration melody, some beats are filled with ♫♫. Notice that the first group of sixteenth notes includes P's, the second N's, and the third both.

0:00 INDEX 1

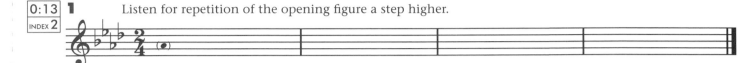

0:13 INDEX 2 **1**　Listen for repetition of the opening figure a step higher.

0:30 INDEX 3 **2**

0:49 INDEX 4 **3**　One beat can be filled with ♫♪.

1:05 INDEX 5 **4**

1:26 INDEX 6 **5**　The notes group themselves around the background harmony.

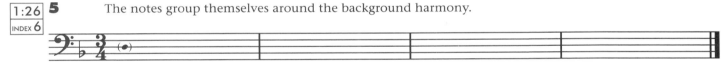

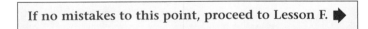

If no mistakes to this point, proceed to Lesson F. ➡

1:45 INDEX 7 **6**

2:01 INDEX 8 **7**

2:17 INDEX 9 **8**

Scoring on Reverse ➡

SCORING

144   80

— _____ Px   — _____ Rx

P-score: R-score:

- If your P-score is 130 or more *and* your R-score is 72 or more, proceed to Lesson F.
- Otherwise, proceed to Lesson EE.

  _____

  You may turn at any time to Short Drill 8 (p. 93) for further practice in recognizing elaborations of melodic triads. ➤

0:00
INDEX 1

1 The groups of ♬♬ all fill the same interval.

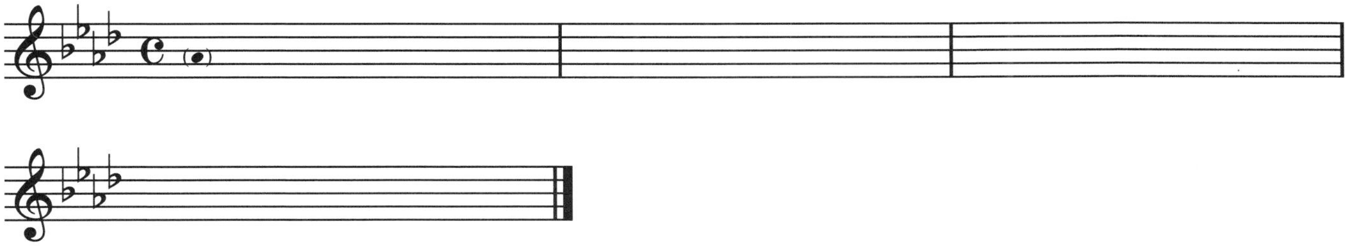

0:22
INDEX 2

2

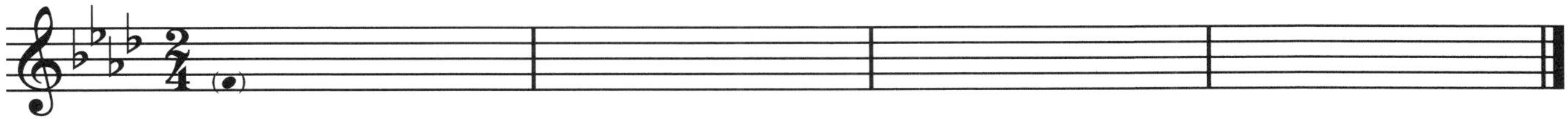

0:38
INDEX 3

3 This melody combines some elements of the previous two.

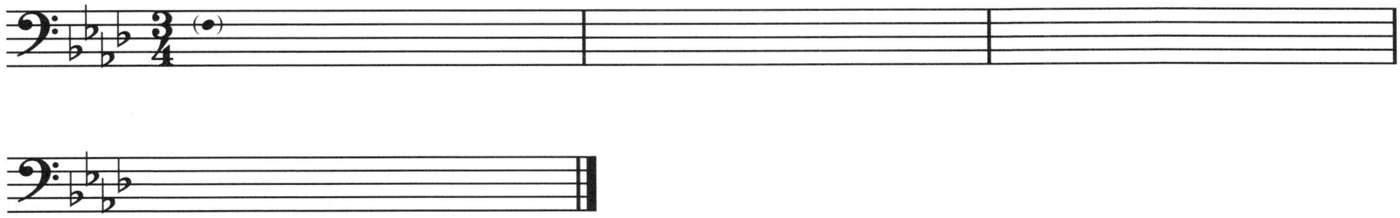

0:58
INDEX 4

4

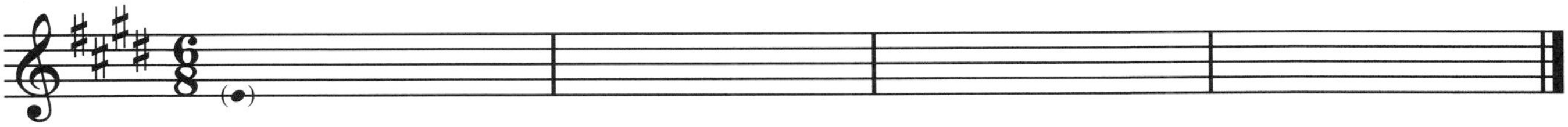

1:16
INDEX 5

5

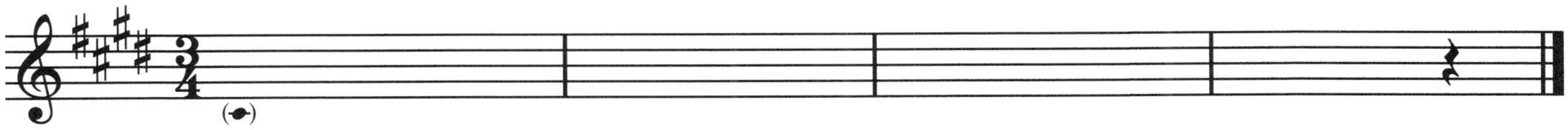

1:34
INDEX 6

6

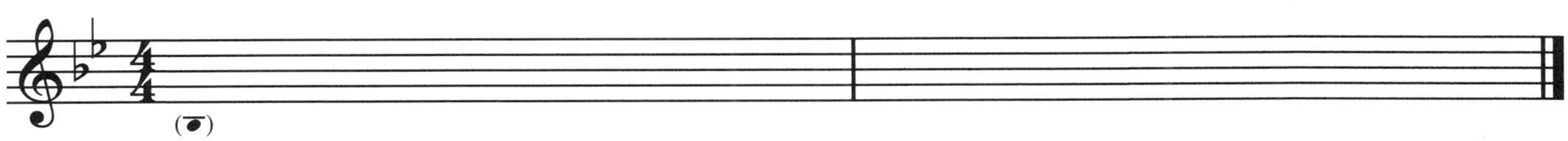

1:50
INDEX 7

7

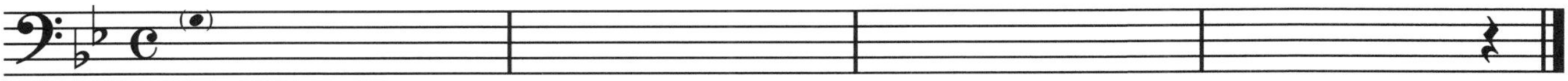

Scoring on Reverse ➧

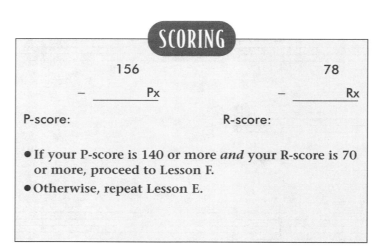

SCORING

156   78

−　——— Px   −　——— Rx

P-score:　　　　　　　　　　　R-score:

- If your P-score is 140 or more *and* your R-score is 70 or more, proceed to Lesson F.
- Otherwise, repeat Lesson E.

CD 1/TRACK 27   Name: _____

In the major mode, the ii chord is outlined.

0:00 INDEX 1

0:12 INDEX 2   **1**

0:26 INDEX 3   **2**   When the background harmony is iv you hear the natural minor ascending.

0:52 INDEX 4   **3**   The rhythm 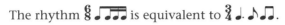 is equivalent to ♩. ♪♫.

1:09 INDEX 5   **4**

1:25 INDEX 6   **5**

If no mistakes to this point, proceed to Lesson G. ➡

1:41 INDEX 7   **6**

2:02 INDEX 8   **7**

2:20 INDEX 9   **8**

Scoring on Reverse ➡

8

7

6

SCORING

155   86

− _____ Px   − _____ Rx

P-score: R-score:

- If your P-score is 140 or more *and* your R-score is 77 or more, proceed to Lesson G.
- Otherwise, proceed to Lesson FF.

5

4

3

2

1

SCORING

129   73

− _____ Px   − _____ Rx

P-score: _____   R-score: _____

- If your P-score is 116 or more *and* your R-score is 66 or more, proceed to Lesson G.
- Otherwise, repeat Lesson F.

The melodies in Lesson G are built on this background harmony:

tonic ➤ dominant preparation ➤ dominant ➤ tonic

0:00 | **1**
INDEX 1

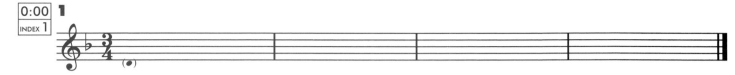

0:15 | **2**
INDEX 2

0:32 | **3**
INDEX 3

0:54 | **4**
INDEX 4

1:11 | **5**
INDEX 5

If no mistakes to this point, proceed to Lesson H. ➤

1:27 | **6**
INDEX 6

1:51 | **7**
INDEX 7

2:07 | **8**
INDEX 8

Scoring on Reverse ➤

SCORING

161		88
− _____ Px		− _____ Rx

P-score: _____   R-score: _____

- If your P-score is 145 or more *and* your R-score is 79 or more, proceed to Lesson H.
- Otherwise, proceed to Lesson GG.

CD 1/TRACK 30

Name: _____

1
0:00
INDEX 1

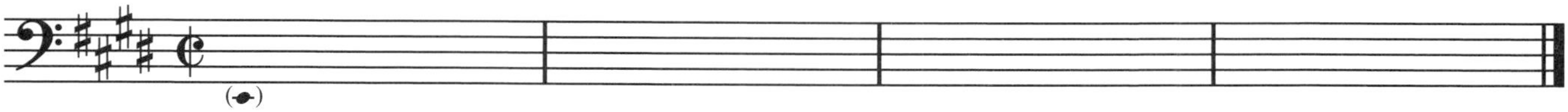

2
0:16
INDEX 2

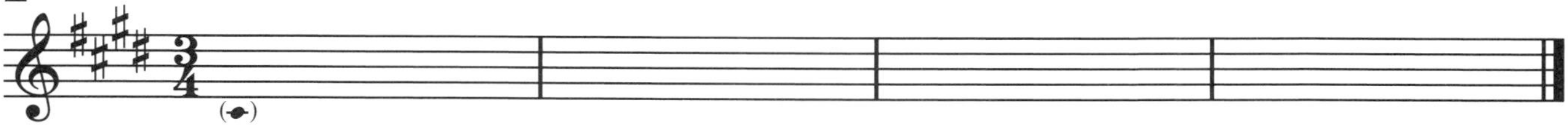

3
0:34
INDEX 3

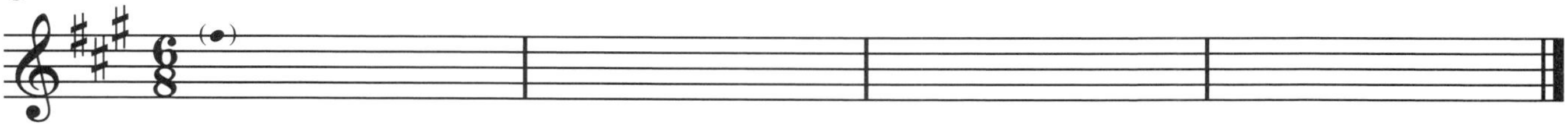

4
0:52
INDEX 4

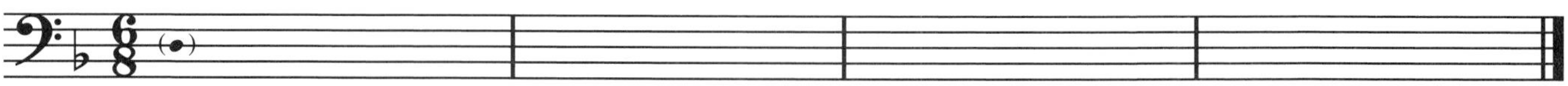

5
1:10
INDEX 5

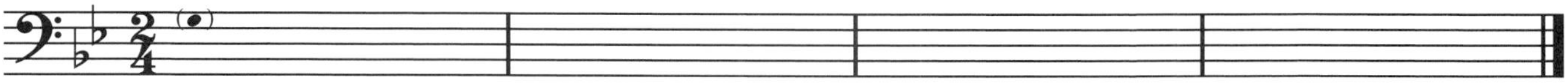

6
1:26
INDEX 6

7
1:43
INDEX 7

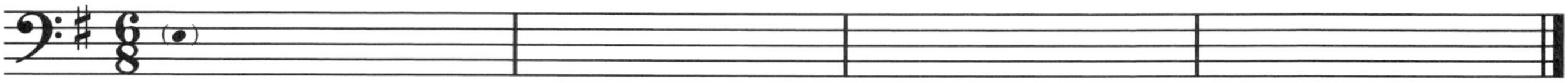

Scoring on Reverse ➡

SCORING

146   60

− _____ Px   − _____ Rx

P-score: R-score:

- If your P-score is 131 or more *and* your R-score is 54 or more, proceed to Lesson H.
- Otherwise, repeat Lesson G.

CD 1/TRACK 31 **Name:** ______________________________

LESSON H: SUMMARY | WORKSHEET

In these melodies, keep in mind the familiar chord and scale patterns, as well as the harmonic background.

0:00
INDEX 1

1

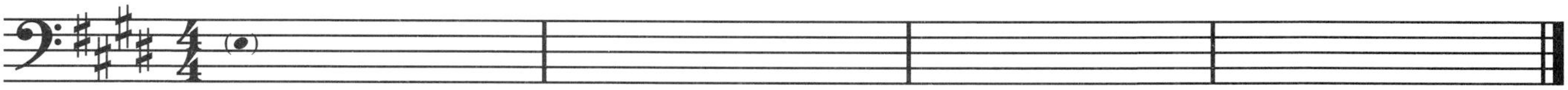

0:23
INDEX 2

2

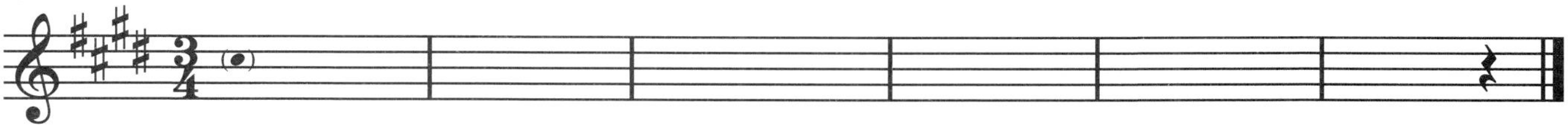

0:39
INDEX 3

3

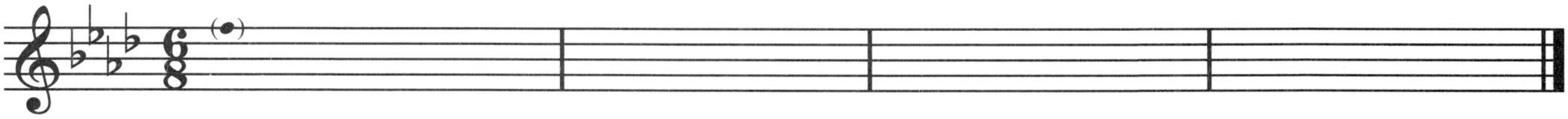

1:00
INDEX 4

4

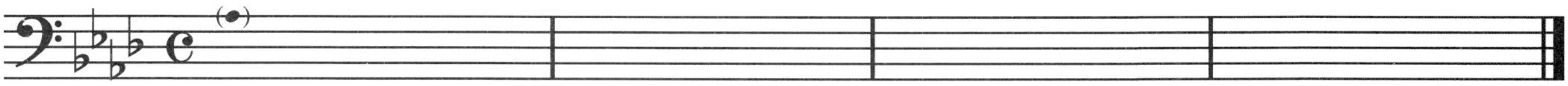

1:19
INDEX 5

5

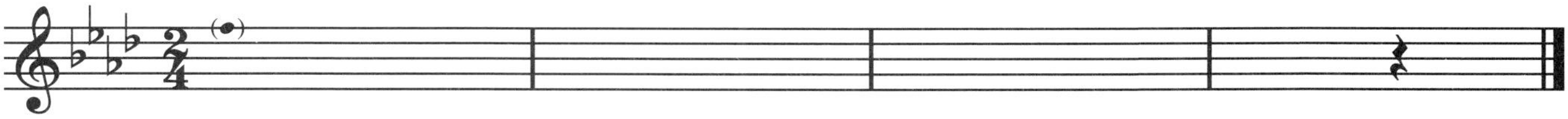

If no mistakes to this point, you have completed Section II.

1:33
INDEX 6

6

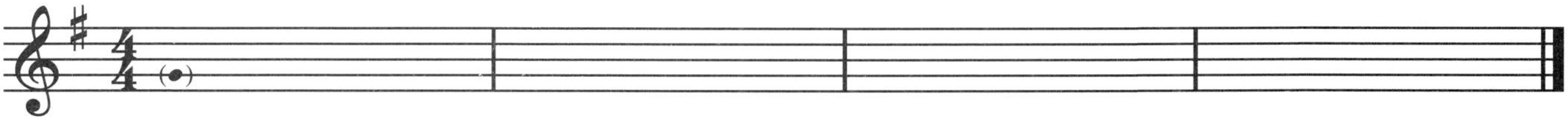

1:53
INDEX 7

7

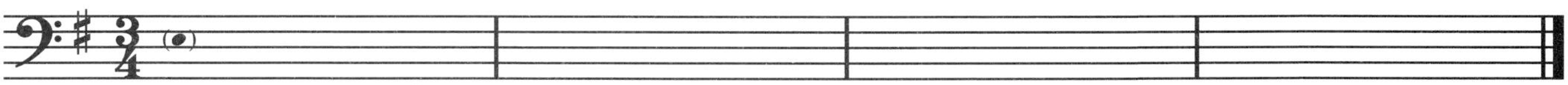

2:12
INDEX 8

8

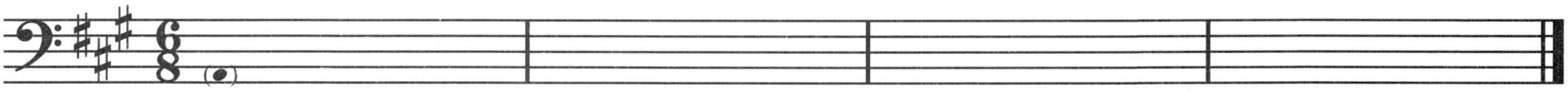

Scoring on Reverse ➡

8

7

6

SCORING

171   97

− _____ Px   − _____ Rx

P-score: R-score:

- If your P-score is 154 or more *and* your R-score is 87 or more, you have completed Section II.
- Otherwise, proceed to Lesson HH.

5

4   **3**

2   **1**

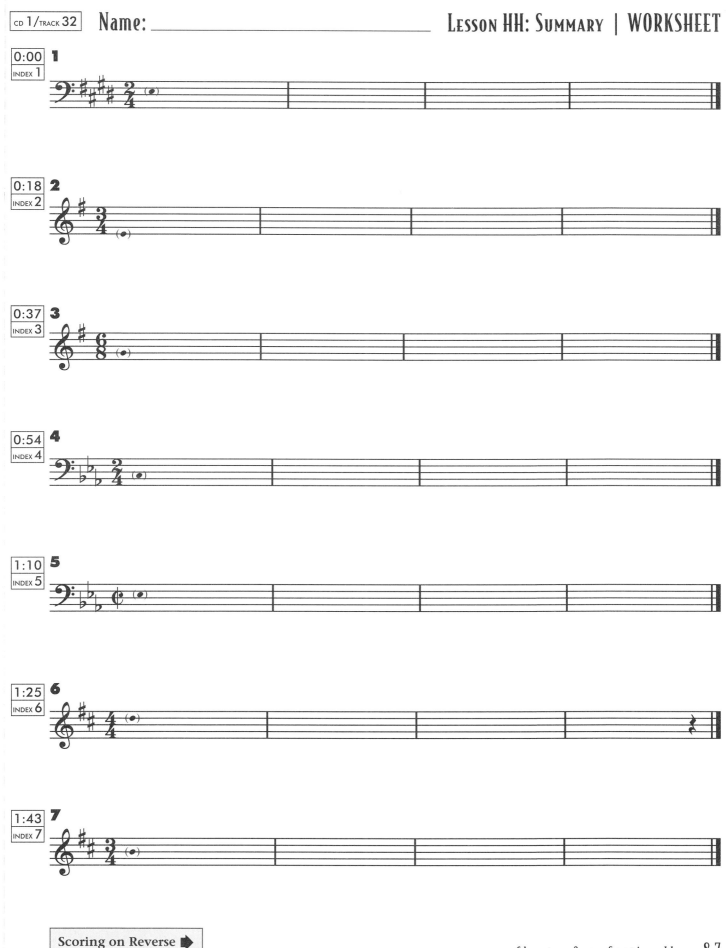

SCORING

138   71

− _____ Px   − _____ Rx

P-score: _____   R-score: _____

- If your P-score is 124 or more *and* your R-score is 64 or more, you have completed Section II.
- Otherwise, repeat Lesson H.

0:00
INDEX 1 **PART ONE**

These exercises focus on the outline of the V⁷ chord in C major. You hear the four notes of the chord seven times, in various orders. Answer by writing a letter that corresponds to one of the patterns given below. Try to do this without stopping the CD.

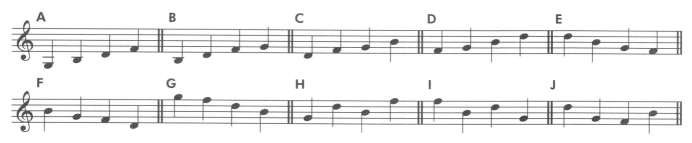

Write your answers below.

1. _____   2. _____   3. _____   4. _____   5. _____   6. _____   7. _____

> **Find the answers for Part One on the reverse of this page by tearing the botton of the page up.** 🔺 **Do not score your answers.**

0:37
INDEX 2 **PART TWO**

These exercises focus on longer patterns featuring the V⁷ chord that are elaborated with P's, N's, and DN's. Listen to each of the seven playings. Answer by writing a letter that corresponds to one of the patterns given below. Here are the choices:

Write your answers below.

1. _____   2. _____   3. _____   4. _____   5. _____   6. _____   7. _____

> **Find the answers for Part Two on the reverse of this page by tearing the top of the page down.** 🔺 **Do not score your answers.**

1. B **2.** F **3.** A **4.** E **5.** G **6.** J **7.** I

PART TWO

1. I **2.** G **3.** D **4.** F **5.** B **6.** H **7.** E

IV, iv, or V?

0:00
INDEX 1 **PART ONE**

Concentrate on distinguishing between the outlines of the triads IV (or iv) and V in C major and C minor. Answer by writing a letter that corresponds to the pattern that you hear. C is always the first note. These are the choices:

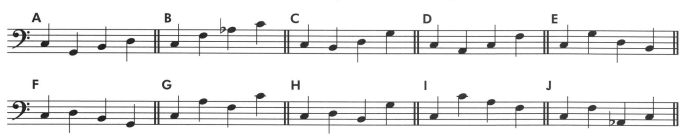

Write your answers below.

1. _____   2. _____   3. _____   4. _____   5. _____   6. _____   7. _____

Tear this page up for answers to Part One. ⬆ Do not score your answers.

0:34
INDEX 2 **PART TWO**

Notated choices are not given. For each exercise, answer IV, iv, or V. C is always the first note.

Write your answers below.

1. _____   2. _____   3. _____   4. _____   5. _____   6. _____   7. _____

Tear this page down for answers to Part Two. ⬇ Do not score your answers.

Elaborating Triads

0:00 INDEX 1 PART ONE

You practice recognizing the difference between the outlines of I (i), IV (iv), and V in C major and C minor, as well as whether the triads are elaborated with P's, N's, or DN's. Answer by writing a letter that corresponds to one of the patterns given below. Here are the choices:

1. _____ 2. _____ 3. _____ 4. _____ 5. _____ 6. _____ 7. _____

> **Tear this page up for answers to Part One.** ⬆ **Do not score your answers.**

0:36 INDEX 2 PART TWO

Notated choices are not given. Answer by writing both the roman numeral of the triad and the type of elaboration—P, N, or DN—that you hear.

	roman numeral	P/N/DN		roman numeral	P/N/DN
1.	_____	_____	5.	_____	_____
2.	_____	_____	6.	_____	_____
3.	_____	_____	7.	_____	_____
4.	_____	_____			

> **Tear this page down for answers to Part Two.** ⬇ **Do not score your answers.**

PART ONE

1. B **2.** C **3.** E **4.** I **5.** A **6.** H **7.** G

PART TWO

1. V	DN	**5.** iv	N
2. I	N	**6.** IV	P
3. i	P	**7.** i	DN
4. I	DN		

Name: ______________________

REVIEW WORKSHEET

1

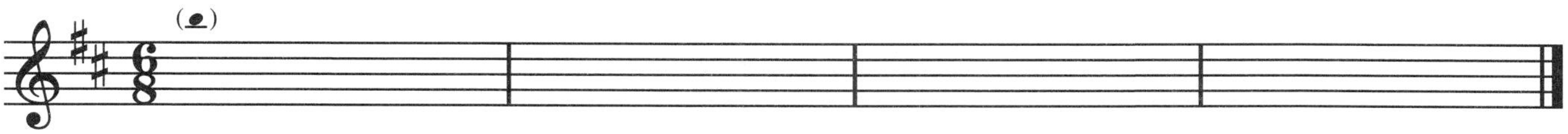

2

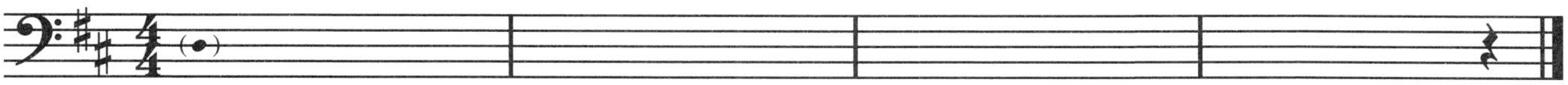

3

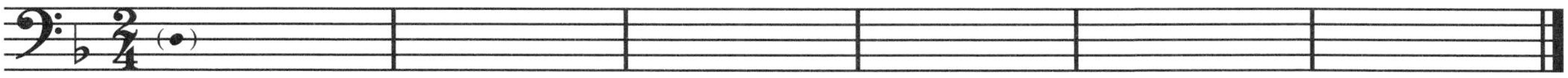

4

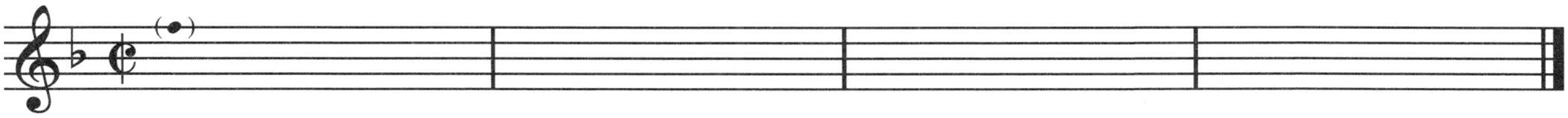

5

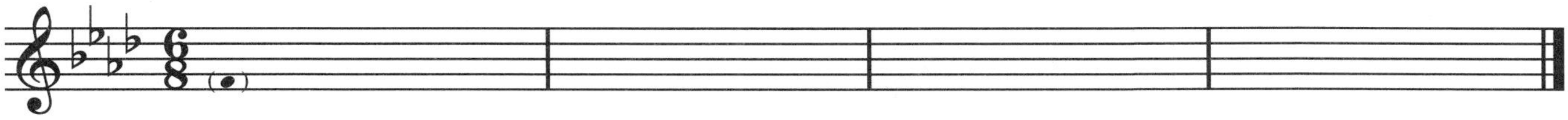

6

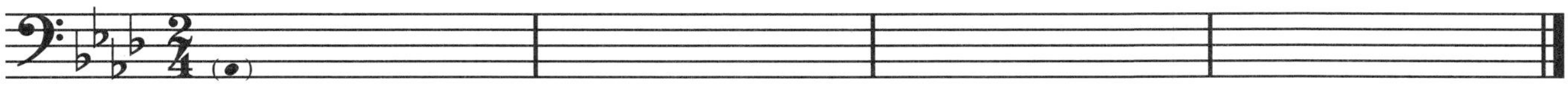

7

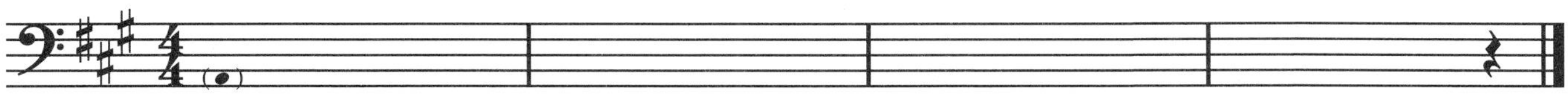

8

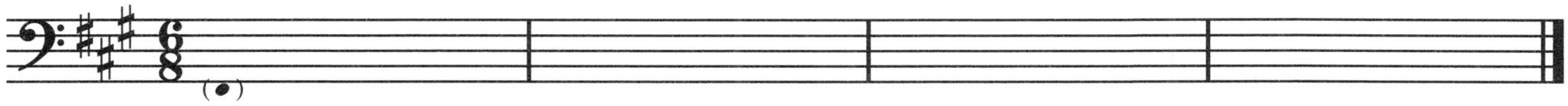

Scoring on Reverse ➡

175   82

– _____ Px   – _____ Rx

P-score: R-score:

For this review you will combine your P-score and
your R-score to get a total score.

P-score   _____

R-score   + _____

Total Score   _____

Now convert your score to a letter grade:

A: 257–231   B: 230–206   C: 205–180   D: 179–154

Your Grade:

Name: _____

1

2

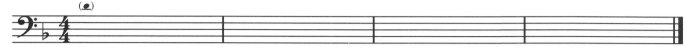

3

4

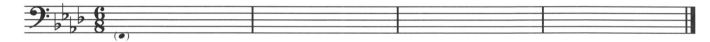

5

SCORING

166

− _____ (Total x)

Final Score: Final Grade:

SECTION III

STUDENT RECORD SHEET

- Circle the Lesson you are to do next: (A)
- After completing that Lesson, draw a line through the circle ~~(A)~~ and circle the Lesson the instructions tell you to do next: (B)
- Keep this sheet up to date. It is intended solely for your guidance.

A	AA
B	BB
C	CC
D	DD
E	EE
F	FF
G	GG
H	HH

Starting date ____________________

Completion date ________________

Keep this page in this book.

HOW TO STUDY SECTION III

All the melodies in the previous two sections began on scale degree 1̂; melodies in this section may begin on 5̂ (starting in Lesson B) or 3̂ (starting in Lesson C). Remember that the prep note is always the tonic, even though the first note of the melody may not be. Since the first note is no longer given on the Worksheets in this section, you will have to determine whether it is 1̂, 3̂, or 5̂ and whether the melody is in the major or minor mode. From the key signature, you can tell that the tonic may be either one of two possible pitches. As you listen to the first playing, quickly decide on the mode.

In addition, starting in Lesson C bar lines are no longer given on the worksheet. Use the time signature as a clue to help you locate the bar lines, and sketch them in quickly as you sing back the melody after the first hearing.

Some two-phrase melodies are introduced in Lesson B. The first phrase, the antecedent, makes a musical statement, which the second, the consequent, continues and concludes. Often the consequent begins by repeating part of the antecedent. Listen for the repetition.

Chromatic neighbor notes are first heard in Lesson F, chromatic double neighbor notes in Lesson G. Such notes are simply chromatic versions of the diatonic N's and DN's with which you are already familiar.

Rhythmic features introduced in Section III include the quarter-note upbeat, the double-eighth-note upbeat (♫), triplets, simple syncopations, and the meters ⅜, ⅝, and ¹²⁄₈. Starting in Lesson D rests are found in the body of many exercises. Mark an x *under* the beat that contains a rest whose duration you have noted incorrectly.

There is no rapid-advance feature in this section. Score every Lesson after you have finished all the exercises in it. Tear up for the first four answers, and down for the last three.

Section III includes a new type of Short Drill that gives you practice in detecting differences in pitch and rhythm. You compare a given version on the page with one that is played with a few changes. There are three such Short Drills in this section; a fourth focuses on upbeats and downbeats.

Name: _____

Lesson A introduces the upbeat. The demonstration melody shows that the first and last measures are rhythmically incomplete but add up to a complete measure.

0:00
INDEX 1

In melodies with upbeats, continue to score the last note as one beat.

0:15
INDEX 2

1   Think of the rhythm as upbeat-downbeat as you sing the melody.

0:40
INDEX 3

2

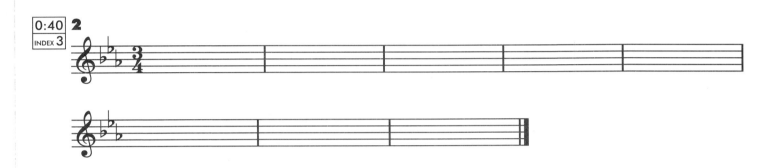

1:02
INDEX 4

3

1:20
INDEX 5

4   Repetition of the rhythmic motive is your clue.

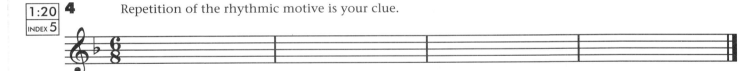

1:36
INDEX 6

5   Concluding rests no longer appear on the Worksheet. In each exercise, score the rest as you do the final note: mark only one x if incorrect.

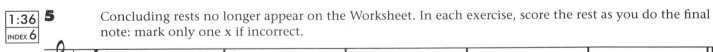

1:52
INDEX 7

6   This excerpt from Brahms's Violin Concerto does not end on $\hat{1}$.

2:15
INDEX 8

7

Scoring on Reverse ➡

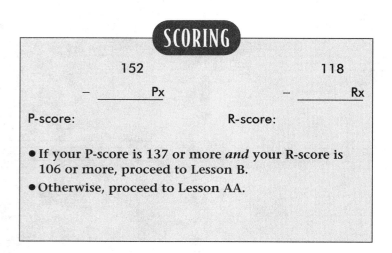

SCORING

152   118

− _____ Px   − _____ Rx

P-score: R-score:

- If your P-score is 137 or more *and* your R-score is
  106 or more, proceed to Lesson B.
- Otherwise, proceed to Lesson AA.

0:00 | **1** | Listen carefully to the duration of the last note.
INDEX 1

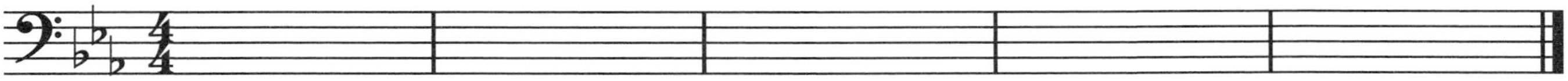

0:16 | **2**
INDEX 2

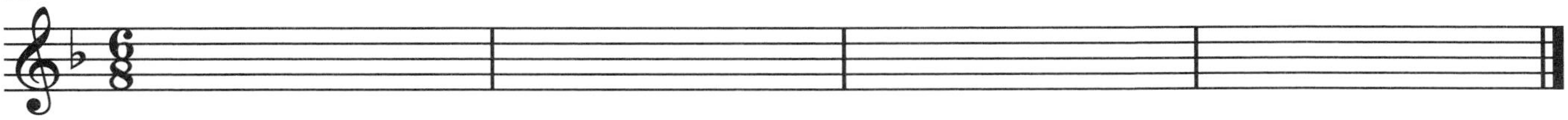

0:32 | **3**
INDEX 3

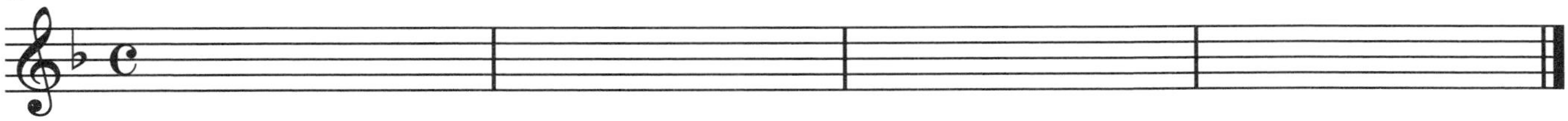

0:47 | **4**
INDEX 4

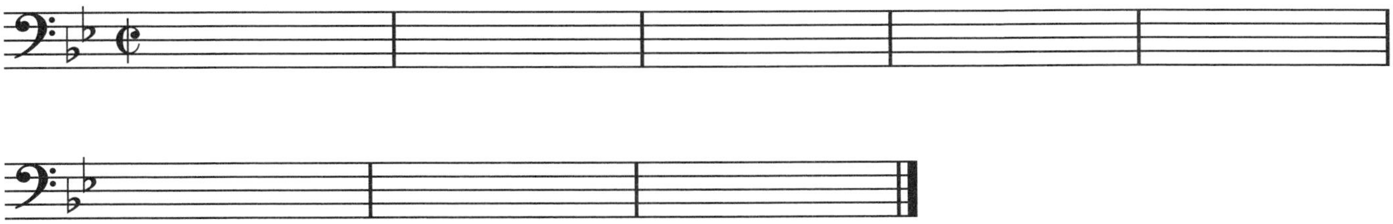

1:05 | **5**
INDEX 5

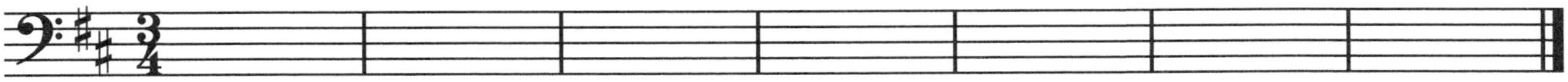

1:21 | **6**
INDEX 6

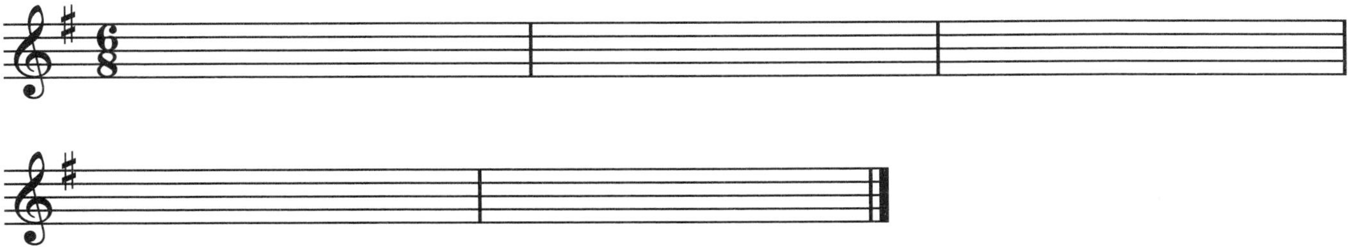

Scoring on Reverse ➤

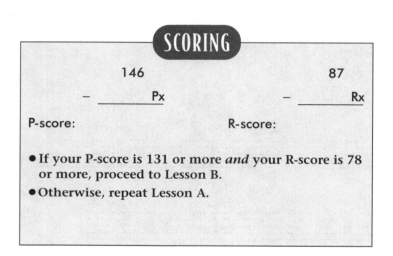

SCORING

146   87

$-$ _____ Px $-$ _____ Rx

P-score: R-score:

- If your P-score is 131 or more *and* your R-score is 78 or more, proceed to Lesson B.
- Otherwise, repeat Lesson A.

Name: _____

Starting with this Lesson, melodies may begin on 5̂. The prep note, however, is always 1̂.

Some of the melodies of this Lesson are built in two phrases, usually described as antecedent and consequent. Together they form a period. The first phrase is a statement, the second continues and completes the thought. Since the consequent often repeats elements of the antecedent, it is a good idea to listen for repetition.

0:00 INDEX 1 — First phrase / Second phrase

0:23 INDEX 2 — **1** The upbeat is 5̂.

0:37 INDEX 3 — **2** The first note isn't 1̂, but the background chord is I.

0:53 INDEX 4 — **3**

1:08 INDEX 5 — **4**

1:31 INDEX 6 — **5** Beethoven wrote most of his scherzos in 3/4.

1:49 INDEX 7 — **6** The melody by Mozart does not end on 1̂.

2:06 INDEX 8 — **7**

Scoring on Reverse ➡

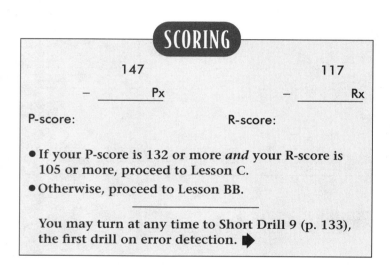

SCORING

147   117

− _____ Px   − _____ Rx

P-score: R-score:

- If your P-score is 132 or more *and* your R-score is 105 or more, proceed to Lesson C.
- Otherwise, proceed to Lesson BB.

_____

You may turn at any time to Short Drill 9 (p. 133), the first drill on error detection. ➡

Name: _____

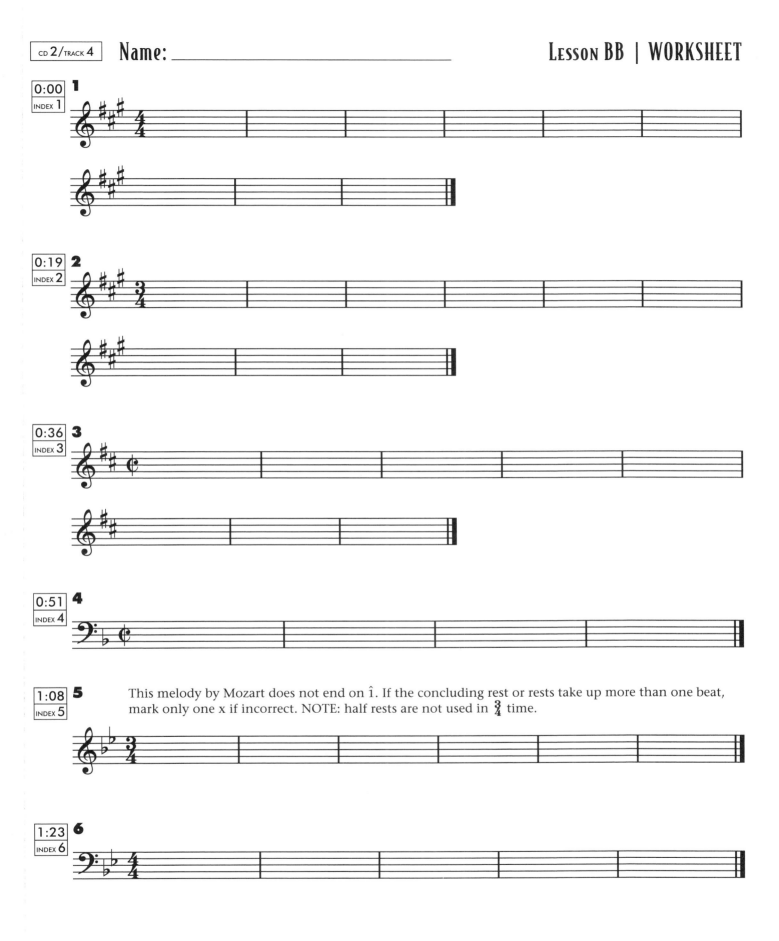

5 This melody by Mozart does not end on 1̂. If the concluding rest or rests take up more than one beat, mark only one x if incorrect. NOTE: half rests are not used in ¾ time.

Scoring on Reverse ➡

Starting with this Lesson, bar lines will not appear on the Worksheet. You must decide whether the first note of the melody is an upbeat or a downbeat. Add bar lines to the demonstration melody, which begins on 3̂. Then close your eyes and listen to this Schubert melody, memorize it, and sing it back.

| 0:00 |
| INDEX 1 |

| 0:17 | **1** |
| INDEX 2 |

In the minor mode, too, a melody may begin on 3̂. Listen for the triad.

| 0:34 | **2** |
| INDEX 3 |

| 0:51 | **3** |
| INDEX 4 |

| 1:11 | **4** |
| INDEX 5 |

| 1:31 | **5** |
| INDEX 6 |

| 1:48 | **6** |
| INDEX 7 |

This melody introduces ⅜ meter. Score the rhythm of each bar as one beat (♩.). Listen for the rising and then descending lines in this melody.

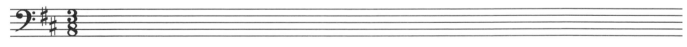

| 2:06 | **7** |
| INDEX 8 |

This melody by Purcell does not end on 1̂. If the concluding rest or rests take up more than one beat, mark only one x if incorrect. NOTE: half rests are not used in ¾ time.

Correct bar lines for demonstration melody:

| **Scoring on Reverse** ➡ |

SCORING

166   102

− ____ Px   − ____ Rx

P-score: R-score:

- If your P-score is 149 or more *and* your R-score is 92 or more, proceed to Lesson D.
- Otherwise, proceed to Lesson CC.

  _____

You may turn at any time to Short Drill 10 (p. 135) for further practice in distinguishing between upbeats and downbeats. ➡

0:00 **1**
INDEX 1

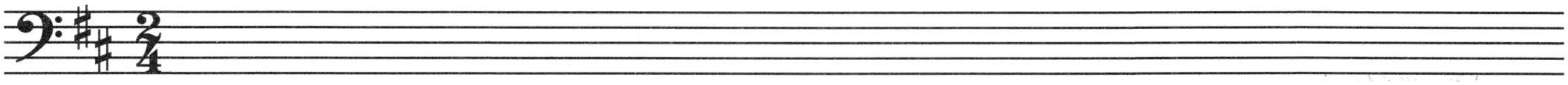

0:15 **2**   This melody does not end on î.
INDEX 2

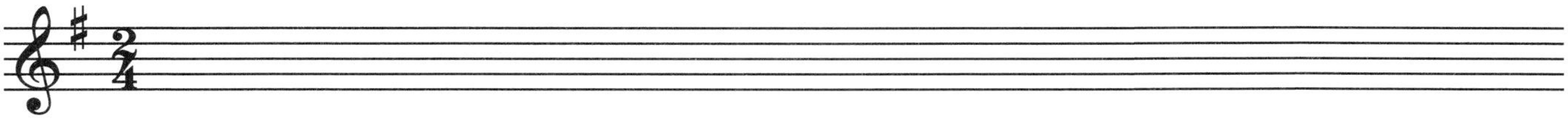

0:27 **3**
INDEX 3

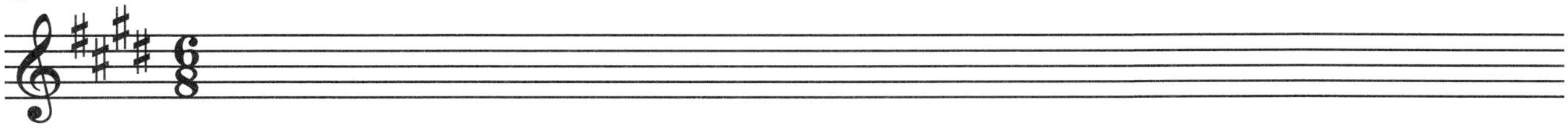

0:43 **4**
INDEX 4

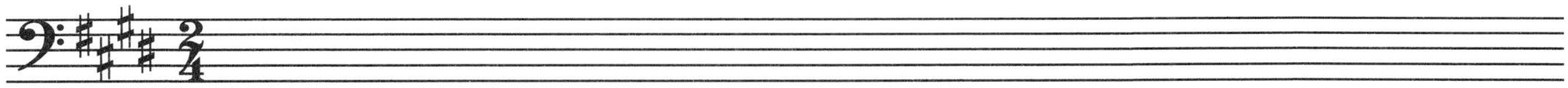

0:57 **5**
INDEX 5

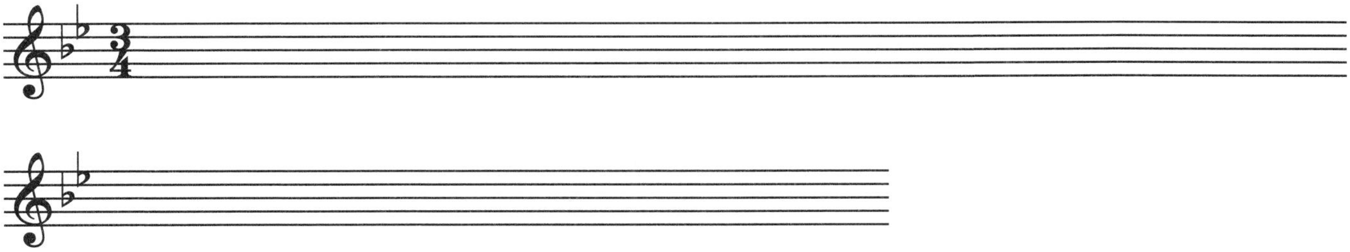

1:13 **6**   Follow the line that rises from î to ŝ and then descends.
INDEX 6

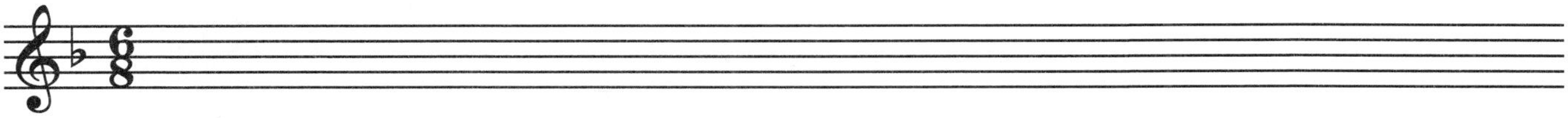

Scoring on Reverse ➡

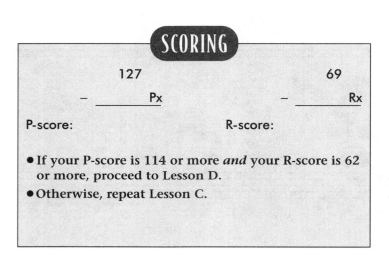

SCORING

127   69

− _____ Px   − _____ Rx

P-score: R-score:

- If your P-score is 114 or more *and* your R-score is 62 or more, proceed to Lesson D.
- Otherwise, repeat Lesson C.

Listen to the difference between eighth notes (two to a beat) and triplets (three to a beat).

 1

 2

 3

4 This melody by Schubert contrasts against ♩. ♪ .

5 This melody by Beethoven begins on 3̂. Listen for repetition.

6 From this point on melodies may include rests. In this German folk tune the two phrases are separated by a quarter rest. Score the rhythm of the rest as you would score a note: only one x for the entire beat.

7 This melody introduces ⅜ meter, which has three beats per measure.

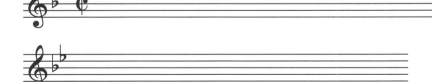

Scoring on Reverse ➡

SCORING

195   106

−　_____　Px   −　_____　Rx

P-score: R-score:

- If your P-score is 176 or more *and* your R-score is 95 or more, proceed to Lesson E.
- Otherwise, proceed to Lesson DD.

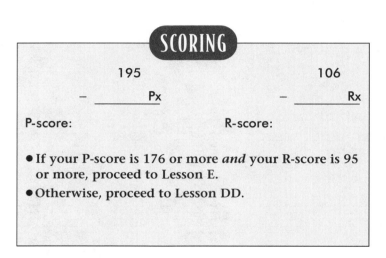

Name: _____ LESSON DD | WORKSHEET

0:00 **1** Listen for the rest that separates the two phrases.
INDEX 1

0:15 **2**
INDEX 2

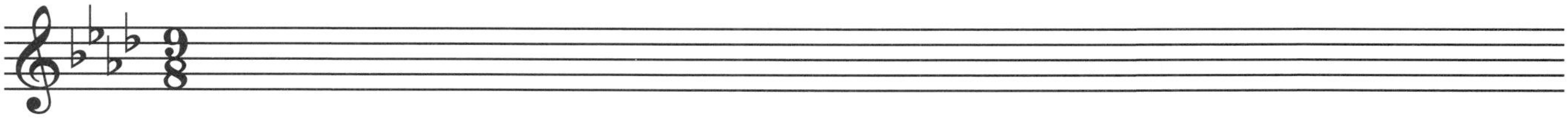

0:34 **3**
INDEX 3

0:51 **4**
INDEX 4

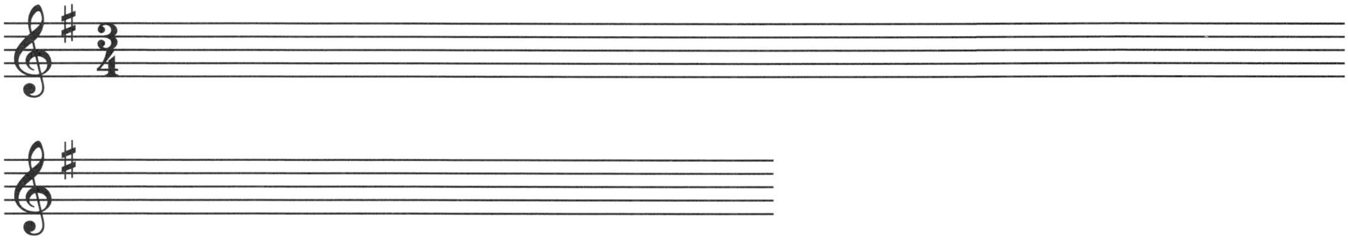

1:08 **5**
INDEX 5

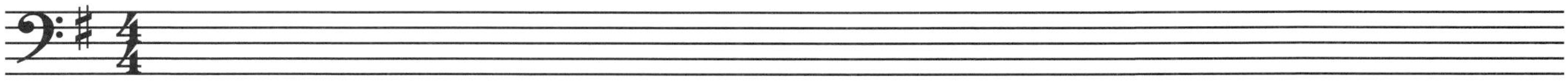

1:25 **6**
INDEX 6

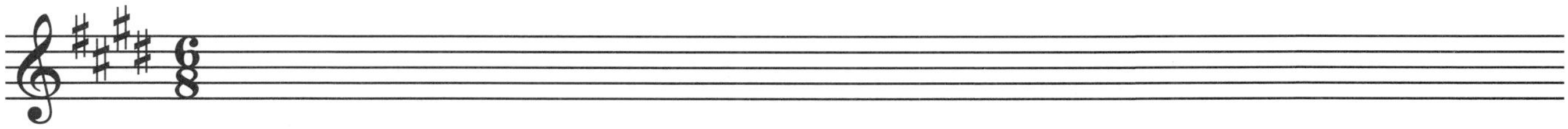

Scoring on Reverse ▶

SCORING

153 99

— _____ Px   — _____ Rx

P-score: _____   R-score: _____

- If your P-score is 138 or more *and* your R-score is 89 or more, proceed to Lesson E.
- Otherwise, repeat Lesson D.

Name: _____

Simple syncopations are introduced in this Lesson.

0:00 **INDEX 1**

0:13 **INDEX 2** **1**   This melody by Dvořák does not end on î.

0:31 **INDEX 3** **2**   Listen closely to the duration of the last three notes.

0:47 **INDEX 4** **3**

1:04 **INDEX 5** **4**

1:22 **INDEX 6** **5**

1:40 **INDEX 7** **6**   Listen for the repetition in this longer melody.

1:57 **INDEX 8** **7**   Rests separate the motives. From this point on, rests may be shorter than one beat. Score the rest as you would score a note: if incorrect, mark only one x for the entire beat.

Scoring on Reverse ➡

SCORING

171   110

− _____ Px   − _____ Rx

P-score: _____   R-score: _____

- If your P-score is 154 or more *and* your R-score is 99 or more, proceed to Lesson F.
- Otherwise, proceed to Lesson EE.

  _____

  You may turn at any time to Short Drill 11 (p. 137), the second drill on error detection. ➡

Name: _____

0:00 **1**
INDEX 1

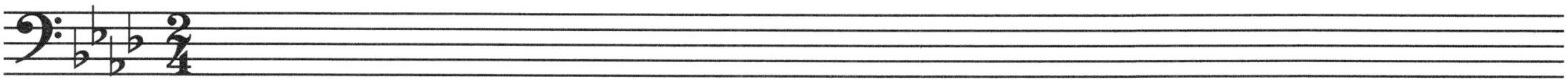

0:16 **2** Here is an example of the harmonic minor used in a melody.
INDEX 2

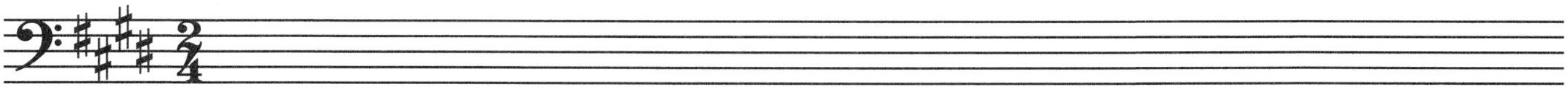

0:31 **3**
INDEX 3

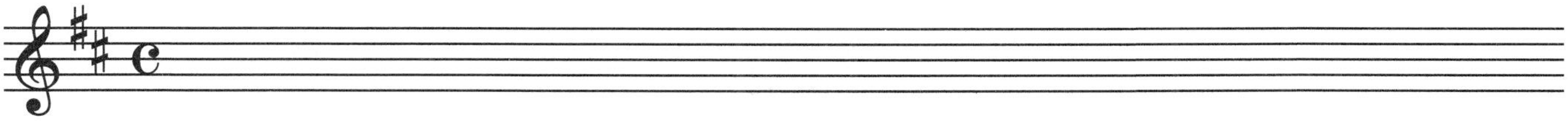

0:45 **4**
INDEX 4

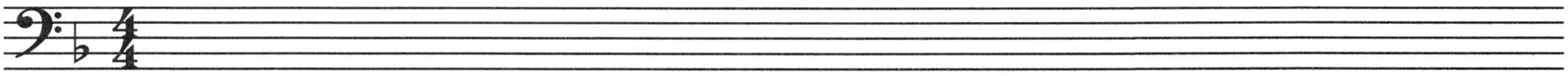

1:01 **5**
INDEX 5

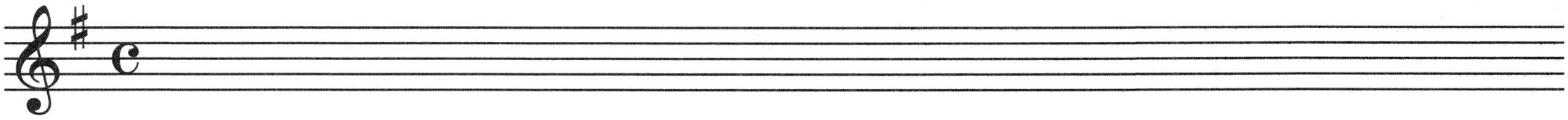

1:18 **6**
INDEX 6

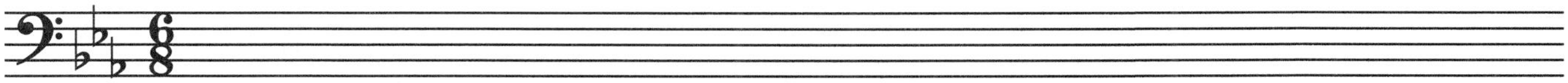

Scoring on Reverse ➡

SCORING

133   82

—   Px   —   Rx

P-score: R-score:

- If your P-score is 120 or more *and* your R-score is 74 or more, proceed to Lesson F.
- Otherwise, repeat Lesson E.

Name: _____ LESSON F | WORKSHEET

This demonstration melody illustrates chromatic N's as well as diatonic ones. Observe that a precautionary accidental is used to restore the diatonic scale.

1   Follow the motive as it descends; Mozart did.

2   Follow the rising line in this melody.

3

4

5   This melody by Donizetti introduces the ♫ upbeat.

6

7

Scoring on Reverse ➡

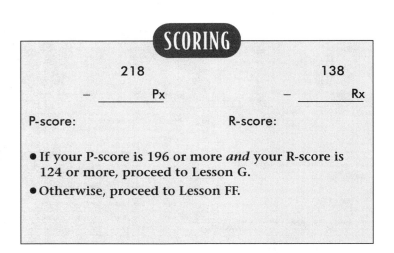

SCORING

218   138

− _____ Px   − _____ Rx

P-score: _____   R-score: _____

- If your P-score is 196 or more *and* your R-score is 124 or more, proceed to Lesson G.
- Otherwise, proceed to Lesson FF.

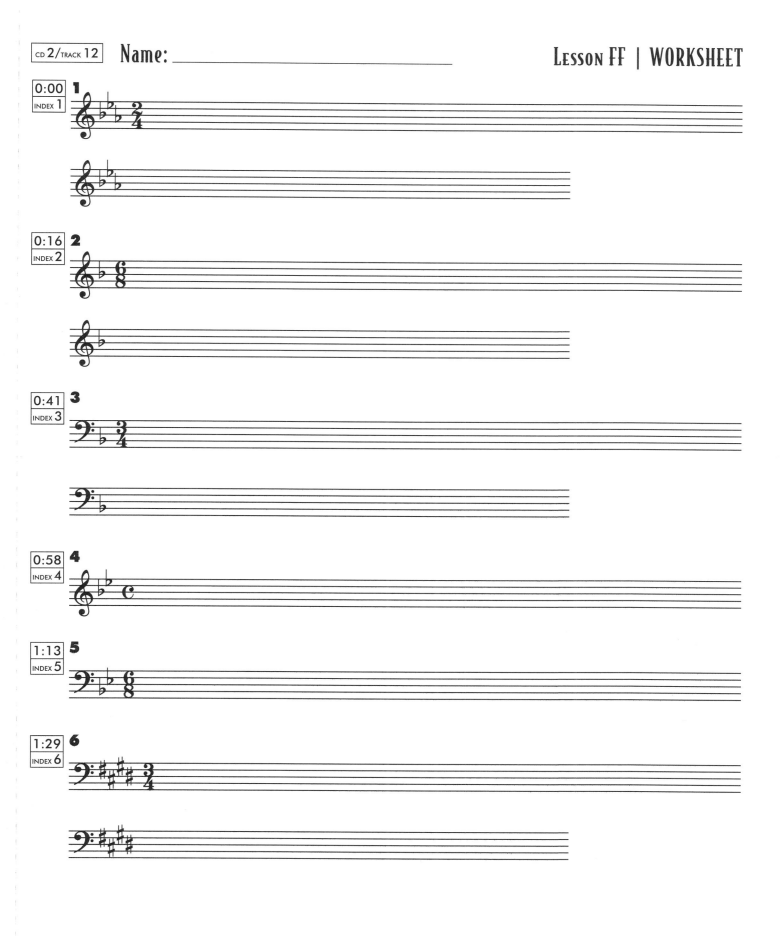

Scoring on Reverse ➡

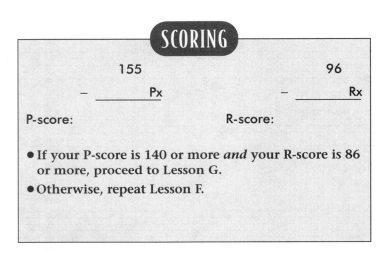

Think of the chromatic DN as a diatonic DN elaborating 1̂ that is transposed to other scale degrees.

0:00 INDEX 1

0:11 INDEX 2 1   Be sure to sing the tonic triad as soon as you hear the prep note.

0:33 INDEX 3 2

0:51 INDEX 4 3

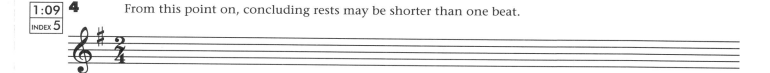

1:09 INDEX 5 4   From this point on, concluding rests may be shorter than one beat.

1:25 INDEX 6 5

1:42 INDEX 7 6   The following melody introduces ⅛ meter, which has four beats per measure.

2:08 INDEX 8 7

Scoring On Reverse ➡

SCORING

172   79

− _____ Px   − _____ Rx

P-score: R-score:

- If your P-score is 155 or more *and* your R-score is 71 or more, proceed to Lesson H.
- Otherwise, proceed to Lesson GG.

_____

You may turn at any time to Short Drill 12 (p. 139), the third drill on error detection. ➡

0:00 **1**
INDEX 1

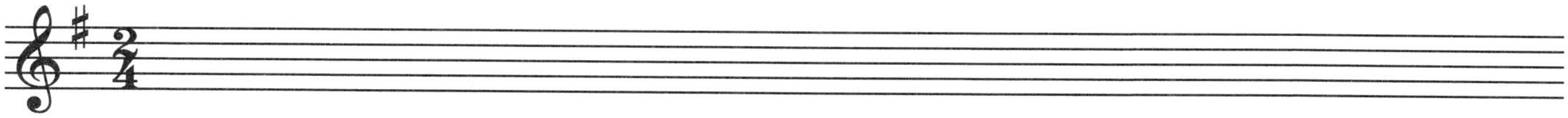

0:12 **2**   Listen carefully for the rests within the phrase.
INDEX 2

0:30 **3**
INDEX 3

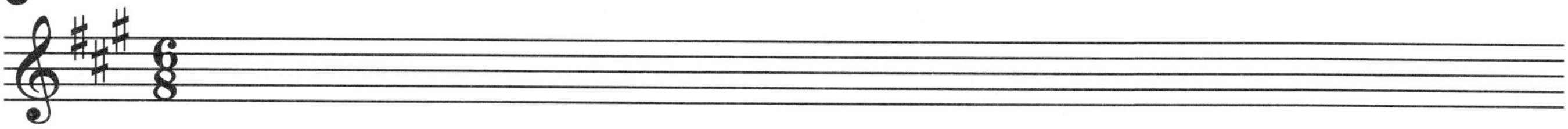

0:46 **4**
INDEX 4

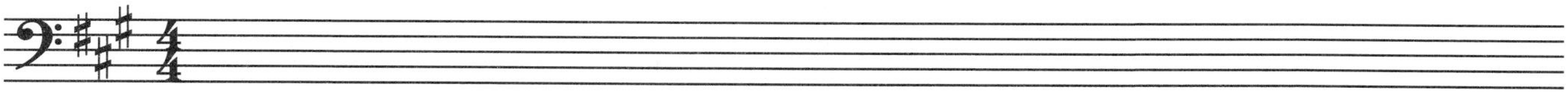

1:01 **5**
INDEX 5

1:18 **6**
INDEX 6

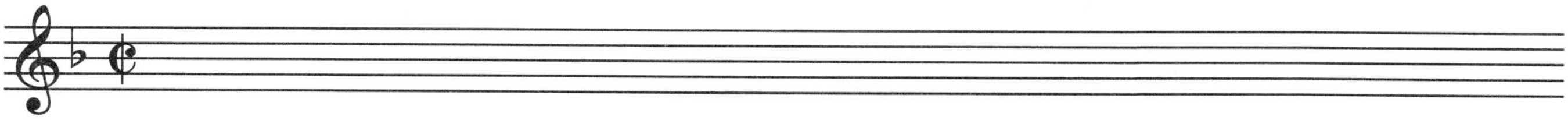

Scoring on Reverse ➡

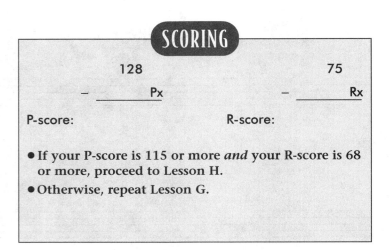

SCORING

128   75

$-$ _____ Px $-$ _____ Rx

P-score: R-score:

- If your P-score is 115 or more *and* your R-score is 68 or more, proceed to Lesson H.
- Otherwise, repeat Lesson G.

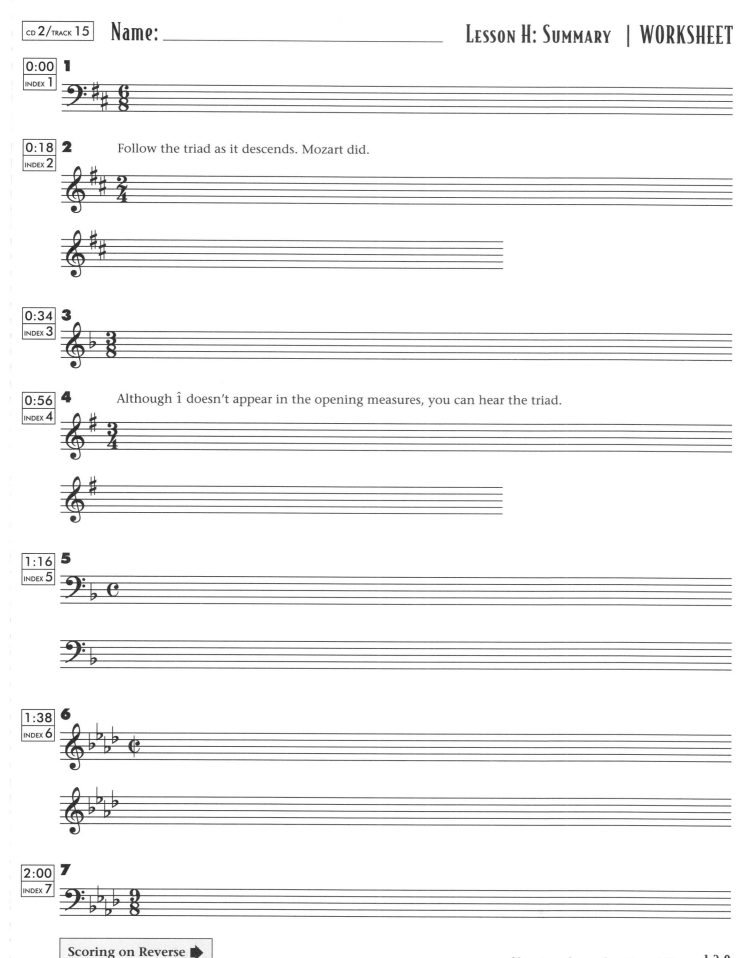

0:00 INDEX 1   **1**

0:18 INDEX 2   **2**   Follow the triad as it descends. Mozart did.

0:34 INDEX 3   **3**

0:56 INDEX 4   **4**   Although î doesn't appear in the opening measures, you can hear the triad.

1:16 INDEX 5   **5**

1:38 INDEX 6   **6**

2:00 INDEX 7   **7**

Scoring on Reverse ➡

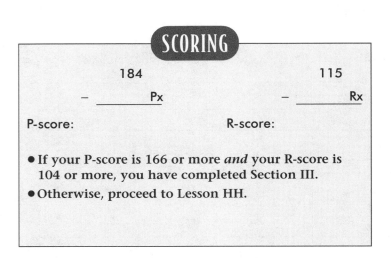

SCORING

184   115

− _____ Px   − _____ Rx

P-score: _____   R-score: _____

- If your P-score is 166 or more *and* your R-score is 104 or more, you have completed Section III.
- Otherwise, proceed to Lesson HH.

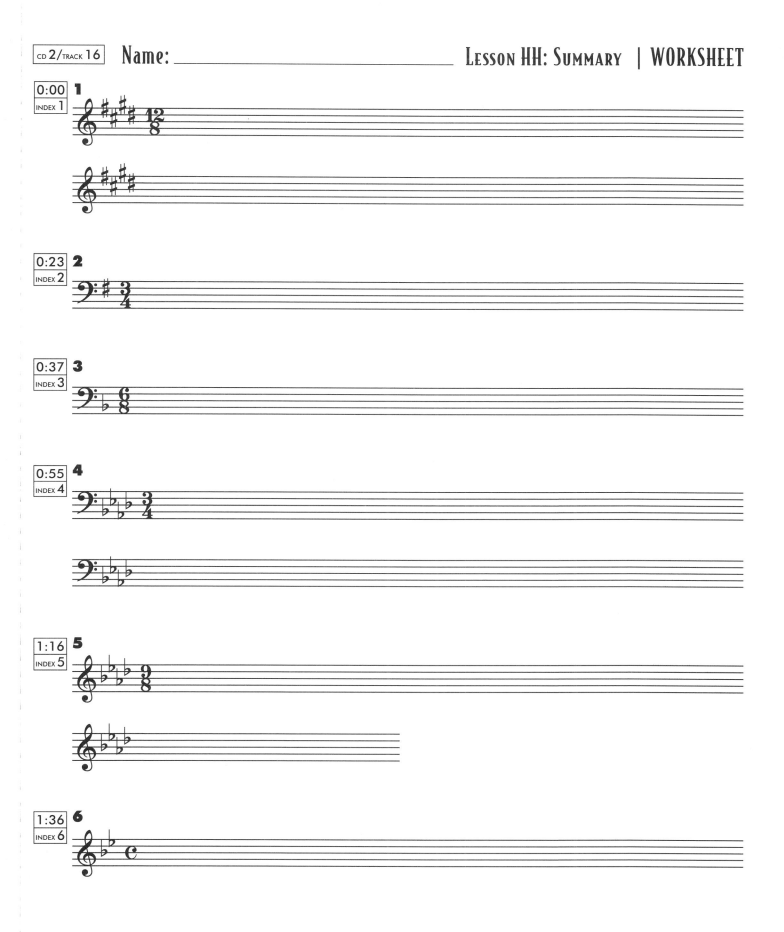

Hearing Differences 1

In this Short Drill you identify differences in pitch and rhythm. The melodies below represent one version; the melodies that you hear represent another. As each melody is played, listen for discrepancies between what you see on the printed page and what you hear. Use the staff that is provided below the printed melody to pinpoint the differences in pitch and rhythm. You may also choose to write the entire melody as you hear it. Mark differences in pitch with an x above the note in the printed version. Mark differences in rhythm with an x under the beat or beats in which the discrepancy occurs.

Tear the page up for Exercises 1–2 and down for Exercises 3–4 and compare your answers with the given answers. If you do not detect all the discrepancies in one hearing, listen to the exercises again until you are able to detect all of them.

Tear this page Up for Exercises 1–2. ⬆ Do not score your answers.

Tear this page Down for Exercises 3–4. ⬇ Do not score your answers.

Upbeats and Downbeats

Sing each melody and decide where the strong beats are. Do you hear an upbeat? Then add the bar lines. If any of your answers is incorrect, compare it carefully with the correct answer and sing the melody again.

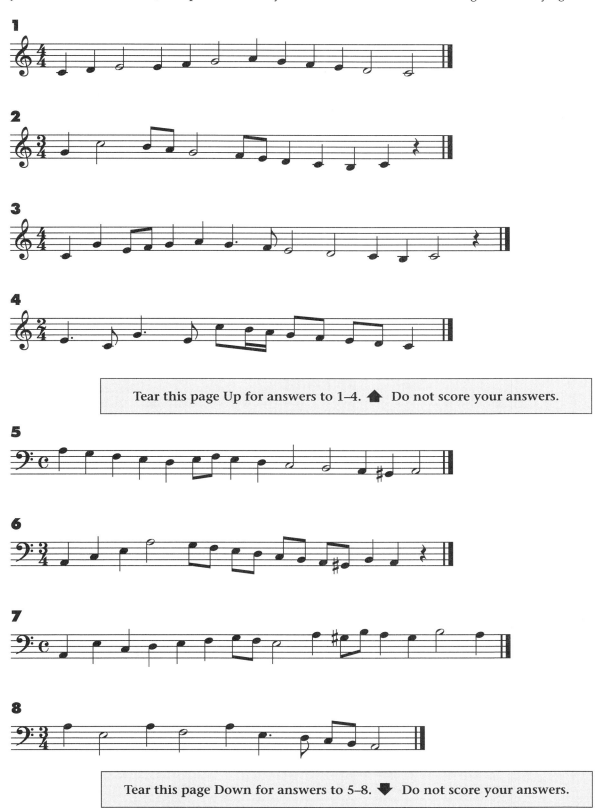

Tear this page Up for answers to 1–4. ⬆ Do not score your answers.

Tear this page Down for answers to 5–8. ⬇ Do not score your answers.

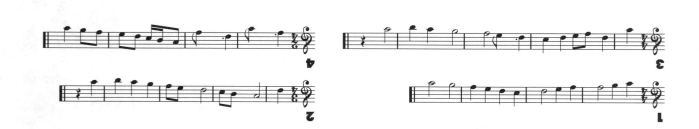

For this Short Drill follow the same procedure that you used for Short Drill 9. If you do not detect all the discrepancies in one hearing, listen to the exercises again until you are able to detect all of them.

Tear this page Up for Exercises 1–2. ⬆ **Do not score your answers.**

Tear this page Down for Exercises 3–4. ⬇ **Do not score your answers.**

Hearing Differences 3

For this short drill follow the same procedure that you used for Short Drill 10. If you do not detect all the discrepancies in one hearing, listen to the exercises again until you are able to detect all of them.

Tear this page Up for Exercises 1–2. ⬆ Do not score your answers.

Tear this page Down for Exercises 3–4. ⬇ Do not score your answers.

Name: _____

1

2

3

4

5

6

7

Scoring on Reverse ▶

Name: ______________________ **TEST WORKSHEET**

1

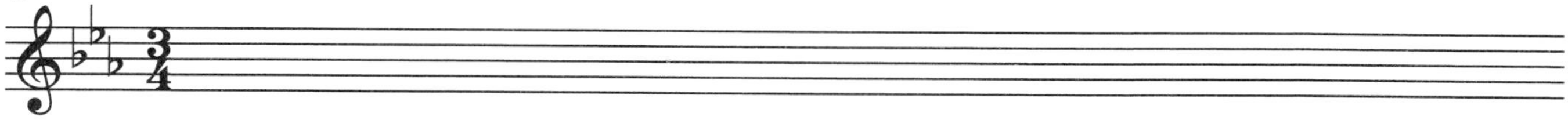

2

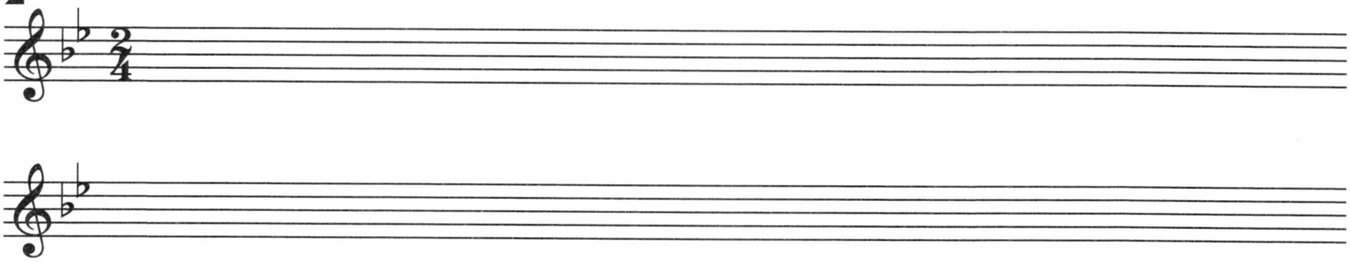

3

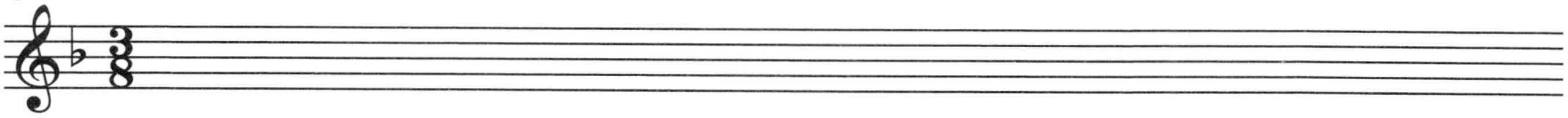

4

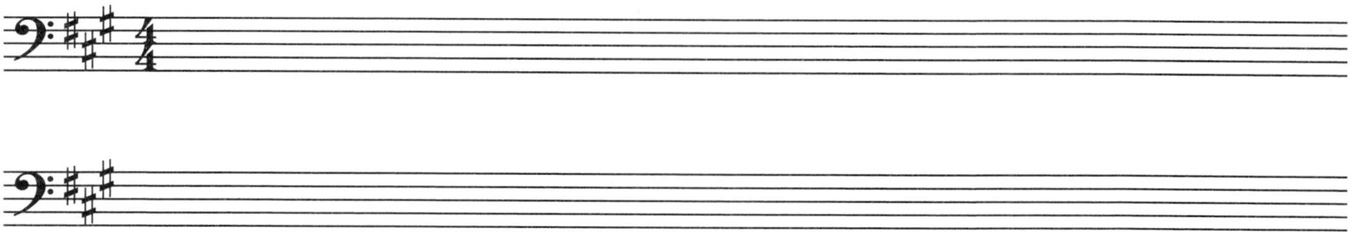

5

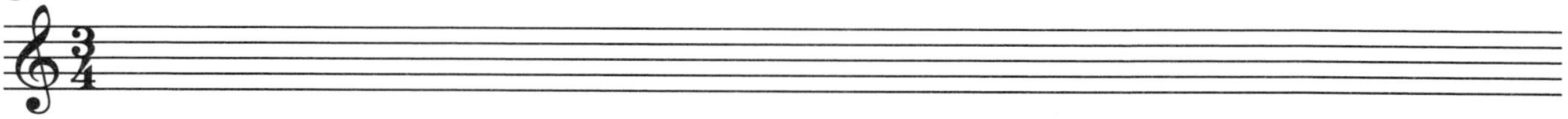

SCORING

241

– ________ (Total x)

Final Score:

Final Grade:

SECTION IV

STUDENT RECORD SHEET

- Circle the Lesson you are to do next: (A)
- After completing that Lesson, draw a line through the circle ~~(A)~~ and circle the Lesson the instructions tell you to do next: (B)
- Keep this sheet up to date. It is intended solely for your guidance.

A	AA
B	BB
C	CC
D	DD
E	EE
F	FF
G	GG
H	HH

Starting date ____________________

Completion date ________________

Keep this page in this book.

HOW TO STUDY SECTION IV

Many of the melodies of Section IV are longer and more complex than those of the previous sections. Nevertheless, the same approach—memorizing the melody and writing it from memory—is the best way to proceed. In doing so, you will improve on the skills you have developed in earlier sections.

In the two-phrase melodies, the antecedent usually ends on a scale degree other than $\hat{1}$, most often $\hat{2}$. The consequent often ends $\hat{3}$–$\hat{2}$–$\hat{1}$, which may be elaborated with N's or DN's. Remember to listen for repetition.

New pitch elements include chromatic passing tones, introduced in Lesson B, the ♭2 and large skips, in Lesson F, and chromatic melodies using eleven different pitches, in Lesson G.

New rhythm elements include ties, introduced in Lesson C, and additional upbeat patterns, introduced in several of the Lessons.

For those Lessons that appear on two pages, complete all exercises in the Lesson before scoring your answers. The answer to any exercise appears on the reverse of the page on which that exercise is found.

As in Section III, many of the melodies in this section are drawn from the standard repertory of classical music. You are beginning to make the transition from the classroom to the concert hall.

Starting in this Lesson, many melodies are longer in length. Listen for repetition; in the two-phrase melodies, the consequent will often repeat some of the opening material of the antecedent. Study this example of a long but simple melody by Haydn (tied notes will be introduced in Lesson D). Remember to make a picture of it in your mind as you memorize its sound. When you can sing the melody without looking at the page, proceed to the exercises.

0:00 | INDEX 1

0:21 | INDEX 2

1   Each six-measure phrase in Verdi's melody is made up of two short units, separated by rests.

0:54 | INDEX 3

2   The upbeat ♪♩ equals one beat.

1:23 | INDEX 4

3   This melody consists of two parallel phrases; listen for the different endings.

Lesson A continues on page 149. ➡

4

The repetition of the motive results in skips to chromatic incomplete neighbor notes.

5

6

Starting in this section, melodies contain five ♯'s or ♭'s.

SCORING

Reminder: Score rests as part of the R score, still scoring each *beat* that includes the rest. The ▬ is one beat in ¢, the 𝄾· is one beat in $\frac{3}{8}$, $\frac{6}{8}$, $\frac{9}{8}$, and $\frac{12}{8}$.

235   173

− _____ Px   − _____ Rx

P-score: R-score:

- If your P-score is 212 or more *and* your R-score is 156 or more, proceed to Lesson B.
- Otherwise, proceed to Lesson AA.

_____

You may turn at any time to Short Drill 13 (p. 189) for practice in speed hearing. ➤

9

5

4

Name: _____

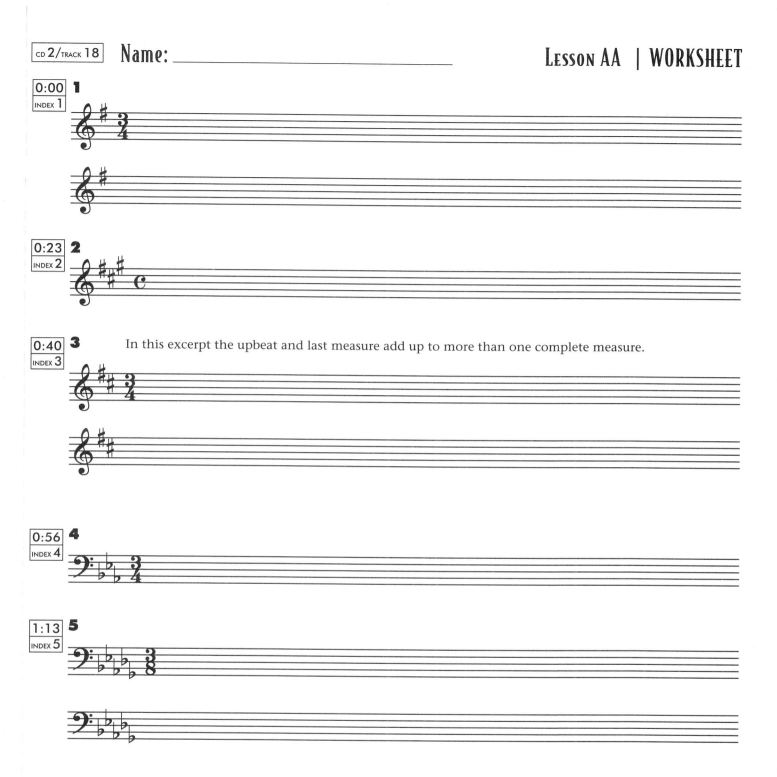

1 0:00 INDEX 1

2 0:23 INDEX 2

3 0:40 INDEX 3

In this excerpt the upbeat and last measure add up to more than one complete measure.

4 0:56 INDEX 4

5 1:13 INDEX 5

Scoring on Reverse ➡

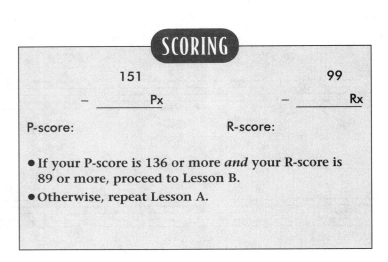

SCORING

151   99

— _____ Px   — _____ Rx

P-score: R-score:

- If your P-score is 136 or more *and* your R-score is 89 or more, proceed to Lesson B.
- Otherwise, repeat Lesson A.

A chromatic P divides a whole step into two half steps. Note the precautionary accidental in the following melody:

0:00
INDEX 1

0:11
INDEX 2

1 This melody includes chromatic P's, N's, and DN's.

0:29
INDEX 3

2 From this point on, melodies in simple meter may begin with an ♪ upbeat. In melodies with upbeats of less than one beat, score the upbeat *and* the last note or rest of the melody as if each were a full beat.

0:51
INDEX 4

3 The triplet in this melody takes up a quarter of a beat, fitting the space of an ♪.

1:07
INDEX 5

4 In ⁶⁄₈ meter the upbeat ♪ takes up one third of a beat.

Lesson B continues on page 155.

1:31 INDEX **6**   **5**   Rather than repeat part of the antecedent exactly, the consequent transposes it.

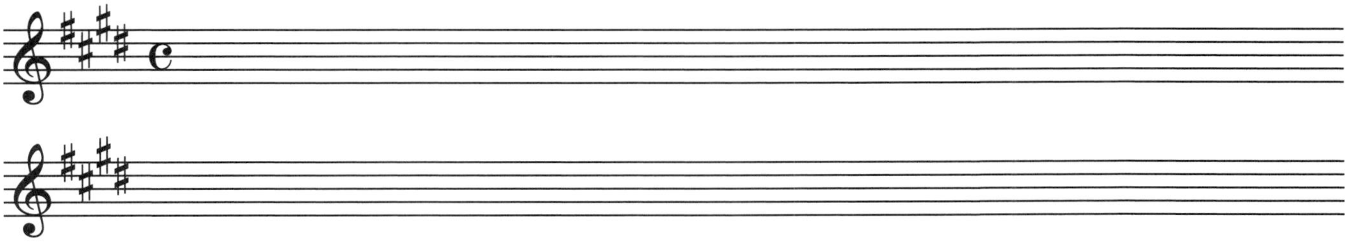

1:53 INDEX **7**   **6**

SCORING

204   144

— _____ Px   — _____ Rx

P-score: _____   R-score: _____

- If your P-score is 184 or more *and* your R-score is 130 or more, proceed to Lesson C.
- Otherwise, proceed to Lesson BB.

———————————

You may turn at any time to Short Drill 14 (p. 193) for further practice in chromatic P's, N's, and DN's.

➡

0:00 INDEX 1   **1**

0:15 INDEX 2   **2**

0:38 INDEX 3   **3**

0:55 INDEX 4   **4**

1:09 INDEX 5   **5**

Scoring on Reverse ➡

Name: _____

Many melodies are built on repetition of a motive. A short pattern is stated, then repeated higher or lower, unifying the melody. Listen for the repetition and determine how much higher or lower it is. Stretch your memory by singing the entire melody by heart.

1

2

3

4   Schumann's lovely melody uses inversion.

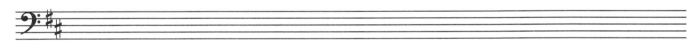

Lesson C continues on page 161. ➤

1:50
INDEX 6

5 In $\frac{3}{8}$ meter the upbeat ♪ takes up one third of a beat.

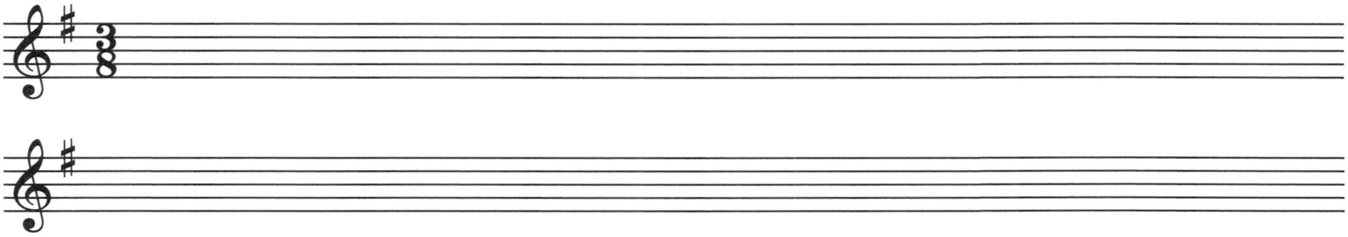

2:09
INDEX 7

6 Score the pitch of the grace note but not the rhythm.

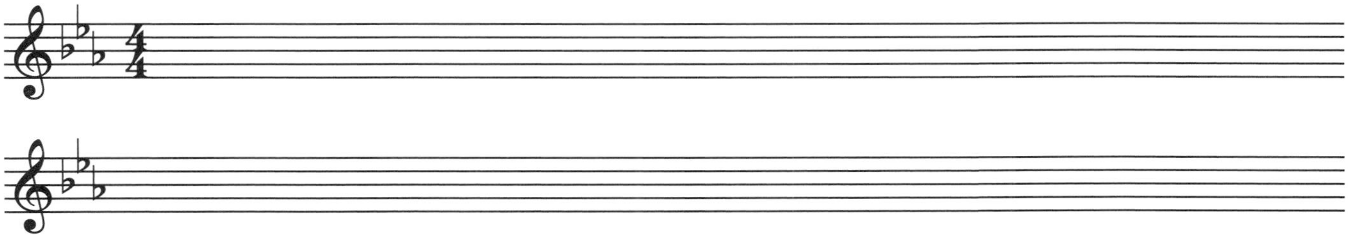

Scoring on Reverse ➡

SCORING

211
P-score:
— _____ Px

111
R-score:
— _____ Rx

- If your P-score is 190 or more *and your* R-score is 100 or more, proceed to Lesson D.
- Otherwise, proceed to Lesson CC.

0:00 **1**
INDEX 1

0:20 **2**
INDEX 2

0:37 **3**
INDEX 3

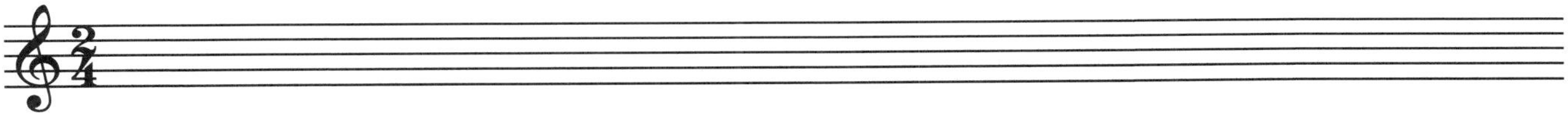

0:52 **4**
INDEX 4

1:14 **5**
INDEX 5

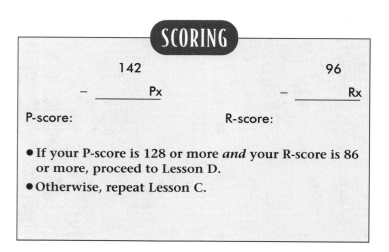

SCORING

142   96

— _____ Px   — _____ Rx

P-score: _____   R-score: _____

- If your P-score is 128 or more *and* your R-score is 86 or more, proceed to Lesson D.
- Otherwise, repeat Lesson C.

This Lesson introduces tied notes. Try to establish the beat with the first two notes in this demonstration melody.

Score tied notes as if there were no ties, in both pitch and rhythm.

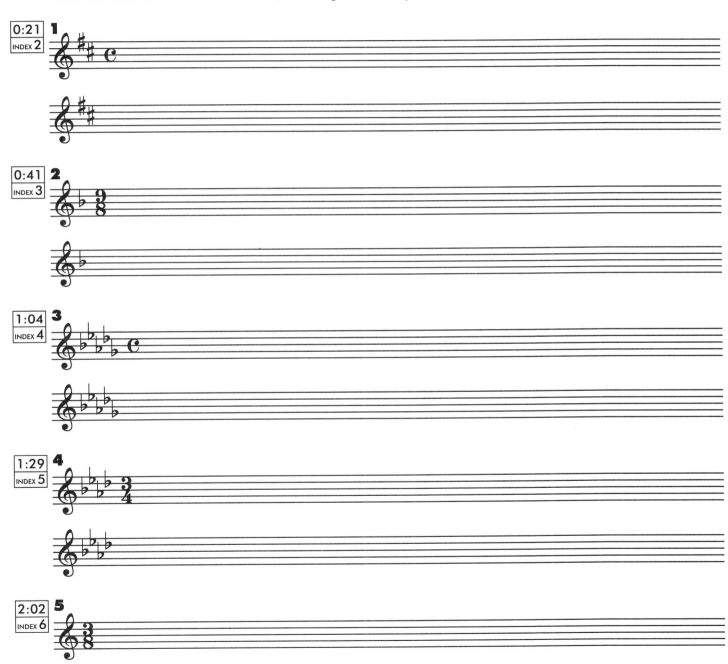

The triplets in this melody occur in the space of one beat in ¢ meter.

Scoring on Reverse ➡

SCORING

198   126

– _____ Px   – _____ Rx

P-score: _____   R-score: _____

- If your P-score is 148 or more *and* your R-score is 113 or more, proceed to Lesson E.
- Otherwise, proceed to Lesson DD.

Name: _____

0:00 INDEX 1 **1**

0:20 INDEX 2 **2**

0:40 INDEX 3 **3**

0:58 INDEX 4 **4**

1:25 INDEX 5 **5**

Scoring on Reverse ➡

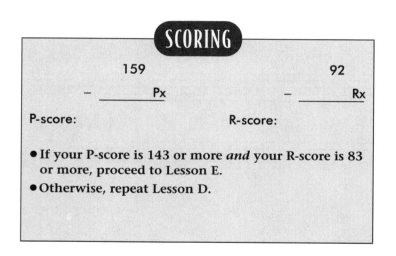

SCORING

159 92

− _____ Px − _____ Rx

P-score: R-score:

- If your P-score is 143 or more *and* your R-score is 83 or more, proceed to Lesson E.
- Otherwise, repeat Lesson D.

Listen to the way in which the consequent phrase, while certainly an answer to the antecedent, varies the idea.

1

2

3   Listen to the difference between tied eighth notes and tied triplets.

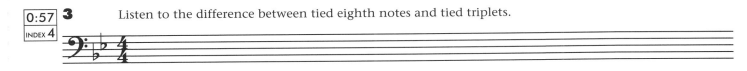

4   Introducing ♪♪♪♪ upbeats.

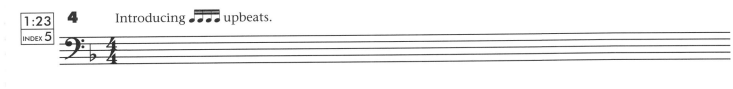

5   In ¢ meter the upbeat ♫ takes up one half of a beat.

6   Many slow movements in the classical style employ 3/8 meter.

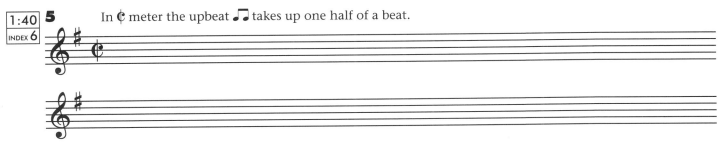

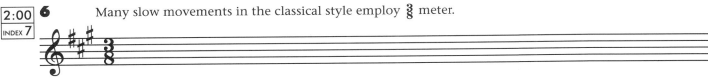

Scoring on Reverse ➡

SCORING

160   96

$-$ _____ Px $-$ _____ Rx

P-score: R-score:

- If your P-score is 144 or more *and* your R-score is 86 or more, proceed to Lesson F.
- Otherwise, proceed to Lesson EE.

CD 2/TRACK 26

Name: ______________________

0:00
INDEX 1

1

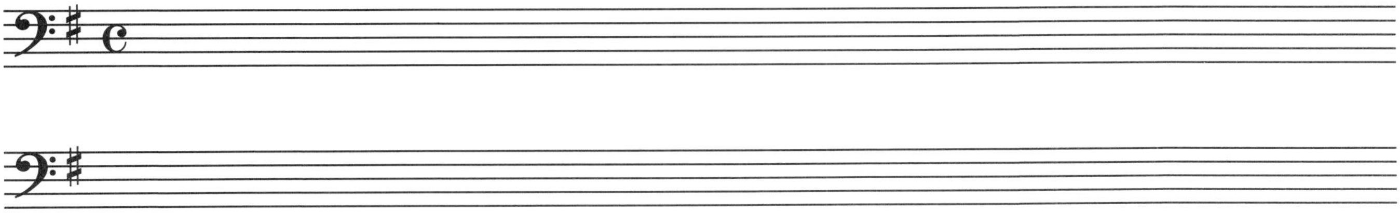

0:29
INDEX 2

2

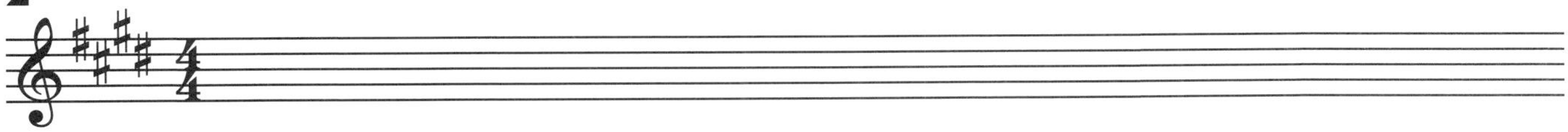

0:48
INDEX 3

3

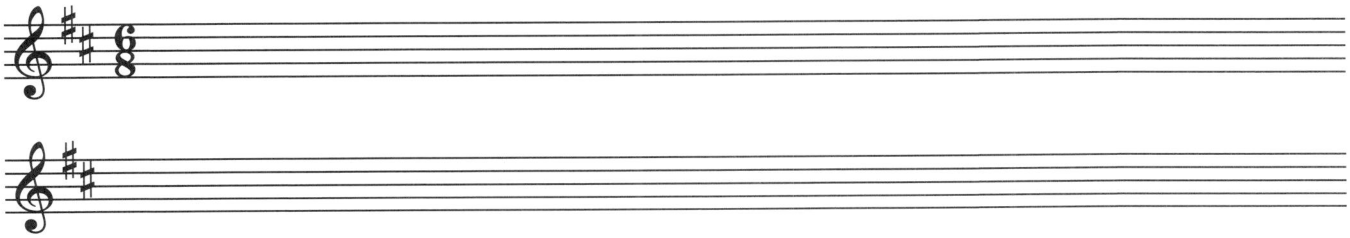

1:13
INDEX 4

4

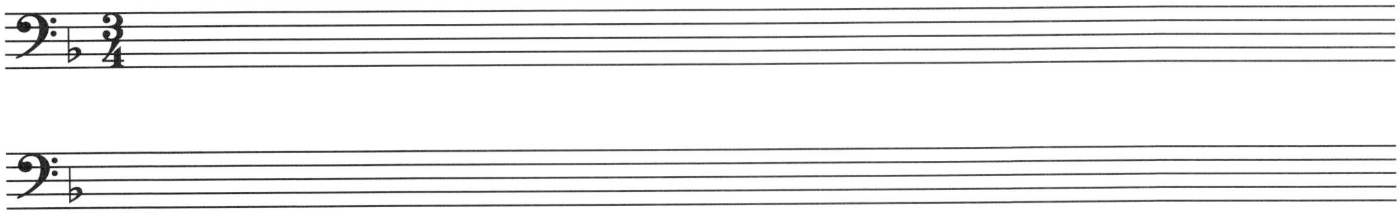

1:35
INDEX 5

5

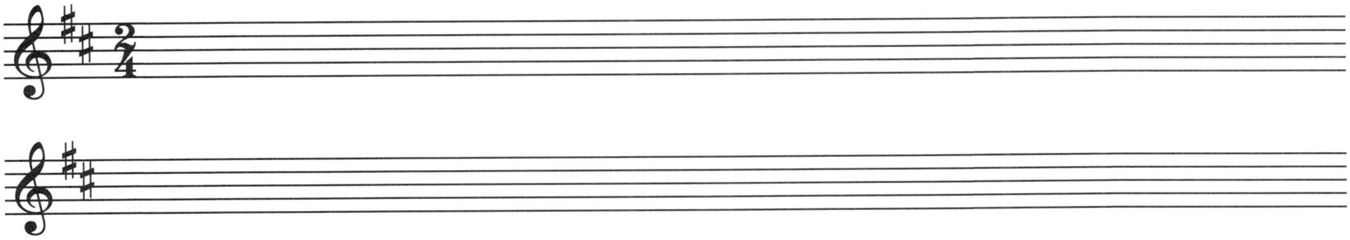

Scoring on Reverse ➡

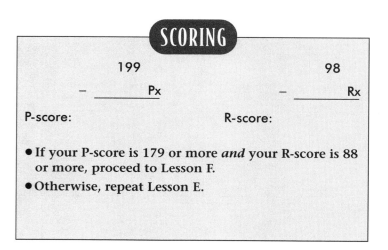

SCORING

199   98

− _____ Px   − _____ Rx

P-score: R-score:

- If your P-score is 179 or more *and* your R-score is 88 or more, proceed to Lesson F.
- Otherwise, repeat Lesson E.

This melody from Mozart's Requiem illustrates the use of both major and minor 7ths.

0:00 INDEX 1

1 This dramatic theme by Haydn includes a ♭2̂.

0:13 INDEX 2

2 Follow the descending line.

0:35 INDEX 3

3 The long-range harmony is i–III–V–i. For the double grace note, score pitch but not rhythm.

0:56 INDEX 4

4

1:27 INDEX 5

5 Although the motive changes with each repetition, it is still easy recognizable.

1:50 INDEX 6

6

2:15 INDEX 7

Scoring on Reverse ➡

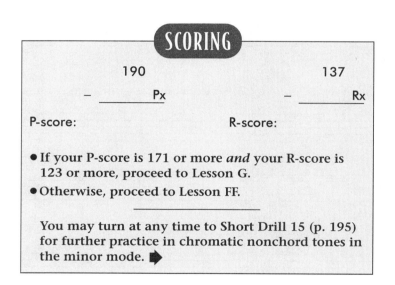

SCORING

190   137

$-$ _____ Px $-$ _____ Rx

P-score: R-score:

- If your P-score is 171 or more *and* your R-score is 123 or more, proceed to Lesson G.
- Otherwise, proceed to Lesson FF.

You may turn at any time to Short Drill 15 (p. 195) for further practice in chromatic nonchord tones in the minor mode. ➡

Name: _____   LESSON FF | WORKSHEET

0:00 **1**
INDEX 1

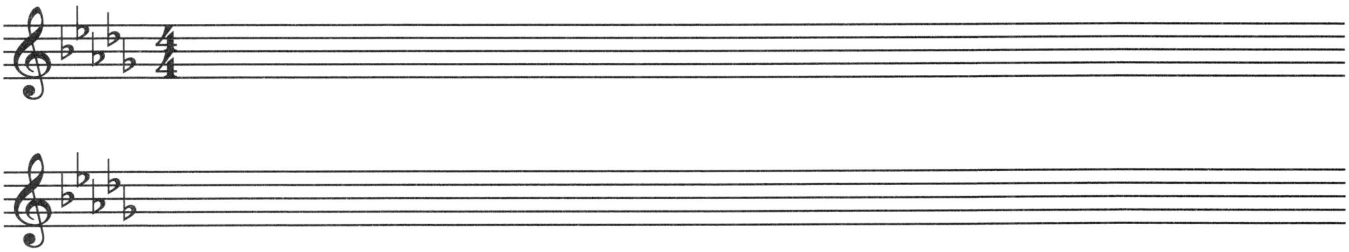

0:25 **2**
INDEX 2

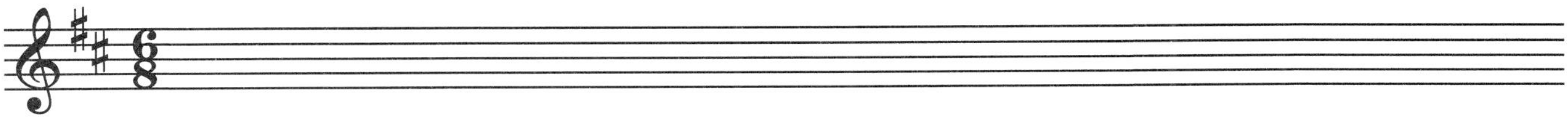

0:49 **3**
INDEX 3

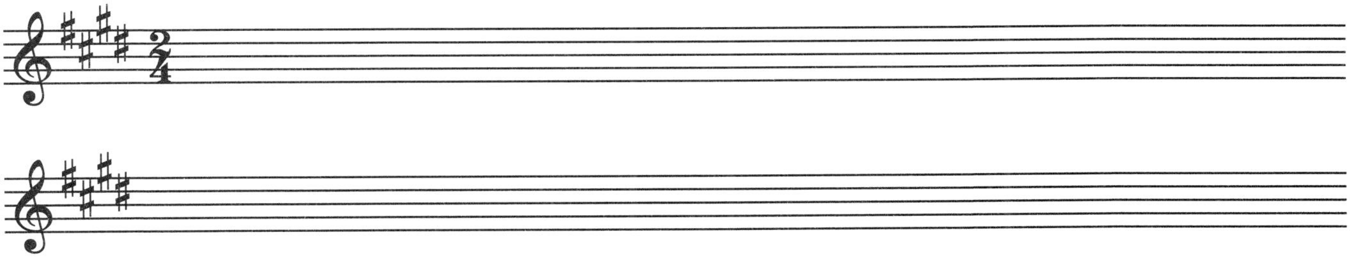

1:06 **4**
INDEX 4

1:27 **5**
INDEX 5

SCORING

209   108

– _____ Px   – _____ Rx

P-score: _____   R-score: _____

- If your P-score is 188 or more *and* your R-score is 97 or more, proceed to Lesson G.
- Otherwise, repeat Lesson F.

This demonstration melody includes eleven different notes.

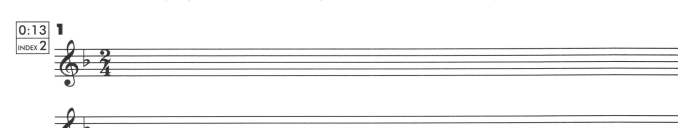

2 In this excerpt the upbeat and the last measure add up to more than one complete measure.

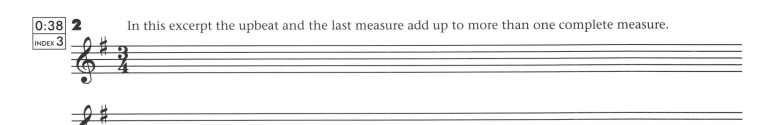

4 Wagner's meter sign is equivalent to ¢.

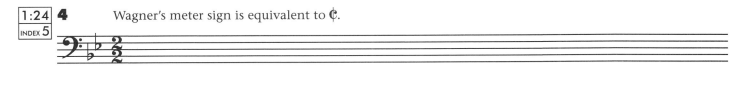

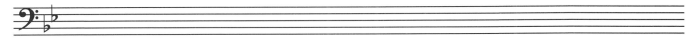

Lesson G continues on page 179. ➡

5   This fugue subject by Bach uses long note values.

1:48 INDEX 6

6

2:10 INDEX 7

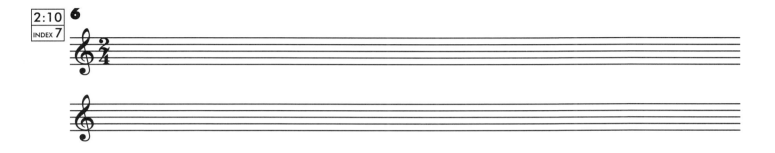

SCORING

213   119

− _____ Px   − _____ Rx

P-score: _____   R-score: _____

- If your P-score is 192 or more *and* your R-score is 107 or more, proceed to Lesson H.
- Otherwise, proceed to Lesson GG.

_____

You may turn at any time to Short Drill 16 (p. 199) for further practice in speed hearing melodies from music literature. ➡

1

0:00
INDEX 1

2

0:15
INDEX 2

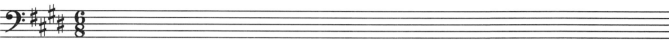

3

0:35
INDEX 3

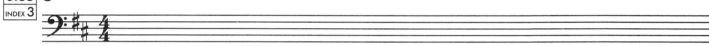

4

0:51
INDEX 4

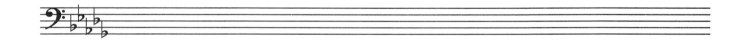

5

1:09
INDEX 5

Scoring on Reverse ➡

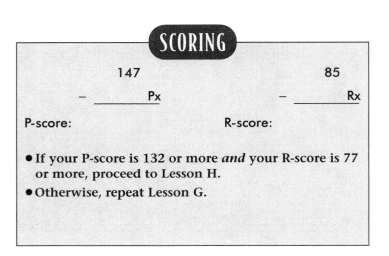

SCORING

147

85

− _____ Px

− _____ Rx

P-score: _____

R-score: _____

- If your P-score is 132 or more *and* your R-score is 77 or more, proceed to Lesson H.
- Otherwise, repeat Lesson G.

Listen to this two-phrase melody by Chopin as many times as you need to in order to memorize it. Try to learn it by listening, not by looking. To help you concentrate on listening, cover the melody or close your eyes.

0:00
INDEX **1**

0:34
INDEX **2**
1 $\frac{2}{4}$ meter is rarely used in slow movements, but this melody by Beethoven is an exception.

1:05
INDEX **3**
2

1:35
INDEX **4**
3

2:01
INDEX **5**
4

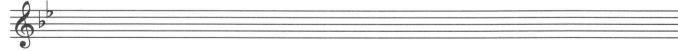

Lesson H continues on page 185. ➡

5

6

SCORING

261   127

− _____ Px   − _____ Rx

P-score: _____   R-score: _____

- If your P-score is 235 or more *and* your R-score is 114 or more, congratulations! You have completed Section IV.

- Otherwise, proceed to Lesson HH.

0:00 INDEX 1 **1**

0:24 INDEX 2 **2**

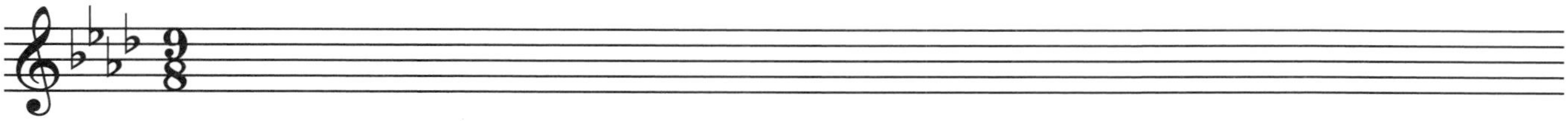

0:41 INDEX 3 **3**

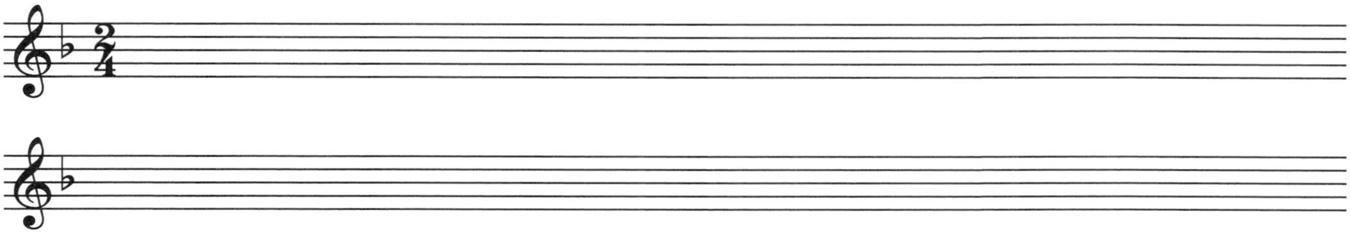

1:00 INDEX 4 **4**

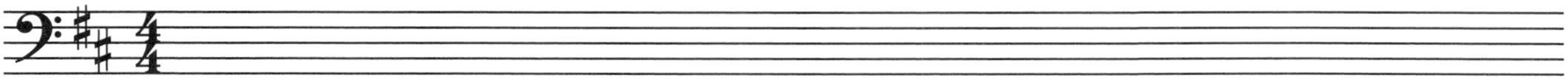

1:17 INDEX 5 **5**

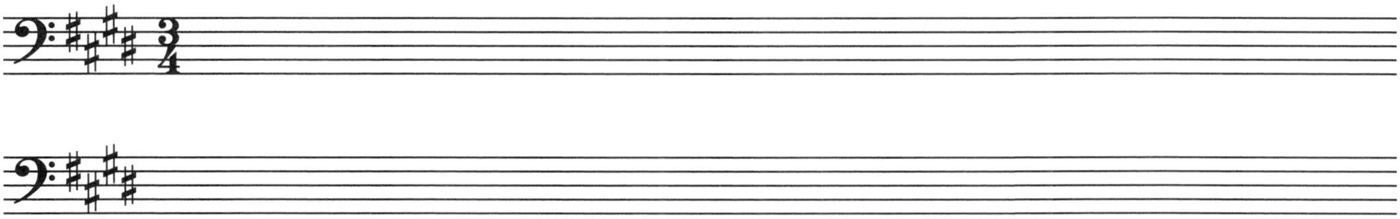

Scoring on Reverse ➡

CD 2/TRACK 36

Speed Hearing

0:00
INDEX 1

PART ONE

These short melodies in C major are played very fast. Try to hear and remember all the notes in a single hearing.

1

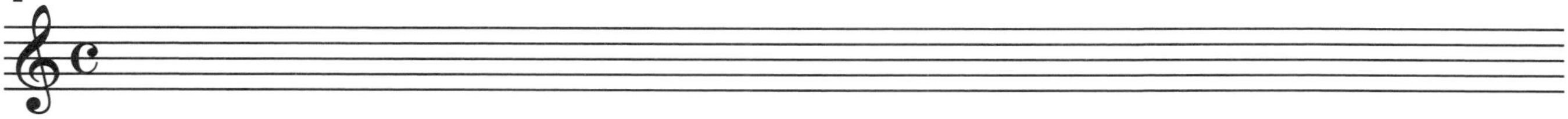

2

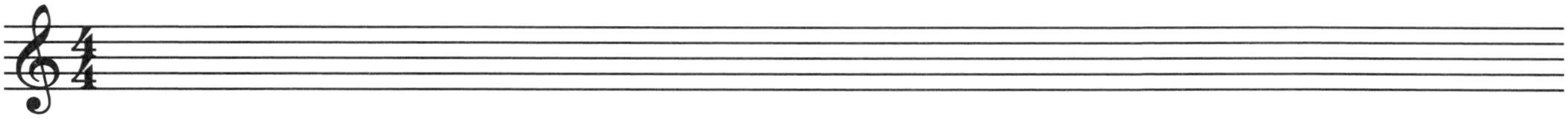

3

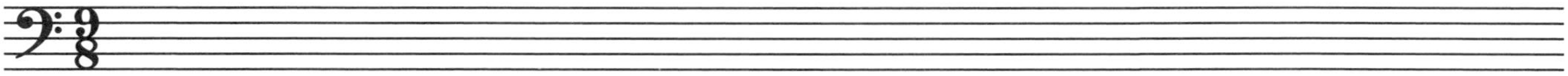

For the answers to 1–3, tear the page up from the bottom. ⬆ Do not score your answers.

4

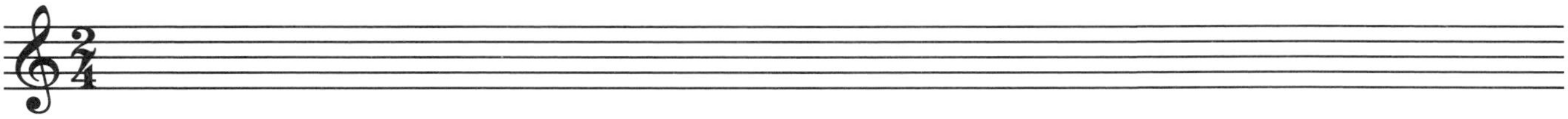

5

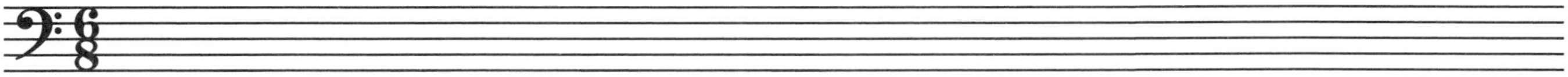

For the answers to 4–5, tear the page down from the top. ⬇ Do not score your answers.

Speed Hearing

| 0:48 |
| INDEX 2 | **PART TWO**

Follow the same procedure for these short melodies in C minor.

1

2

3

For the answers to 1–3, tear the page up from the bottom. ⬆ Do not score your answers.

4

5

For the answers to 4–5, tear the page down from the top. ⬇ Do not score your answers.

Chromatic P's, N's, and DN's

Each of these little melodies includes chromatic N's, P's, or DN's. Be aware of these elaborations as you listen. Try to identify each kind as you sing back and write the melody. Try to write each entire melody in a single hearing.

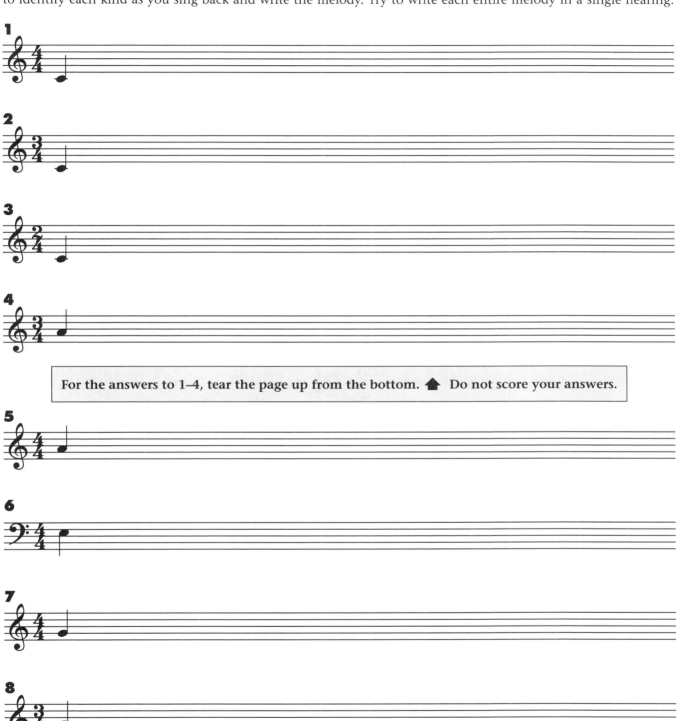

For the answers to 1–4, tear the page up from the bottom. ⬆ Do not score your answers.

For the answers to 5–8, tear the page down from the top. ⬇ Do not score your answers.

Chromatic Tones in the Minor Mode

0:00
INDEX 1 **PART ONE**

Focus on chromatic motion from $\hat{5}$ to $\hat{8}$ in the minor mode. Sing each short melody and write it as quickly as you can.

1

2

3

For the answers to 1–3, tear the page up from the bottom. ⬆ Do not score your answers.

4

5

6   This is the bass of an air by Purcell.

For the answers to 4–6, tear the page down from the top. ⬇ Do not score your answers.

Chromatic Tones in the Minor Mode

0:44
INDEX 1 **PART TWO**

Focus on chromatic motion from î to ŝ in the minor mode. Again, sing back and write quickly.

1

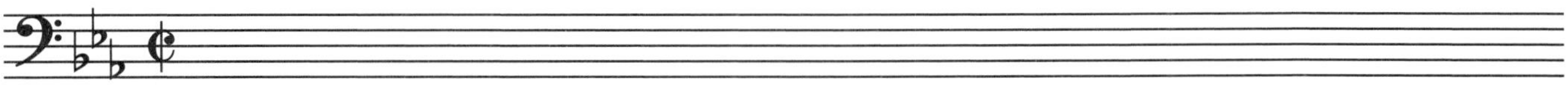

2

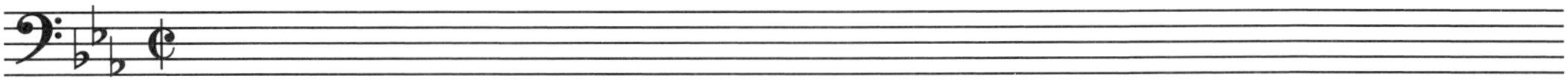

3

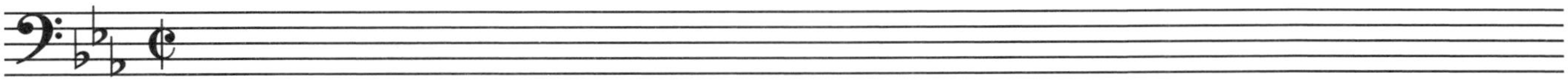

4

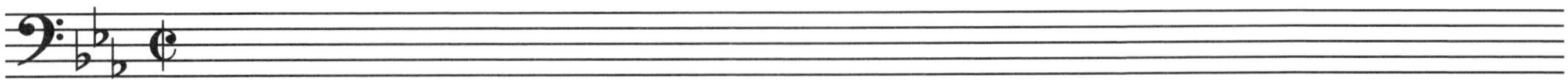

For the answers to 1–4, tear the page up from the bottom. ⬆ Do not score your answers.

5

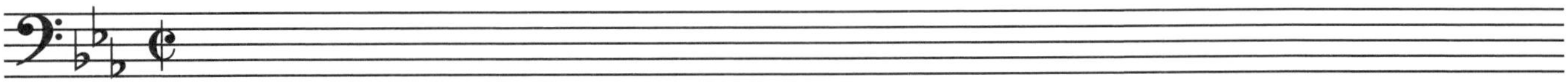

6

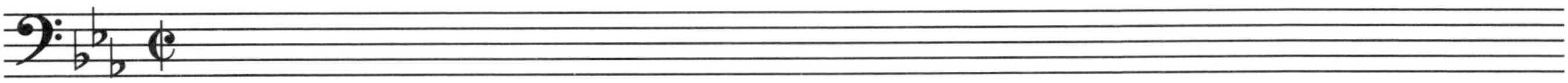

7

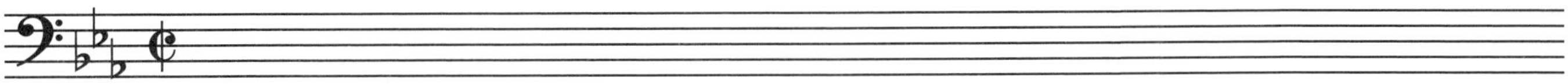

For the answers to 5–7, tear the page down from the top. ⬇ Do not score your answers.

Speed Hearing Music from the Literature

These melodies, taken from the standard repertory, are played at the tempo you would hear in concert or recorded performance. As always, the way to hear many notes quickly is to hear repeated patterns or to recognize the harmonic background. Listen to each melody once, sing it back, and then write it. Stretch your memory!

For the answers to 1–2, tear the page up from the bottom. ⬆ Do not score your answers.

For the answers to 3–4, tear the page down from the top. ⬇ Do not score your answers.

1

2

3

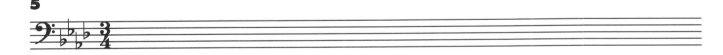

4

5

6

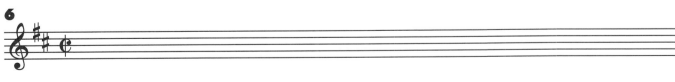

Name: _____

1

2

3

4

5

SCORING

243

− _____ (Total x)

Final Score: _____   Final Grade: [ ]

CHAPTER TWO

HARMONIC DICTATION

ABOUT THIS CHAPTER

Chapter Two consists of a series of Lessons in harmonic dictation, organized into four large sections. Section I includes nine single-letter Lessons, nine double-letter Lessons, a Review, and a Test; sections II, III, and IV each include eight single-letter Lessons, eight double-letter Lessons, a Review, and a Test. There are no Short Drills in this chapter (however, please note that the Short Drills for Chapter One, Sections I and II are found on CD 3).

Each single-letter Lesson starts with an Introduction that presents the essential harmonic features of that Lesson. Double-letter Lessons follow the same procedure as single-letter Lessons but do not include introductory material. You are reminded to review the introductory material for that Lesson, however, should you be required to complete the double-letter Lesson.

THE BIG PICTURE:
LISTEN TO THE LONG RANGE!

The aim of this chapter is to help you develop the ability to recognize quickly the important chord progressions of tonal music when you hear them. The exercises in Chapter Two begin with the simplest and shortest chord progressions, then move step by step to longer progressions, the kind of harmony that you find in the standard repertory of tonal music.

When you listen to people speaking you don't listen to one word at a time: you hear words in groups. Similarly, you can hear music in general and chord progressions in particular in coherent groups. This program shows you how to do that, starting with the shortest groups.

Hearing large-scale harmonic motion involves hearing chords in groups. How do we group the chords? According to their harmonic function. When learning to follow harmonic motion, we try to listen for the two most important functions in tonal music: the tonic and the dominant. Almost all tonal pieces begin with the statement of the tonic, move to the dominant, and close with a restatement of the tonic. The dominant is almost always preceded by some type of preparatory or pre-dominant chord. In this program we will outline the basic flow of tonal music using the abbreviations "**T**" for tonic, "**P**" for preparatory or pre-dominant chord, and "**D**" for dominant:

T P D T

It should be understood that **T** and **D** in some cases may represent individual chords and in others groups of chords. **P** is almost always represented by a single chord in this program. Hearing a group of chords as belonging to a single function is a way to develop long-range listening.

HOW TO STUDY THE LESSONS
IN CHAPTER TWO

Each Lesson in Chapter Two has an Introduction and a Worksheet. Answers and scoring instructions are on the back of the Worksheet. The Introduction presents the new material of the Lesson, using the same kinds of progressions that you will hear in the exercises on the Worksheet. Start each Lesson by studying the Introduction at a piano or other keyboard. This material is not heard on the CDs; rather, you should play through it as many times as you need to absorb it. The Lesson's Worksheet lists a new CD track number at the top of the page in the following notation: CD 3/TRACK 12. Each exercise within the Lesson starts at the time indicated in the box to the left of that exercise or at the new index number listed below the time.*

We suggest that you listen to each exercise no more than three times, and use one (or more) of the following three listening strategies:

- On the first hearing, write the roman numerals that identify the chords below the staff but *above* the gray band. On the second hearing, write the soprano and bass notes on the staff. On the third hearing, write **T**, **P**, or **D** *in* the gray band to indicate harmonic function, and complete the exercise.
- On the first hearing, write the harmonic functions. On the second hearing, write the soprano and bass. On the third hearing, fill in the inner voices and write the chord identifications.
- On the first hearing, write the soprano and bass on the staff. On the second hearing, write the inner voices. On the third hearing, write the chord identifications and harmonic functions below the staff.

Remember that each exercise will be played only three times in the Review and Test at the end of each section, so it's good to get into the habit of completing each exercise in three listenings from the beginning.

You proceed through the program in the following way:

1. Study the Introduction at the piano or another keyboard. Read the explanation carefully, then play each example slowly. As you play, listen for the bass line, the soprano line, and then for the inner voices; listen for the identity of the chords; listen for their function. For further practice, sing one part while playing the other three. Make sure that you have absorbed all the material of the Introduction before you proceed to the exercises.
2. Each exercise begins with the sounding of the tonic triad; in Sections I and II, the tonic triad is the first chord of the exercise, which is given on the Worksheet. As soon as you hear this triad, press the Pause button and sing it up and down: $\hat{1}$–$\hat{3}$–$\hat{5}$–$\hat{3}$–$\hat{1}$, or sing the scale of the key. This will orient you in the key of the exercise. Then listen carefully to the entire exercise before writing anything down. Concentrate specifically on the outer voices, the chord identities, or the harmonic functions. Then write all that you can remember before playing the exercise again.

3. To play the progression again, press the Rewind button on your CD player until the counter indicates the starting time of the exercise, or press the appropriate index number on your CD player. On the second and third hearings, complete the exercise, then go on to the next exercise and follow the same procedure.
4. Continue the exercises until the Worksheet is completed.
5. After the last exercise, mark your answers. For correct answers to Exercises 1–4, tear the Worksheet *up* from the bottom and fold along the dotted line. For the correct answers to the remaining exercises, tear *down* from the top and fold along the dashed line. Mark and score your answers according to the instructions given below.
6. Mark your Student Record Sheet accordingly, sign the Worksheet, remove it, and hand it in if your teacher requests it.

SCORING THE HARMONIC DICTATION

When you have completed a Lesson, fold the page according to the instruction given above. Compare your answers with the printed answers. Score the first exercise for pitch: mark an x *over* or *beside* any incorrect pitch. Score the roman numeral designations: mark an x *under* any incorrect or omitted number. Score the designations of harmonic function: mark an x *under* any **T**, **P**, or **D** that is incorrectly placed. Mark the remaining exercises in the same manner. (Suggestion: Use a colored pen or pencil to mark the x's. That will make it easier to find them when you tally your score at the end of the Lesson.)

When you have scored all the exercises in the Lesson, add all the x's in the Lesson together and write the total in the space provided on the reverse of the Worksheet. Subtract your total x's from the number given to determine your score.

If your total score is 90 percent or more you are directed to the next single-letter Lesson. Otherwise, you are directed to the double-letter Lesson at the same level.

Here are three illustrations of the scoring procedure:

1. The soprano in the third chord is F, not D. An x is marked over the incorrect soprano note. The roman-numeral identification is V^7, not V. An x is marked under the incorrect roman numeral, for a total of 2x.

Printed answer

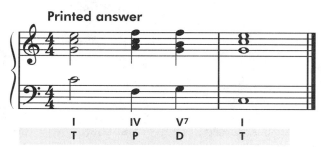

*Not all CD players accommodate index numbers. If yours does not, use the timings that are indicated to the left of the exercise.

Worksheet

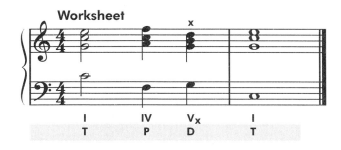

	I	IV	V x	I
	T	P	D	T

2. The second chord is ii⁶, not IV. An x is marked over the incorrect alto note (D, not C) and under the incorrect roman numeral designation, for a total of 2x.

Printed answer

	I	ii⁶	V	I
	T	P	D	T

Worksheet

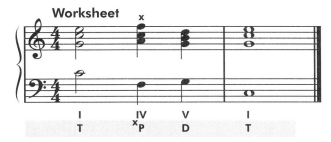

	I	IV	V	I
	T	P	D	T

3. The second chord is ii⁶, not ii. The next-to-last chord is V, not V⁷. And the **D** and **P** are both placed incorrectly. The total number of x's is 4.

Printed answer

	I	ii⁶	V	I
	T	P	D	T

Worksheet

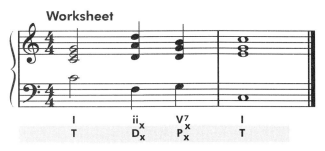

	I	ii	V⁷	I
	T	D	P	T

WHEN TO USE *CASPAR*

CASPAR offers four complete exercises at each of the levels in every section of Chapter Two. You may choose to do these exercises to improve your listening skills. Although the chord progressions in *CASPAR* are similar to those in this program, the different approach of the computer-based program may prove beneficial to you.

STUDENT RECORD SHEET

- Circle the Lesson you are to do next: (A)
- After completing that Lesson, draw a line through the circle (A) and circle the Lesson the instructions tell you to do next: (B)
- Keep this sheet up to date. It is intended solely for your guidance.

A	AA
B	BB
C	CC
D	DD
E	EE
F	FF
G	GG
H	HH
I	II

Starting date _____

Completion date _____

Keep this page in this book.

HOW TO STUDY SECTION I

Before starting Section I, be sure you have read carefully the introductory materials on pages 1–2 and 205–207. Study the Introduction to each Lesson carefully. We recommend that you do so at any convenient place where a piano or other keyboard is available. Play each example and listen to the voice leading as well as to the chords as a whole. After you have absorbed the Introduction, you are ready to undertake the Lessons.

Section I includes the diatonic chords heard most frequently. Many of them are in $\frac{5}{3}$ position; some are in $\frac{6}{3}$ position. Listening to the bass line will help you to determine the position of the triads. As you work through the Lessons in this section you may wish to consult the following diagram, which shows the diatonic triads built on each scale degree in both major and minor modes. Notice that for the V and VII chords in the minor mode two versions are given.

Triads built on scale degrees in the major mode

I   ii   iii   IV   V   vi   vii°

Triads built on scale degrees in the minor mode

i   ii°   III   iv   v   V   VI   VII   vii°

Listening and Remembering

The way to hear chords in groups is to relate the individual chords to the larger functions of tonic (**T**) and dominant (**D**). In this program these functions, as well as the preparatory or pre-dominant function (**P**), are introduced in Lesson C. Lessons A and B are preliminary Lessons in which you focus on hearing the difference between IV and V, in the progressions I–IV–I and I–V–I. These first two Lessons will also familiarize you with the way this program works.

The **T P D T** labels introduced in Lesson C will be an important part of the program from then on and will always appear in the Introductory examples. In Lessons C, D, and E, **T P D T** are expressed each as single chords; starting in Lesson F these harmonic functions may be expressed by two or more chords in succession.

Until Lesson G, **T** is always heard as I in major or i in minor. Lesson G introduces I6 as a tonic extension. **D** is always heard in this section as V or V7. The first **P** chords that you hear are IV and ii6 in major, iv and ii°6 in minor. Later, the vi chord (VI in minor) is heard first as **P**, in Lesson H, then in Lesson I as one that connects **T** with **P**. This illustrates an important point: the same chord may have different meanings in different contexts.

All exercises in each Lesson are written in meters that reinforce those introduced in the Lessons in Chapter One; do not score rhythm in this chapter, however.

Chord Textures

Two types of chord texture will be used in the exercises for this chapter: (1) piano texture, or close texture; and (2) SATB, or open texture. In the first, the three upper voices are written on the treble clef in close position so that their notes can be played easily with the right hand. The lowest voice is written on the bass clef. This texture resembles that used in accompaniments to many songs:

In the second, the two upper voices, the soprano and alto, are written in the treble clef, with note stems going up for the soprano and going down for the alto. The two lower voices, the tenor and bass, are written in the bass clef, with note stems going up for the tenor and going down for the bass:

To help you determine which of the two textures is used in a particular exercise, the tonic chord that sounds at the beginning of each exercise will employ the same texture as the exercise itself. Always listen carefully to the voicing of this tonic chord!

Scoring

1. Mark any incorrect or omitted pitch with an x *over* or *beside* the note.
2. Mark any incorrect roman numeral x *under* the symbol.
3. Mark any harmonic function that is not located correctly with an x *under* the designation.
4. Do not score rhythm or texture.
5. Enter the number of x's in the space on the reverse of the Worksheet marked "total x."
6. Subtract that number from the given number to obtain your score. Then follow the instruction on how to proceed.

If you do not reach a 90 percent level on a single-letter Lesson, you are directed to the double-letter Lesson. Before doing any double-letter Lesson, be sure to review the Introduction of that single-letter Lesson.

The first step in learning to hear chord progressions is to recognize the difference between two basic chords: IV and V. Lesson A focuses on that distinction. The only progressions you will hear will be I–IV–I and I–V–I in the major mode. Be sure to study the progressions in the Introduction at a keyboard before proceeding to the Worksheet. Play each example as many times as you wish, listening especially to the outer voices. Try to hear the soprano and bass notes at the same time. Be aware of the way in which the individual voices move. In this Lesson you will hear that the upper voices (soprano, alto, and tenor) either move by step or do not move at all, while the bass skips a perfect 4th or perfect 5th, always returning to the note on which it began.

Observe that there are two different textures in these exercises, as in all the Lessons in Chapter Two. You will find both close position, with three voices on the upper staff and one on the lower staff, and open position in the SATB format, with two voices on each staff.

You will see that the soprano sometimes has the root of the triad, sometimes the third, and sometimes the fifth.

Reminder: The first chord of the exercise, which appears on the Worksheet, is sounded one note at a time before the exercise begins. On the Worksheet write the notes that you hear and identify the chords. You can do this in any order. The notes and chord identification of the first chord are provided.

> ☛ **Tip:** Two of the three upper voices move in parallel 3rds, 6ths, or 10ths.

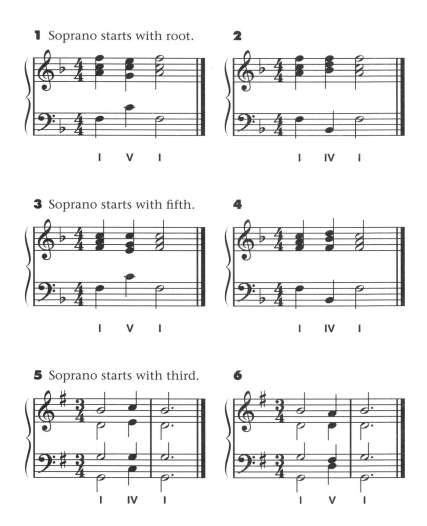

Name: _____

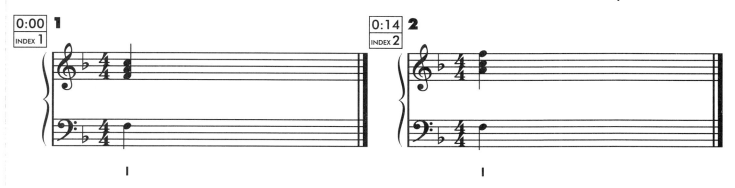

Mark any incorrect pitch with an **x**.
Mark any incorrect chord introduction with an **x**.

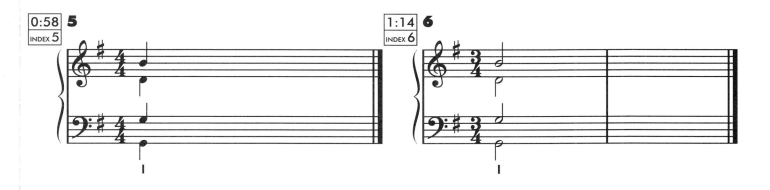

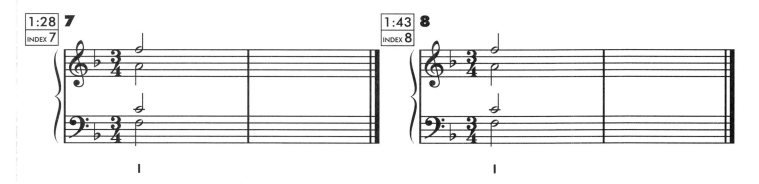

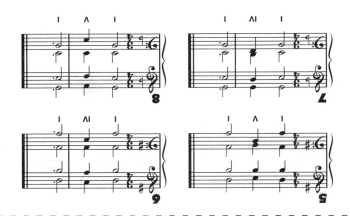

SCORING

80

− _____ Total x

Your Score: _____

- If your score is 72 or more, proceed to Lesson B.
- Otherwise, proceed to Lesson AA.

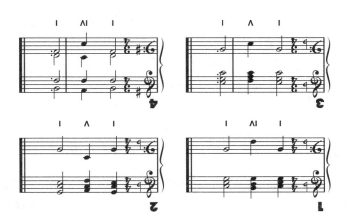

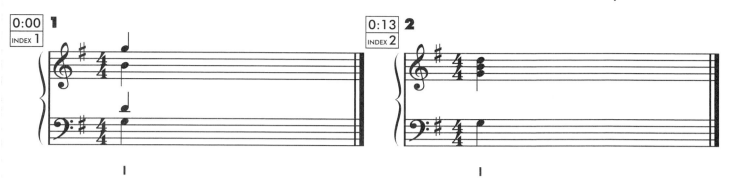

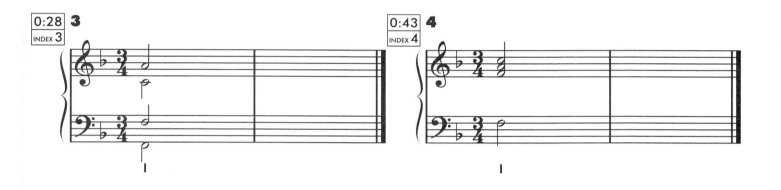

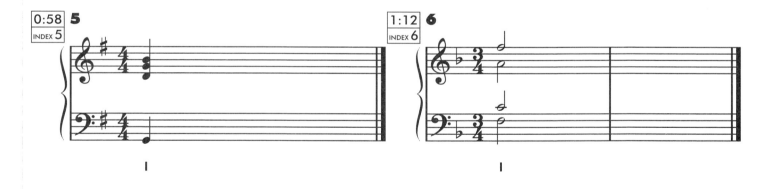

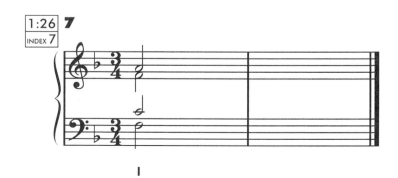

Scoring on Reverse ➡

SCORING

70

−　_____　Total x

Your Score:

- If your score is 63 or more, proceed to Lesson B.
- Otherwise, repeat Lesson A.

The progressions you heard in the major mode in Lesson A are played in the minor mode in this Lesson. For V, you will need to place one accidental before the leading note, to raise $\hat{7}$ of the diatonic scale. The accidental will be a ♯ in some keys and a ♮ in others.

> ☛ **Tip:** Again, all voices end with the same note that they started on.

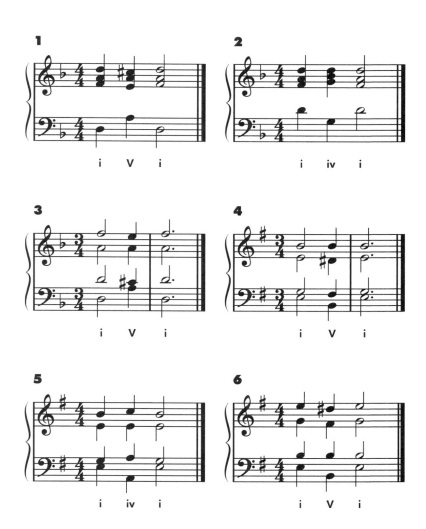

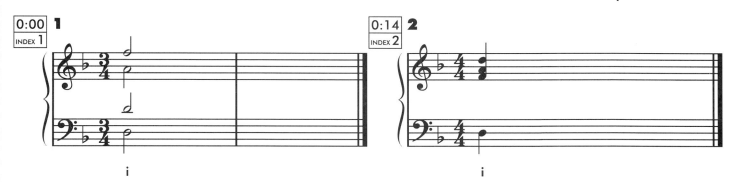

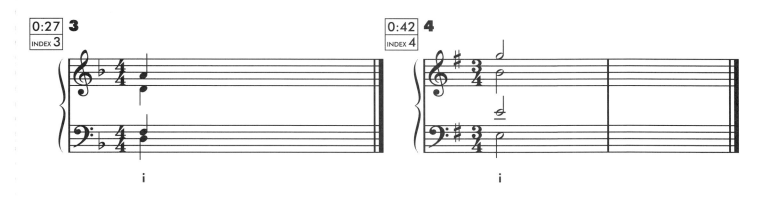

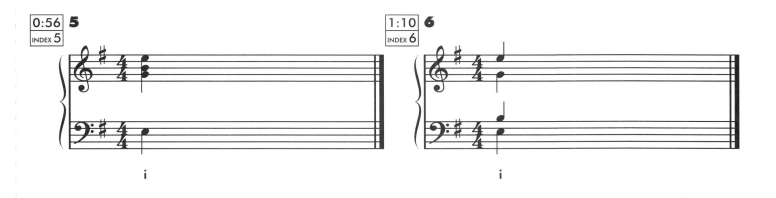

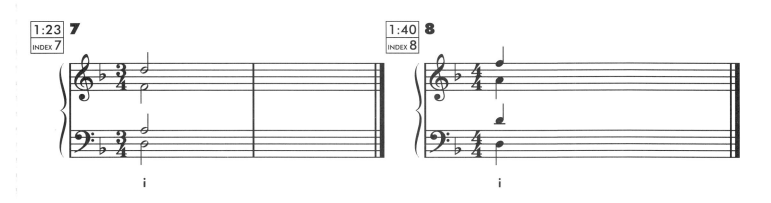

Scoring on Reverse ➡

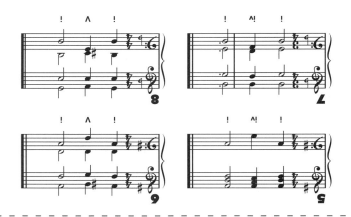

SCORING

80

− _____ Total x

Your Score:

- If your score is 72 or more, proceed to Lesson C.
- Otherwise, proceed to Lesson BB.

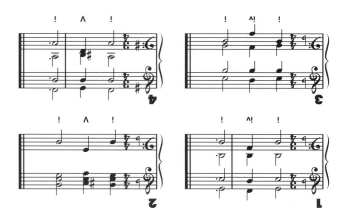

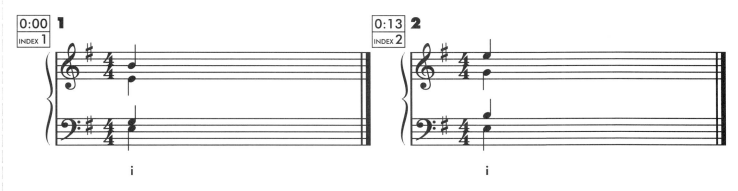

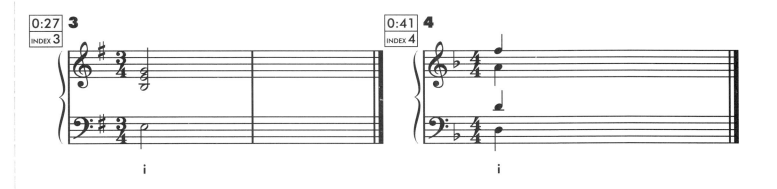

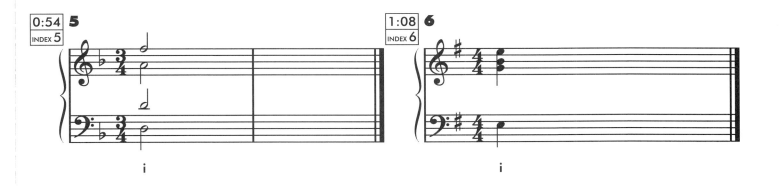

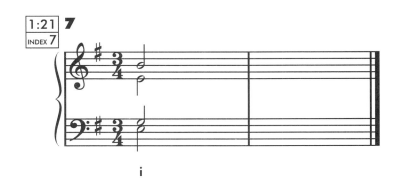

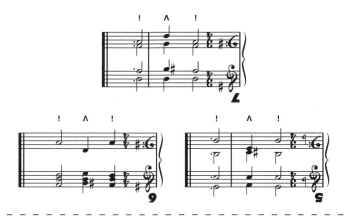

SCORING

70

− _____ Total x

Your Score: _____

- If your score is 63 or more, proceed to Lesson C.
- Otherwise, repeat Lesson B.

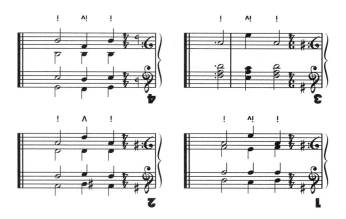

LESSON C | INTRODUCTION

This Lesson begins the focus on basic harmonic motion from tonic to dominant and back to tonic, in the major mode. Before the dominant, a preparatory chord is heard. In this program, the abbreviation for this motion is **T–P–D–T**. From this point on, this large view of the harmony appears in the introductory examples to the Lessons in the gray area below the staff.

In this Lesson, the motion **T–P–D–T** is heard in the major mode in two forms: I–IV–V–I and I–ii6–V–I. In Lessons D and E you learn to hear the difference between the two forms in both the major and minor modes. As you play the illustrations in this Introduction, listen for the difference between IV and ii6. Although the bass note, $\hat{4}$, is the same for both chords,

IV has a major sound and ii6 a minor sound. For further practice, sing one part in each illustration while playing the other three.

In some of these exercises the last note in the bass is an octave lower than the starting note.

On the Worksheet write the notes that you hear, identify the chords, and place **T P D T** correctly. You can do this in any order. The notes, chord identification, and chord function of the first chord are provided.

> ☞ **Tip:** Listen for the chord that is *not* in $\frac{5}{3}$ position.

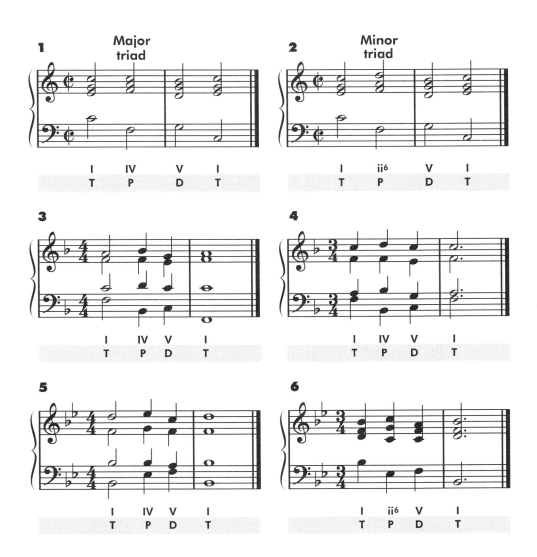

More on Reverse ➡

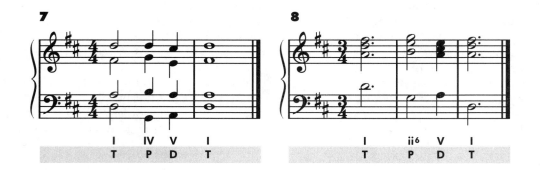

Mark any incorrect pitch with an **x**.
Mark any incorrect chord identification with an **x**.
Mark any incorrectly placed harmonic function with an **x**.

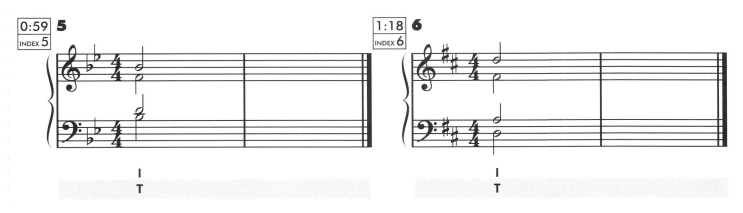

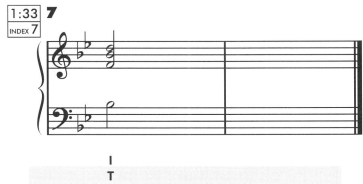

SCORING

126

− _____ Total x

Your Score: _____

- If your score is 113 or more, proceed to Lesson D.
- Otherwise, proceed to Lesson CC.

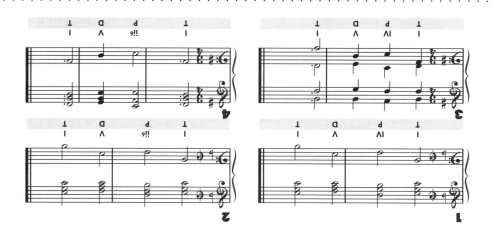

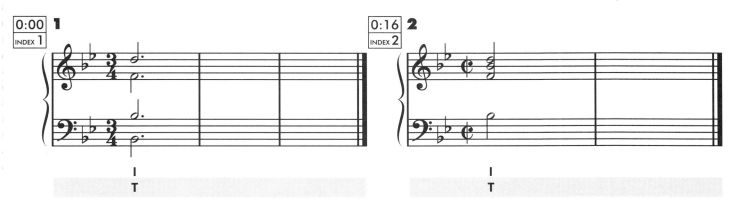

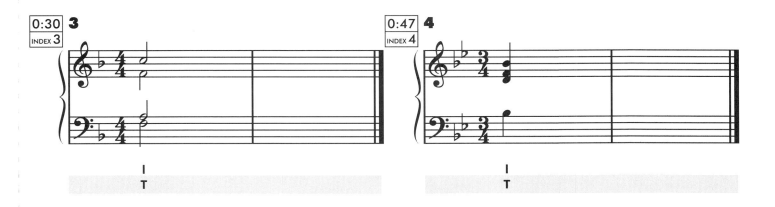

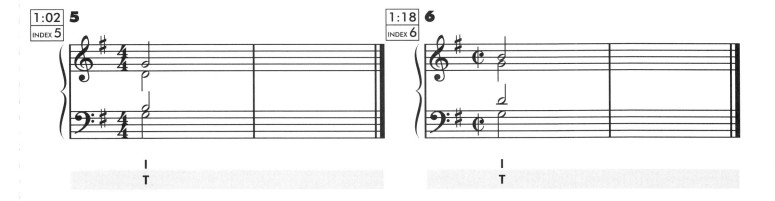

Scoring on Reverse ➡

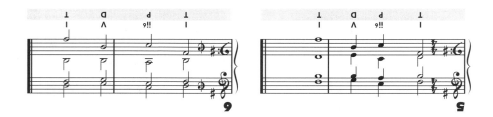

SCORING

108

− _____ Total x

Your Score: _____

- If your score is 97 or more, proceed to Lesson D.
- Otherwise, repeat Lesson C.

In this Lesson you study the same progressions as in Lesson C, but some are in the minor mode: i–iv–V–i and i–ii°⁶–V–i. You can tell from the given chord whether an exercise is in the major or the minor mode. In the minor mode, ii°⁶ is a diminished triad in $^6_3$ position. Remember that V is a major triad and must be spelled accordingly.

☞ **Tip:** The leading note may be heard in any of the three upper voices.

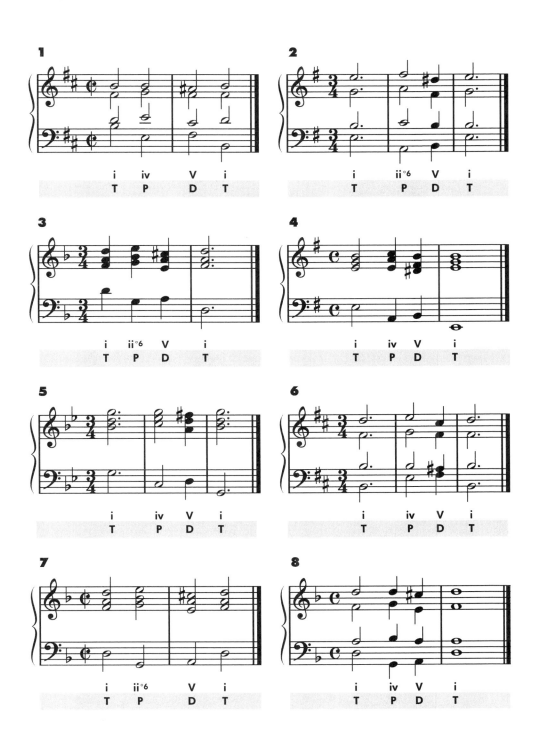

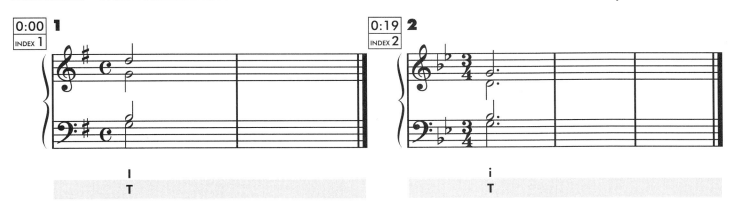

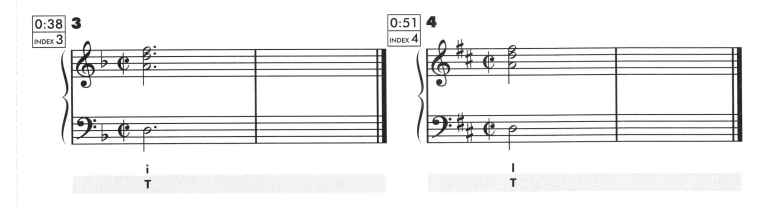

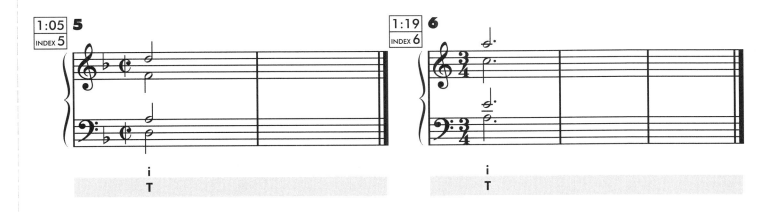

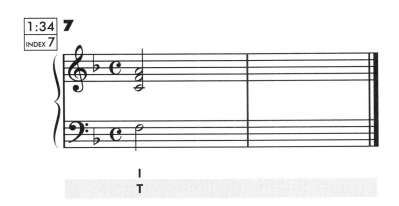

Scoring on Reverse ➡

SCORING

126

− _____ Total x

Your Score:

- **If your score is 113 or more, proceed to Lesson E.**
- **Otherwise, proceed to Lesson DD.**

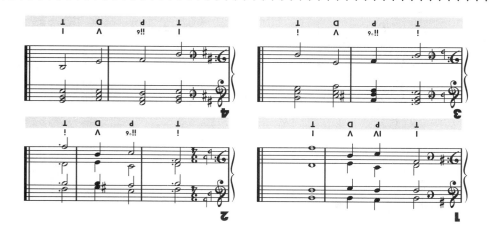

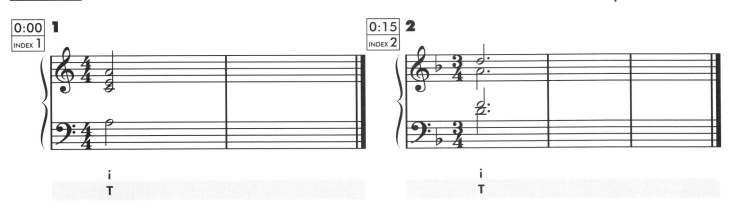

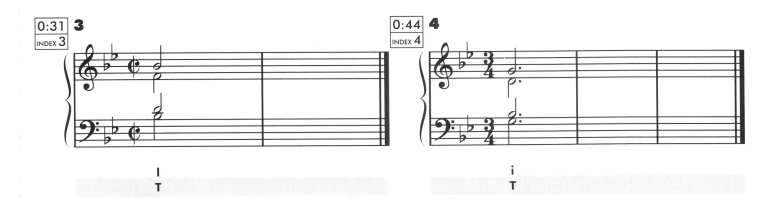

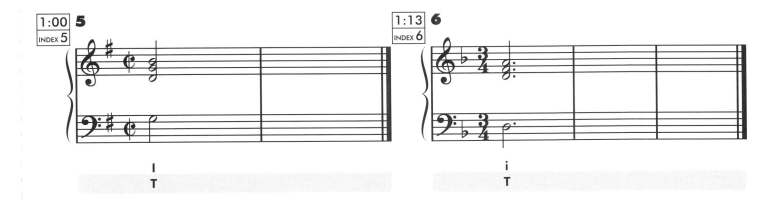

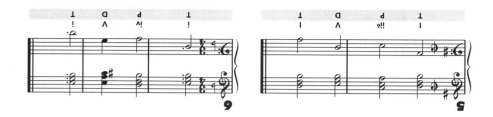

SCORING

108

— _____ Total x

Your Score:

- If your score is 97 or more, proceed to Lesson E.
- Otherwise, repeat Lesson D.

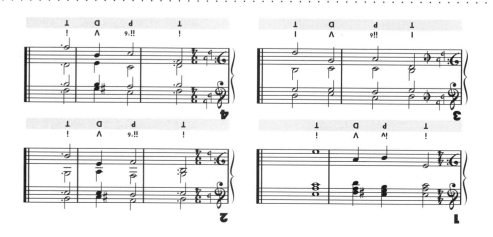

Lesson E | INTRODUCTION

In the standard repertory you hear dominant harmony most often as a V⁷ chord. Lesson E affords you practice in distinguishing between V and V⁷. Exercises are in both major and minor modes. V⁷ is the same chord in both modes. Since it is common practice in tonal music to omit the fifth of V⁷ and double the root, look for examples of that in the illustrations.

Exercises in the minor mode may end with a major tonic triad. When you hear that major triad, be sure to use an appropriate accidental for the third of the chord and I as the chord identification. This is the first of many types of modal mixture that you will encounter in this program.

> ☛ **Tip:** Listen for the downward resolution of the seventh in V⁷, from $\hat{4}$ to $\hat{3}$.

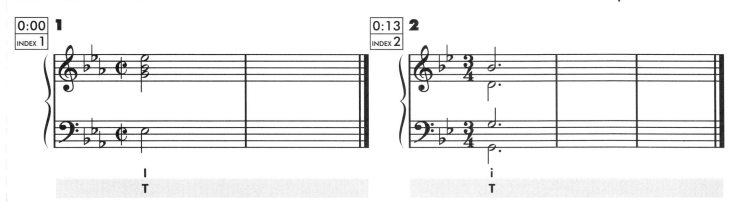

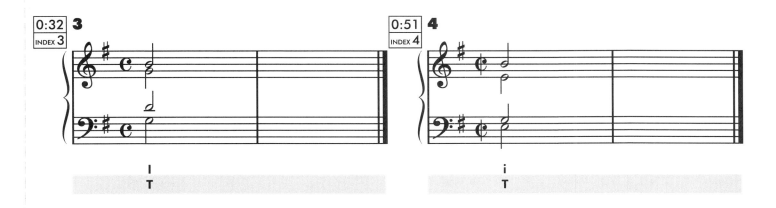

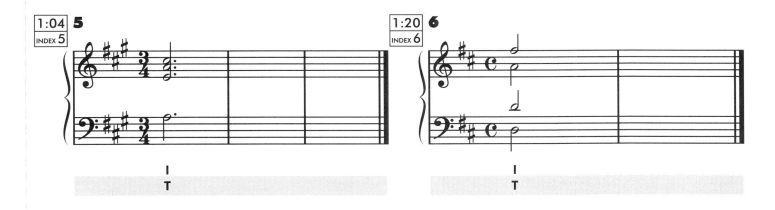

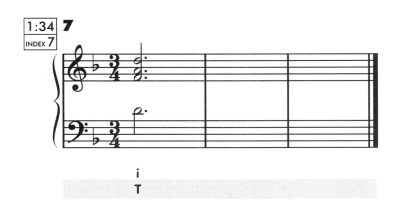

Scoring on Reverse ➡

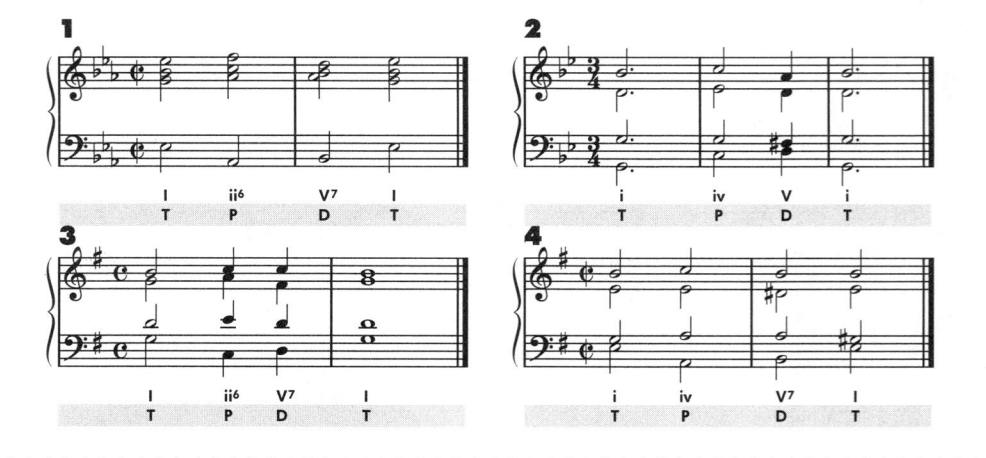

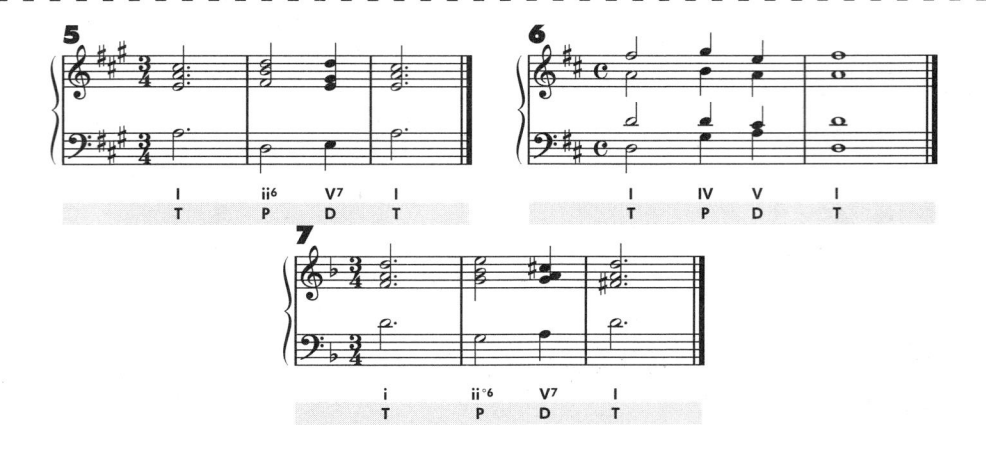

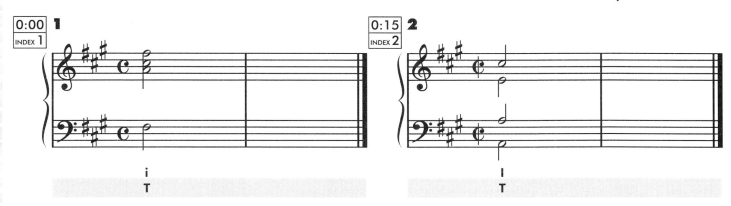

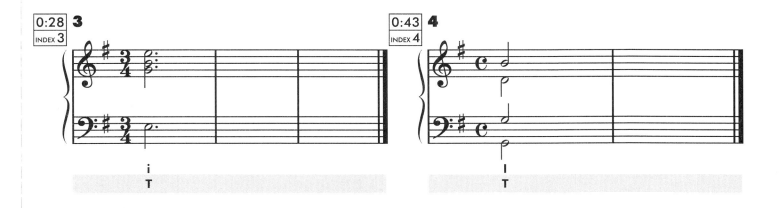

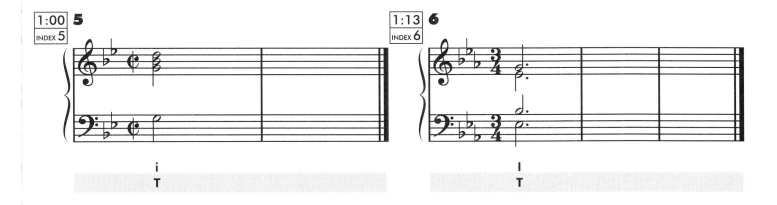

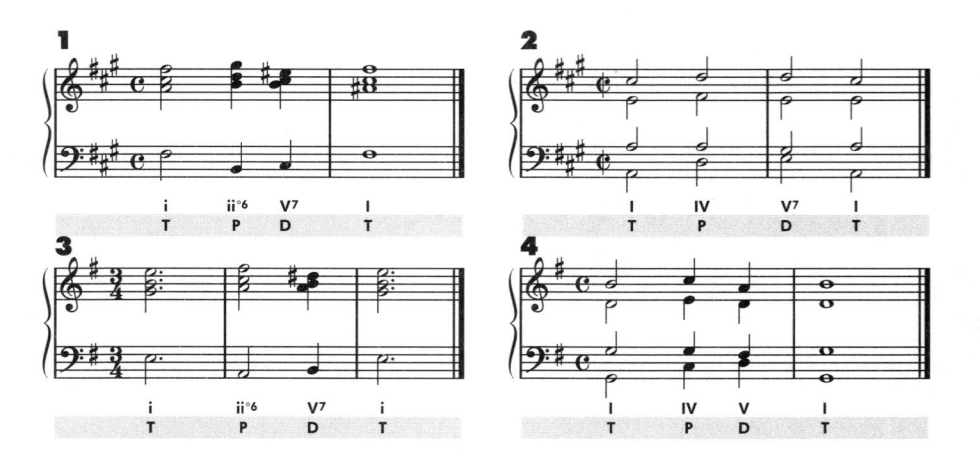

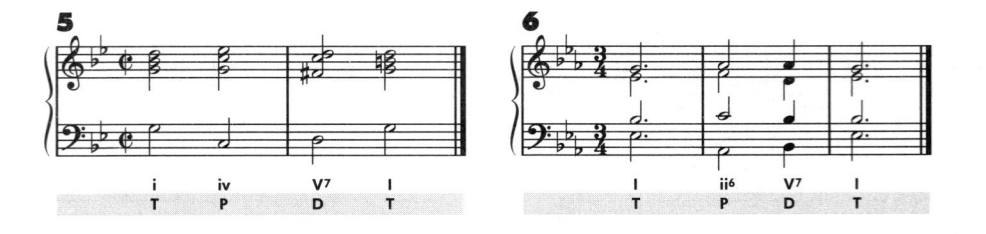

LESSON F | INTRODUCTION

Up to this point you have heard only one chord expressing a harmonic function. In Lesson F you will study a way to hear two or more chords as a group. This begins the kind of listening that leads away from hearing chords one at a time and moves you toward long-range hearing.

The exercises in this Lesson include five chords. No new chords are introduced, but the chords that you have already heard are used in larger combinations. Some of the progressions do not include a **P** chord.

Starting with this Lesson, tonic and dominant functions may include groups of two or three chords. The easiest way to extend **T** or **D** is to repeat the chord. In the simplest extension found in this Lesson the chord repetition occurs over an octave skip in the bass. The position of the upper three voices may change with the octave skip, but the notes of the chord remain the same. The beginnings of Examples 1, 4, and 5 show this.

Another extension of tonic harmony uses IV as a neighbor chord. Example 2 ends with such an extension of tonic harmony, but this can occur at the beginning of a progression, as in Example 3. Since you have previously heard IV (and iv) as a preparatory chord, you can understand that the same chord can have a different function depending on the context. Find the neighbor notes in the upper voices of the IV chord and observe how the bass skips to support these voices. In these two illustrations IV (or iv) is not a dominant preparation but a neighbor chord elaborating I.

You will also find a simple elaboration of the bass line: an octave skip up or down, as at the end of Example 1. These notes should be scored in the same way that you score other pitches.

Dominant harmony may also be extended: In this Lesson two chords, V and V7, are heard as a group, as in Example 6.

On the Worksheet, show the extensions of harmonic function by drawing a straight line under the roman numerals that are grouped together, and place the function symbol underneath the first chord of the group, as in the illustrations below.

When scoring extensions of harmonic functions, mark x if the function symbol is not correctly placed beneath the first chord of the extension. In addition, the line that indicates a harmonic extension must appear under all the chords included in the extension. Mark x (1) if the line does not appear; (2) if it does not include all the chords in the extension; or (3) if it includes chords that are not in the extension. Also, mark x if you have drawn a line where there is no extension. Use the examples in the illustrations as your models.

☞ **Tip:** In the tonic extension of I–IV–I or i–iv–i, listen for two neighbor notes in the upper voices.

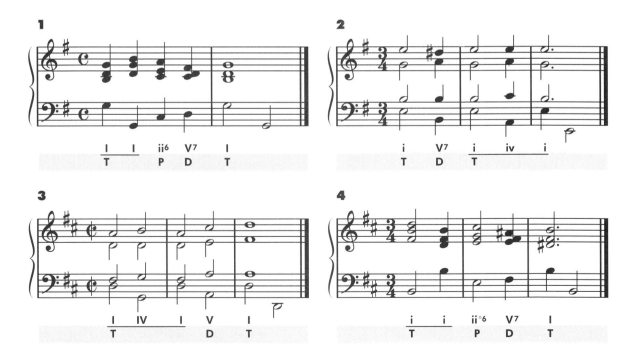

More on Reverse ➡

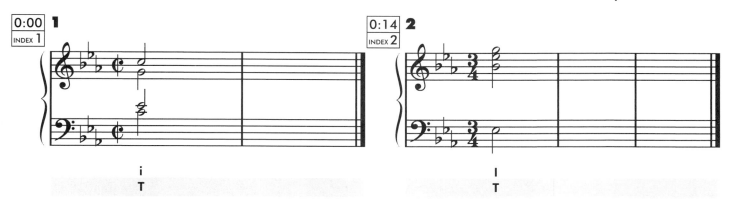

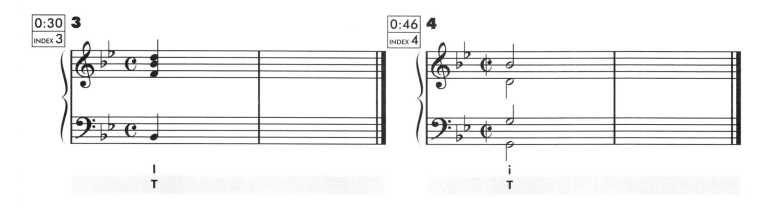

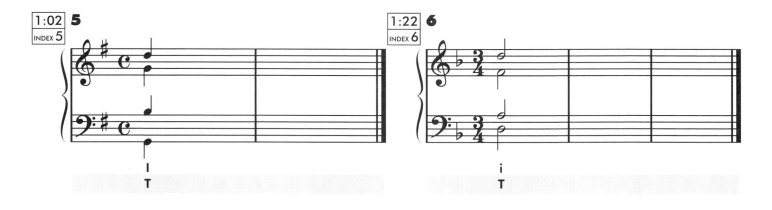

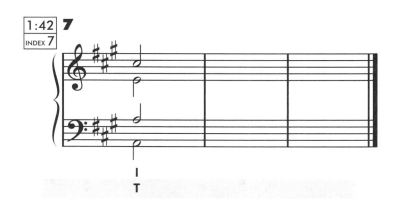

SCORING

168

− _____ Total x

Your Score:

• **If your score is 151 or more, proceed to Lesson G.**
• **Otherwise, proceed to Lesson FF.**

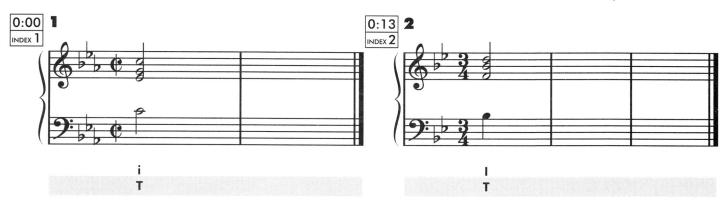

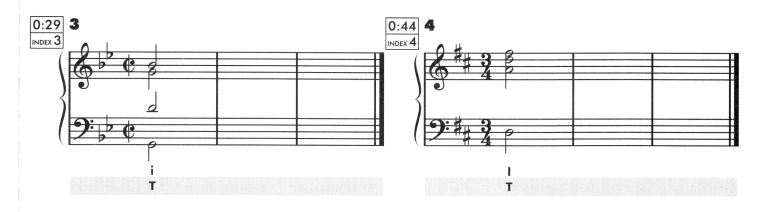

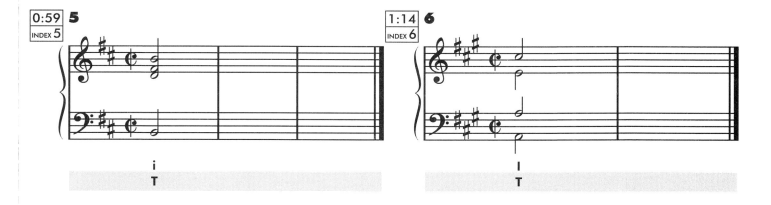

Scoring on Reverse ➡

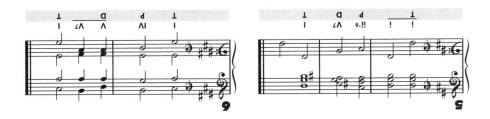

SCORING

146

− _____ Total x

Your Score: _____

- If your score is 131 or more, proceed to Lesson G.
- Otherwise, repeat Lesson F.

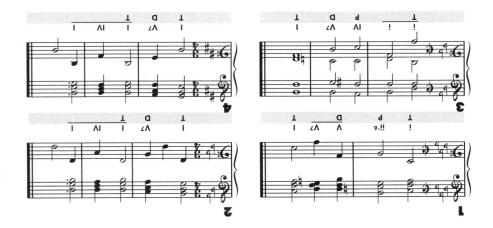

Tonic harmony may be extended to include I–I⁶. In the motion from I to I⁶, the bass rises a 3rd or falls a 6th. Look quickly at the beginning of the illustrations and observe the direction of the bass motion. For such extensions, draw a line under the chord group and mark the harmonic function under the first roman numeral identification.

Remember to score the octave-skip elaboration of the bass line in the same way that you score other pitches.

> **☞ Tip:** Remember that I and I⁶ have the same notes, so that the move from one to the other simply rearranges the same triad. The bass leads the way.

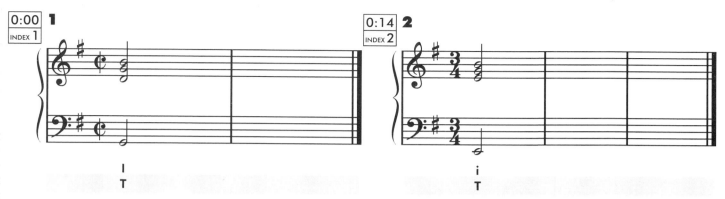

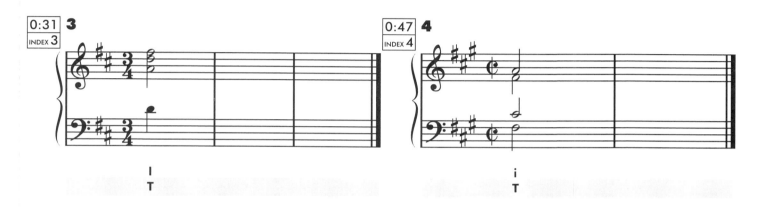

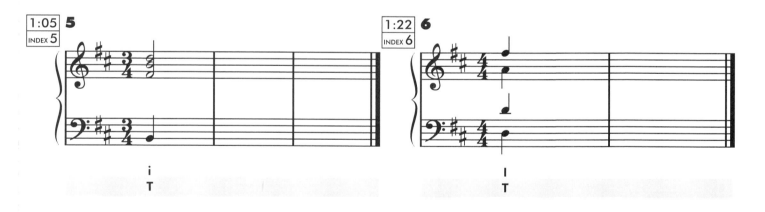

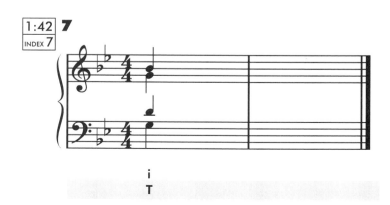

Scoring on Reverse ➡

SCORING

175

− _____ Total x

Your Score: _____

- If your score is 158 or more, proceed to Lesson H.
- Otherwise, proceed to Lesson GG.

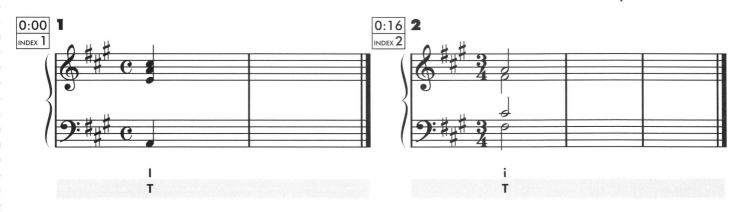

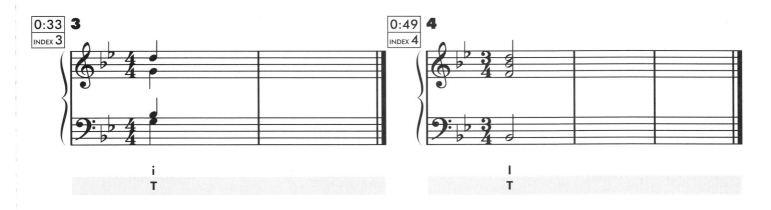

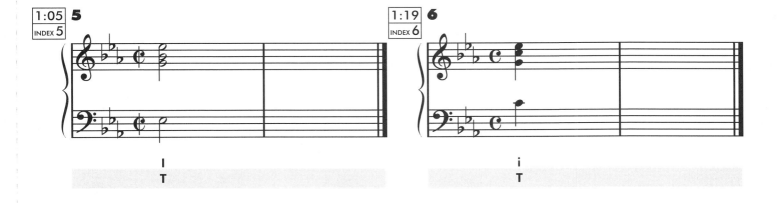

Scoring on Reverse ➡

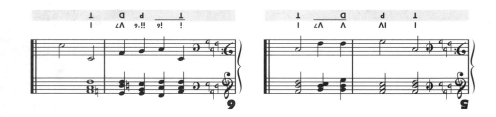

SCORING

147

_____ – _____ Total x

Your Score: _____

- **If your score is 132 or more, proceed to Lesson H.**
- **Otherwise, repeat Lesson G.**

LESSON H | INTRODUCTION

This Lesson and the next introduce the VI chord functioning in two different ways. In Lesson H, vi (or VI) acts as a **P** chord, which connects smoothly to V or V7; listen for the bass moving down a step. The motion from 1̂ to 6̂ isn't always a 3rd down. Find the illustrations in which the bass skips up a 6th rather than down a 3rd.

> ☞ **Tip:** Listen for the doubled third of VI in the minor mode.

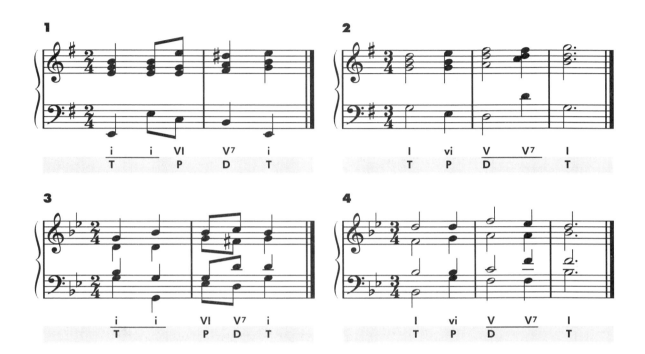

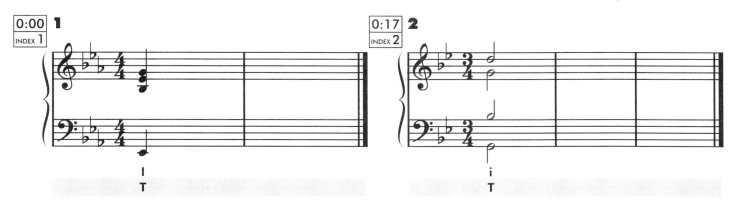

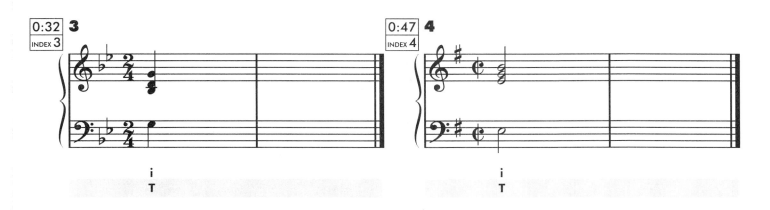

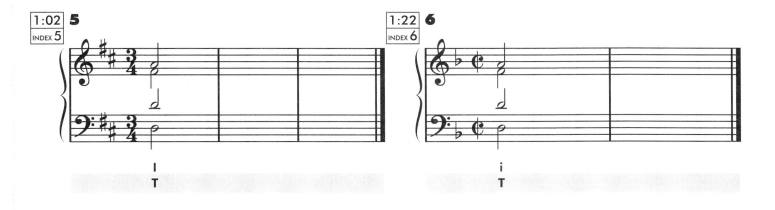

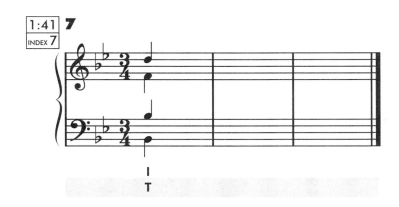

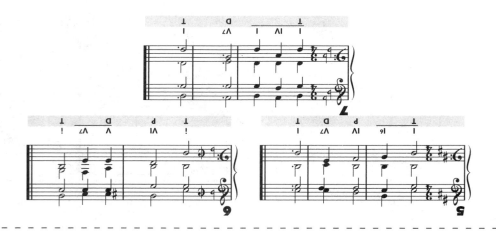

SCORING

168

$-$ _____ Total x

Your Score: _____

- If your score is 151 or more, proceed to Lesson I.
- Otherwise, proceed to Lesson HH.

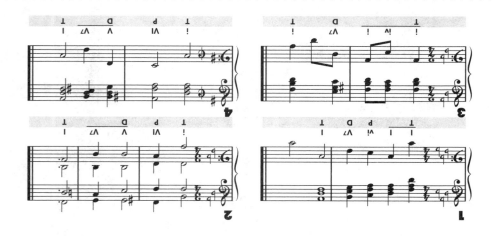

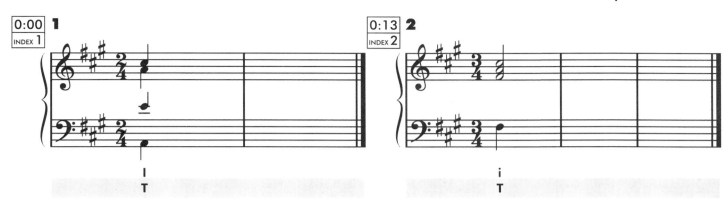

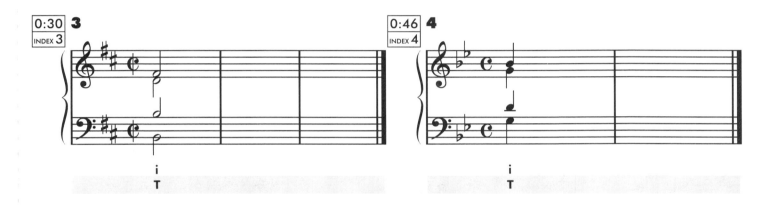

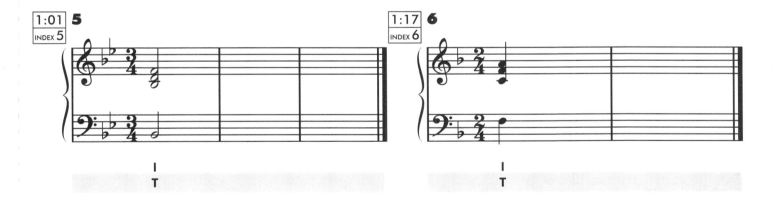

Scoring on Reverse ➡

SCORING

147

− _____ Total x

Your Score:

● If your score is 132 or more, proceed to Lesson I.
● Otherwise, repeat Lesson H.

Lesson I | INTRODUCTION

A familiar bass motion, $\hat{8}$ down to $\hat{4}$, creates the interval of a perfect 5th. That interval may be divided into two 3rds, so that you hear $\hat{8}$–$\hat{6}$–$\hat{4}$. As we have seen in Lesson H, a triad on $\hat{6}$ is the vi (or VI) chord. Here, vi is simply a connection between **T** and **P** and has no independent harmonic function; therefore, on the Worksheet leave the space in the gray band under such a vi blank.

In this pattern, the bass of I–vi or i–VI may also skip up a 6th; find the illustrations that show this skip.

> ☛ **Tip:** Scale degree $\hat{4}$ may support IV or ii6.

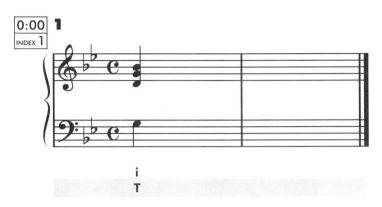

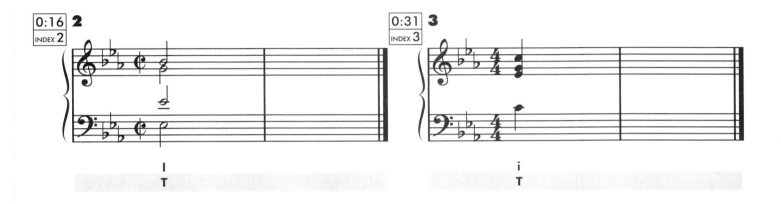

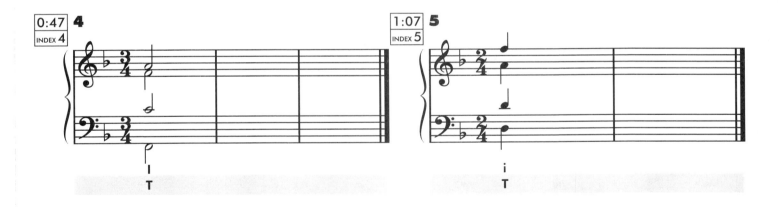

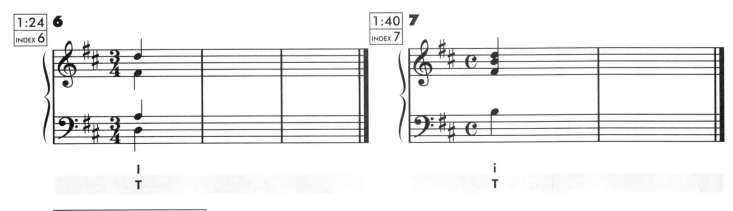

Scoring on Reverse ➡

SCORING

167

− _____ Total x

Your Score:

- If your score is 150 or more, you have finished
  Section I.
- Otherwise, proceed to Lesson II.

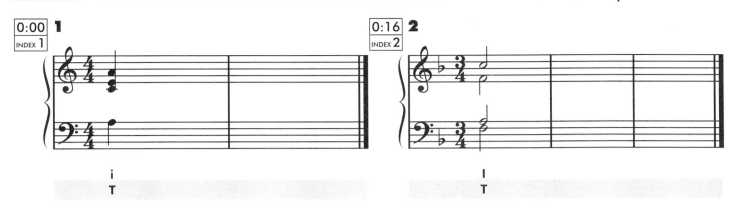

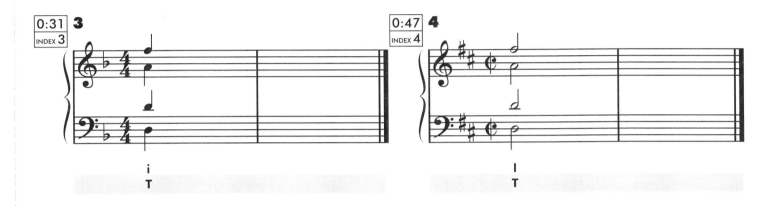

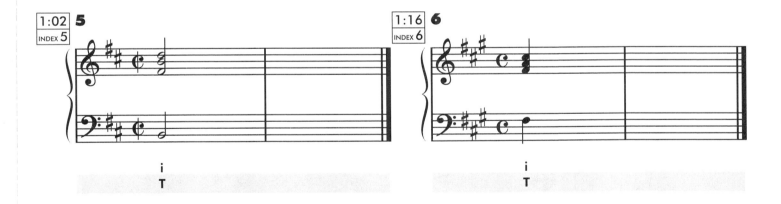

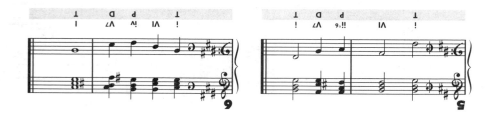

SCORING

140

_____ − _____ Total x

Your Score:

- If your score is 126 or more, congratulations! You have finished Section I.
- Otherwise, repeat Lesson I.

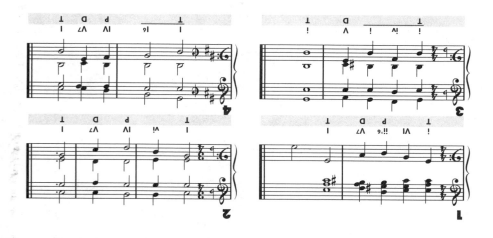

1

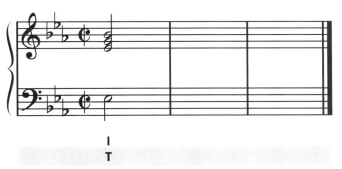

i
T

2

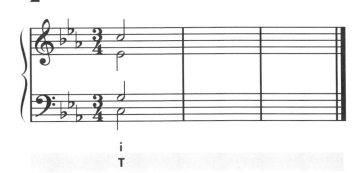

i
T

3

i
T

4

i
T

5

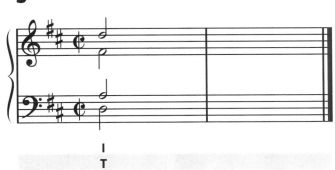

i
T

6

i
T

7

i
T

Scoring on Reverse ➡

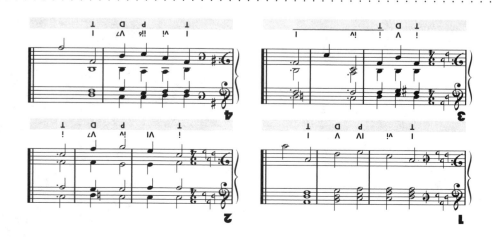

1

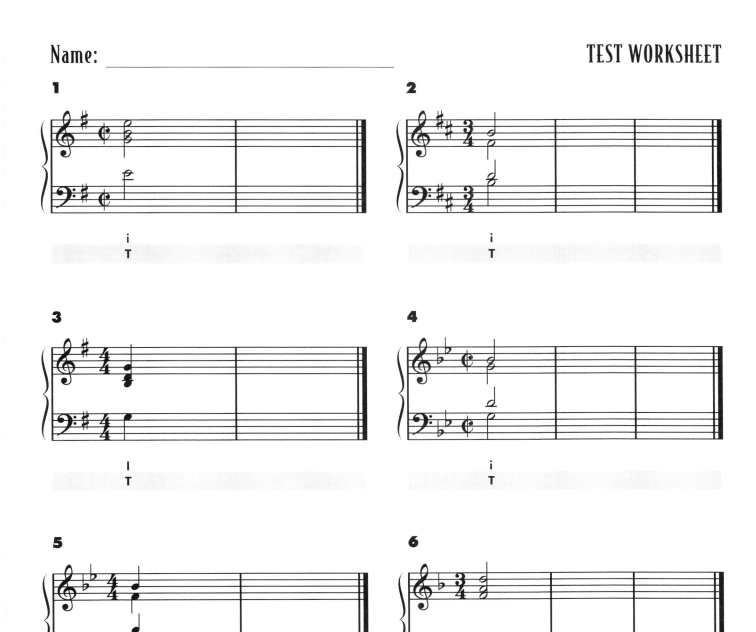

2

3

4

5

6

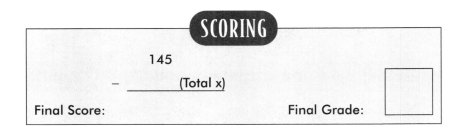

SCORING

145

− _____ (Total x)

Final Score: _____   Final Grade: [ ]

SECTION II

STUDENT RECORD SHEET

- Circle the Lesson you are to do next: (A)
- After completing that Lesson, draw a line through the circle (~~A~~) and circle the Lesson the instructions tell you to do next: (B)
- Keep this sheet up to date. It is intended solely for your guidance.

A	AA
B	BB
C	CC
D	DD
E	EE
F	FF
G	GG
H	HH

Starting date ____________________

Completion date ________________

Keep this page in this book.

HOW TO STUDY SECTION II

The Lessons in Section II include longer extensions of tonic and dominant harmony, as well as a variety of new connecting chords. Differences between major and minor also emerge in this section. For instance, the ii chord in $\frac{5}{3}$ position is normal in the major mode, but you will not hear it in the minor, whereas the III chord is more common in the minor mode. The VII chord is hardly ever heard in the major mode, but in the minor, it occurs quite often, leading to III. You will hear ii6 in both major and minor (in the minor mode, as ii°6).

Two important new chords are introduced in Section II. The $\frac{6}{4}$ chord, a standard feature in cadences and introduced in Lesson D, is understood as part of the dominant harmony. Although all the **P** chords heard up to this point are triads, the four-note chord ii$\frac{6}{5}$ is introduced as a strong dominant preparation in Lesson H.

The importance of the melodic element in harmony is illustrated by passing and neighbor motion. When a double-neighbor motion in the bass elaborates $\hat{5}$, as you will study in Lesson C, you hear an extension of dominant harmony.

Three different positions of the V7 chord, as well as the vii°6, extend tonic harmony through passing or neighbor motion. Although most of these tonic extensions bear the number V, none express the dominant function. The ways in which these chords elaborate tonic harmony is explained step by step in Lessons E, F, and G.

Remember that the horizontal line under the roman-numeral identifications indicates an extension of either tonic or dominant, which in this section may include as many as five chords. Keep up the effort to hear all the chords in such a group as a single entity.

Beginning with this section the roman numeral and function of the first chord are not given. The first chord is printed just as in Section I, however. As in Section I, the prep chord, which is always the tonic chord, is sounded before the exercise begins.

This Lesson introduces two new progressions. In the first, in the major mode, you will hear I–IV–ii–V–I. This progression introduces ii in $\frac{5}{3}$ position, serving as the dominant preparation; IV is simply a connection. In the second progression, in the minor mode, III links the opening tonic and the dominant preparation: i–III–**P**–**D**–**T**. In both progressions the bass normally moves up at the beginning, but a downward move is also possible.

REMINDER: Many exercises in the minor mode end with a major triad.

Tip: Practice hearing the difference—only one note—between III and i⁶ in minor. In the minor-mode illustrations, play III as written, then play the progression again, replacing III with i⁶ to hear the difference between the major triad and the minor one.

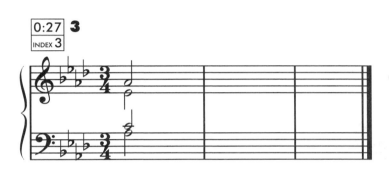

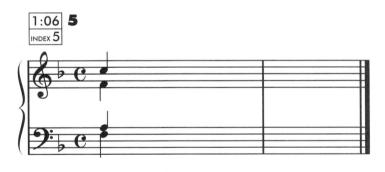

Scoring on Reverse ➡

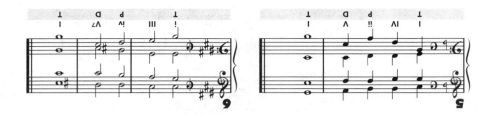

SCORING

151

— _____ Total x

Your Score:

- If your score is 136 or more, proceed to Lesson B.
- Otherwise, proceed to Lesson AA.

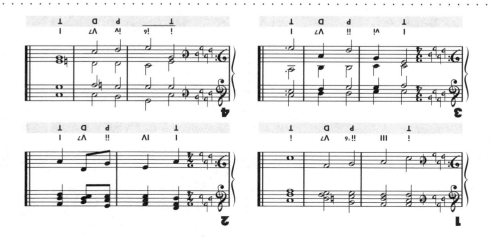

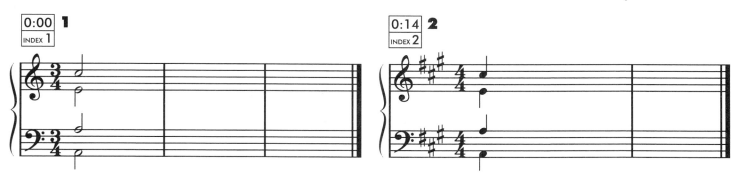

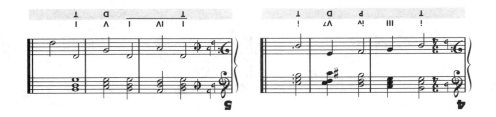

SCORING

128

− _____ Total x

Your Score: _____

- If your score is 115 or more, proceed to Lesson B.
- Otherwise, repeat Lesson A.

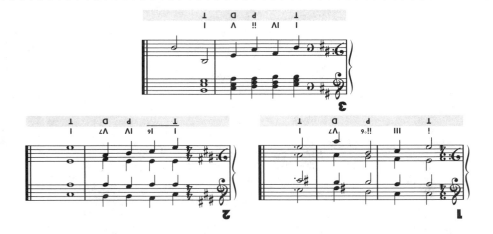

In the minor mode, III is often preceded by VII. Listen for the bass motion from $\hat{7}$ to $\hat{3}$. In Example 1, you hear that motion as an ascending 4th. In Example 2, you hear that motion as a descending 5th. VII and III rarely have a definable harmonic function but rather serve as connections on the way from **T** to **P** or **D**.

Octave skips in the bass may be heard in **D** as well as **T** chords. The concluding bass note may be elaborated with the skip $\hat{8}–\hat{5}–\hat{1}$.

> ☞ **Tip:** You will hear contrary motion between soprano and bass for the most part. Be aware of that, but also of the occasional appearance of similar motion. You may learn to hear this better by playing only the soprano and bass of each example.

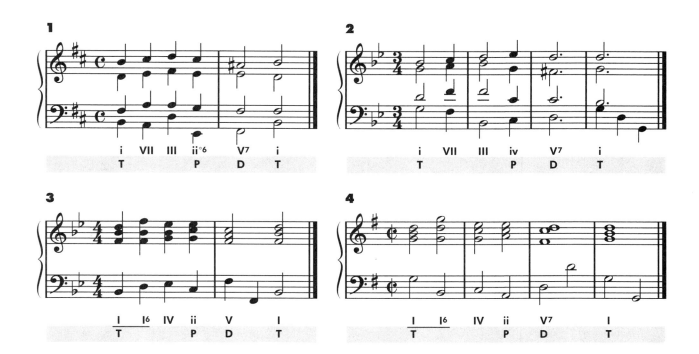

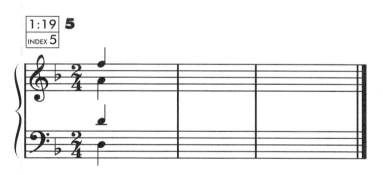

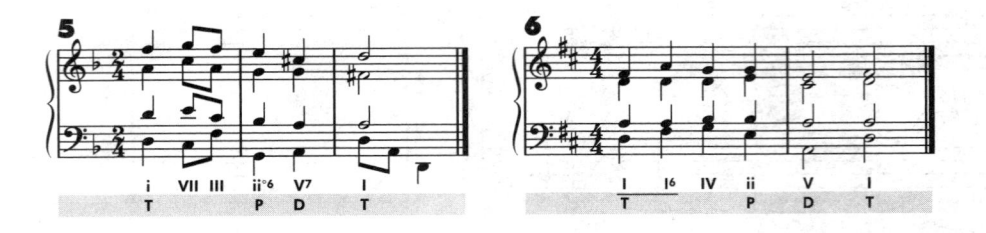

SCORING

194

_____ − _____
Total x

Your Score: _____

- If your score is 175 or more, proceed to Lesson C.
- Otherwise, proceed to Lesson BB.

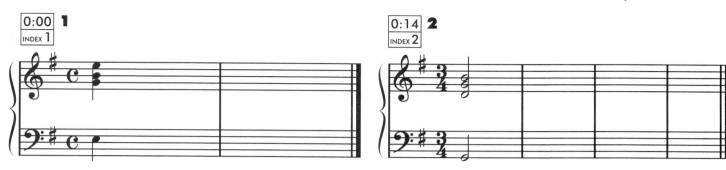

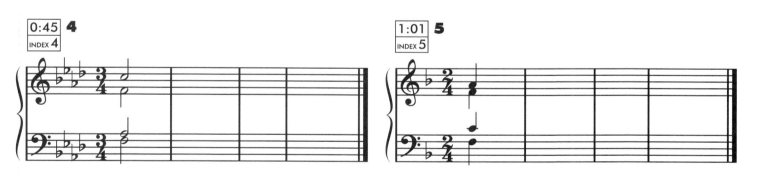

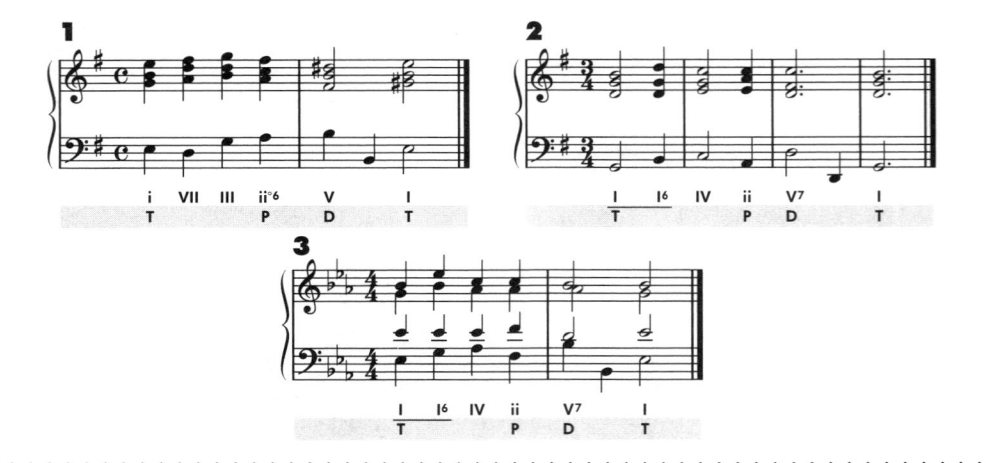

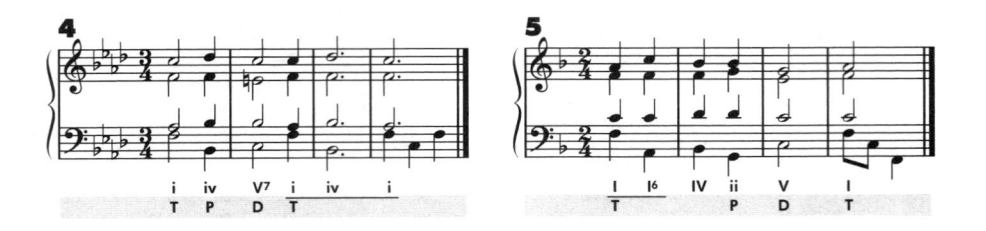

The dominant function is expressed as a four-note group, of which the first and fourth chords are V or V⁷ and the two chords in between are other, elaborative chords. What organizes this group is a double neighbor in the bass. In Example 1, the double-neighbor figure is boxed.

In Example 1, listen for the doubled 3rd in the VI chord. When the complete V⁷ resolves deceptively to VI, the doubled third (indicated in the example by ar-rows) prevents parallel 5ths and octaves. The triad with a doubled third has a special sound, particularly characteristic of this progression.

> ☞ **Tip:** On first hearing, try to decide whether the bass ends at the same pitch level at which it began, or an octave or two higher or lower.

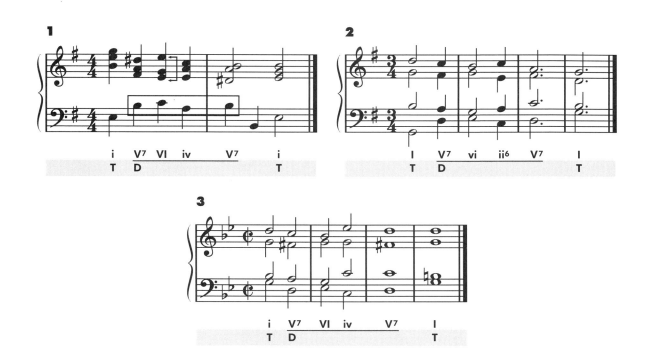

0:00 **1**
INDEX 1

0:15 **2**
INDEX 2

0:38 **3**
INDEX 3

0:58 **4**
INDEX 4

1:22 **5**
INDEX 5

1:38 **6**
INDEX 6

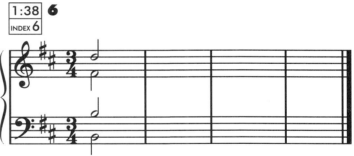

Scoring on Reverse ▶

SCORING

191

− _____ Total x

Your Score: _____

- If your score is 172 or more, proceed to Lesson D.
- Otherwise, proceed to Lesson CC.

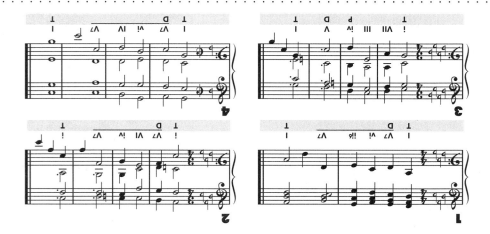

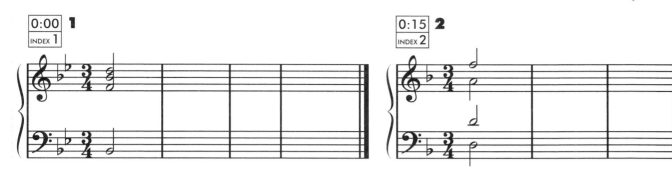

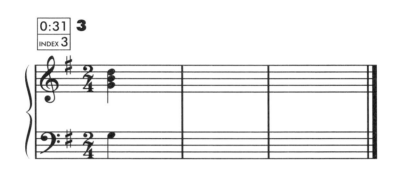

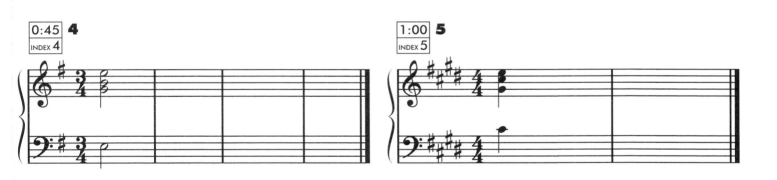

In tonal harmony, the dominant function is often expressed by two chords. The first is a $^6_4$ chord. Resolution of the 4th above the bass to a 3rd in the second chord brings the V or V⁷. In this program, no roman numeral is attached to $^6_4$ chords. All the examples in this introduction show the abbreviation $^6_4$ followed by either V or V⁷. In each case the **D** for dominant function appears beneath the chord pair.

Listen for the 4th of the $^6_4$ resolving to the 3rd of the V or V⁷. Focus on this by isolating two voices, the bass and the voice a 4th (or an 11th) above the bass. Play the dissonant interval and its resolution. Then play the two chords that contain those intervals.

Most of these examples review the bass descent in 3rds to $\hat4$, which supports the preparatory chords ii⁶ or IV. Each of these then leads to the dominant, usually initiated by the $^6_4$ chord.

> ☛ **Tip:** As the $^6_4$ chord moves to V or V⁷, does the bass remain stationary or does it skip an octave?

0:00 **1**
INDEX 1

0:21 **2**
INDEX 2

0:42 **3**
INDEX 3

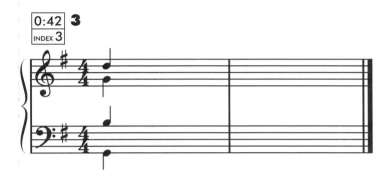

1:02 **4**
INDEX 4

1:17 **5**
INDEX 5

1:33 **6**
INDEX 6

Scoring on Reverse ➡

SCORING

186

—_____ Total x

Your Score: _____

- If your score is 167 or more, proceed to Lesson E.
- Otherwise, proceed to Lesson DD.

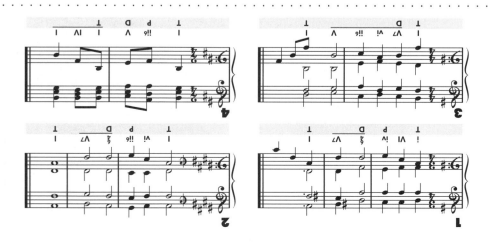

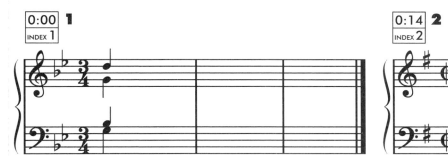

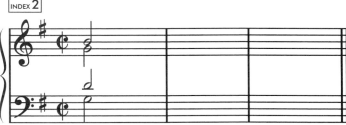

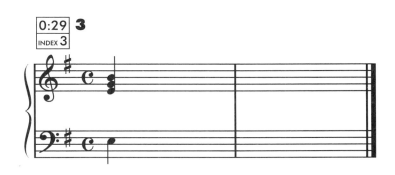

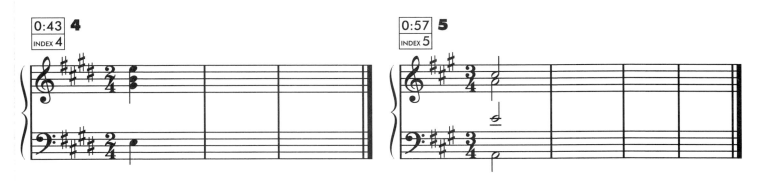

Scoring on Reverse ➡

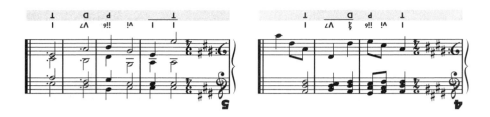

SCORING

159

— _____ Total x

Your Score:

- If your score is 143 or more, proceed to Lesson E.
- Otherwise, repeat Lesson D.

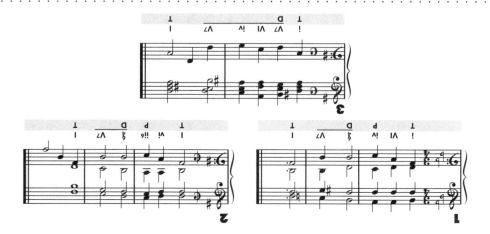

You will now hear a simple extension of tonic harmony, a three-chord group in which the second chord is V⁶ or V⁶₅. That elaborative chord is supported by a neighbor note in the bass, indicated in Example 1 with an N. Play the bass line of each example first and listen for the neighbor-note motion. Also, distinguish between V⁶ and V⁶₅: There is only one note difference. V⁶ may also serve as a connection on the way to vi, as in Example 6.

This Lesson also introduces a passing motion in an upper voice, which connects V to I; in Examples 5 and 6 notice the doubled root of the dominant, the upper voice of which passes from 8̂ to 7̂ in its journey to the third of the tonic triad.

Review the ⁶₄ chord within the dominant in these examples.

> ☞ **Tip:** The neighbor-note motion in the bass that underpins I–V⁶₅–I is often mirrored by contrary motion in an upper voice.

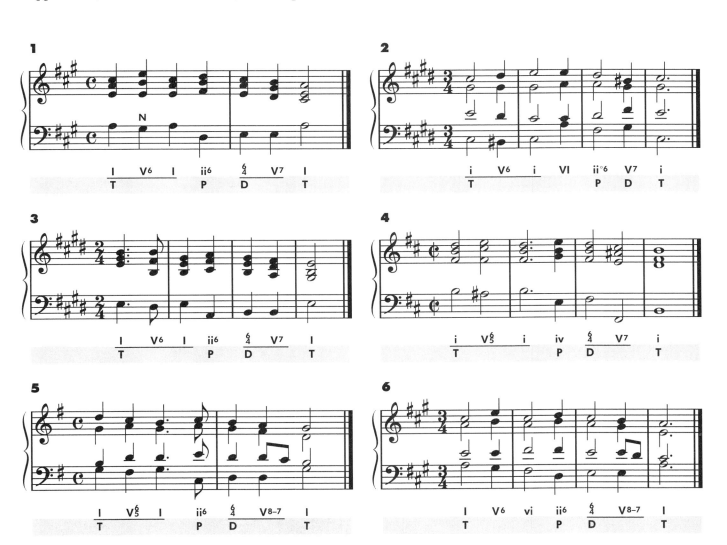

0:00 **1**
INDEX 1

0:15 **2**
INDEX 2

0:35 **3**
INDEX 3

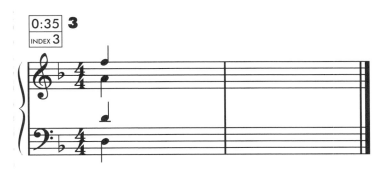

0:55 **4**
INDEX 4

1:15 **5**
INDEX 5

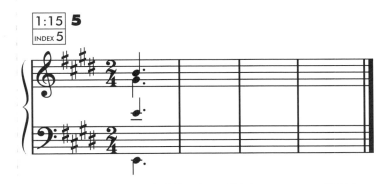

1:31 **6**
INDEX 6

Scoring on Reverse ▶

SCORING

220

− _____   Total x

Your Score: _____

- **If your score is 198 or more, proceed to Lesson F.**
- **Otherwise, proceed to Lesson EE.**

Name: _____

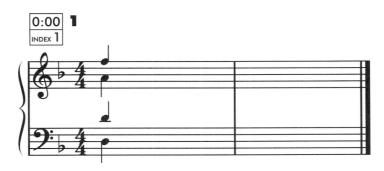

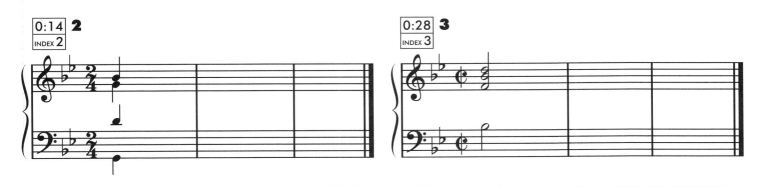

SCORING

177

—   Total x

Your Score:

- If your score is 159 or more, proceed to Lesson F.
- Otherwise, repeat Lesson E.

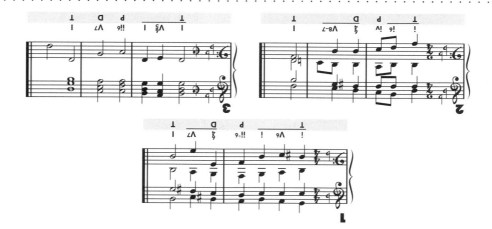

You have studied the two-chord group I–I⁶ as an extension of tonic harmony. Those two chords may be connected by vii°⁶ or V⁴₃. The bass line fills the 3rd with steps. Listen to the bass in Example 1. The motion from 1̂ to 5̂ is completely stepwise. The first three notes of that bass motion support the extension of tonic harmony. When V⁴₃ occurs in the minor mode, be sure to write an accidental to indicate the leading note.

☛ **Tip:** In the motion that connects I to I⁶ there is often voice exchange between the bass and an upper voice.

0:00 **1**
INDEX 1

0:23 **2**
INDEX 2

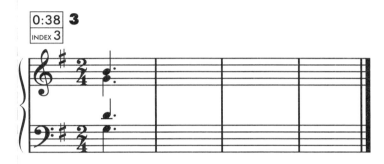

0:38 **3**
INDEX 3

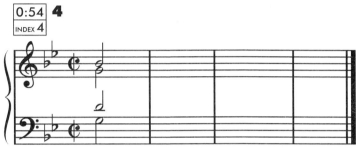

0:54 **4**
INDEX 4

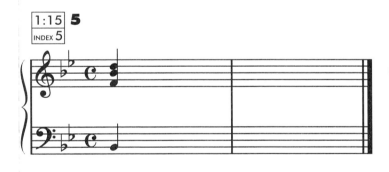

1:15 **5**
INDEX 5

1:30 **6**
INDEX 6

Scoring on Reverse ➡

SCORING

223

− _____ Total x

Your Score:

- **If your score is 201 or more, proceed to Lesson G.**
- **Otherwise, proceed to Lesson FF.**

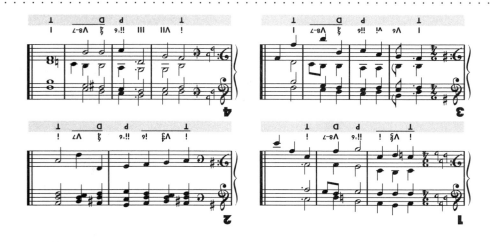

Name: _____ LESSON FF | WORKSHEET

0:00 **1**
INDEX 1

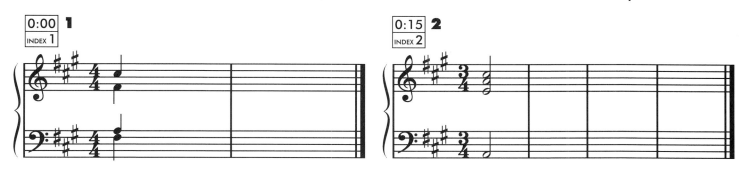

0:15 **2**
INDEX 2

0:31 **3**
INDEX 3

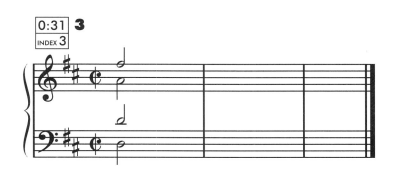

0:46 **4**
INDEX 4

1:02 **5**
INDEX 5

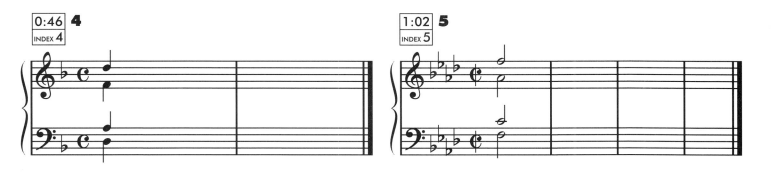

Scoring on Reverse ➡

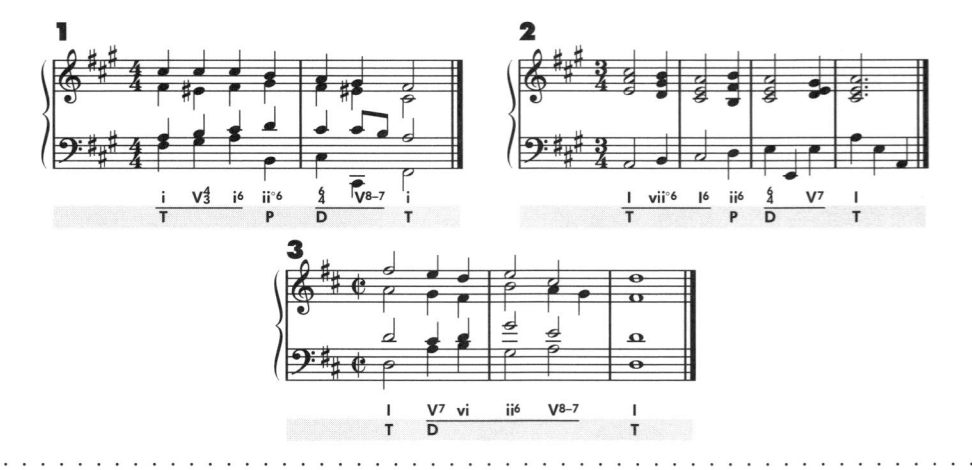

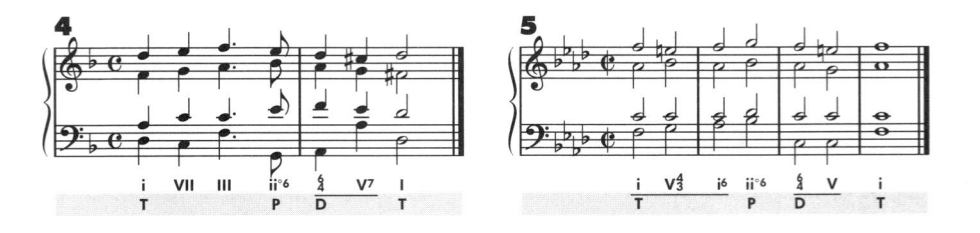

SCORING

182

_____ − _____ = Total x

Your Score:

- If your score is 164 or more, proceed to Lesson G.
- Otherwise, repeat Lesson F.

LESSON G | INTRODUCTION

Another way to connect I to I6 is by V2. If you look at the opening examples, you will see that the bass begins with an upward skip of a 4th. You will hear that 4̂ is dissonant with two of the notes above it. Listen for the resolution of that dissonance, and you will hear the bass of I6.

In Example 3, both V2 and V6/5 help build a longer tonic extension. This may also be done with V4/3. Try to hear the first five chords of Example 3 as a single unit, the extension of tonic harmony.

In the minor mode, you hear i–VII6–III, which also initiates a stepwise bass motion. You can see this in Example 4.

☛ **Tip:** Now you have studied more than one progression with the same bass line: 1̂–2̂–3̂–4̂–5̂. Without looking at the page, play this bass line in any key, then play at least two different chord progressions with that bass line.

0:00 **1**
INDEX 1

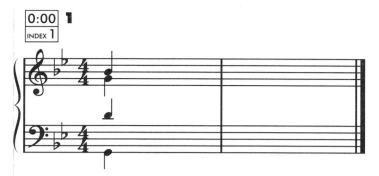

0:20 **2**
INDEX 2

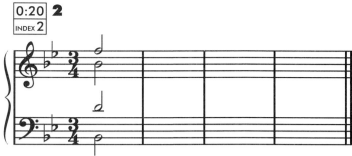

0:46 **3**
INDEX 3

1:01 **4**
INDEX 4

1:17 **5**
INDEX 5

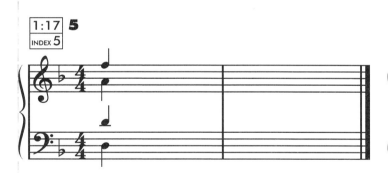

1:34 **6**
INDEX 6

Scoring on Reverse ➡

SCORING

223

— _____ Total x

Your Score:

- If your score is 201 or more, proceed to Lesson H.
- Otherwise, proceed to Lesson GG.

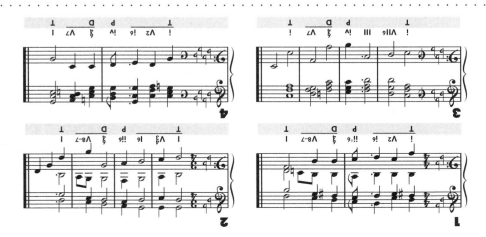

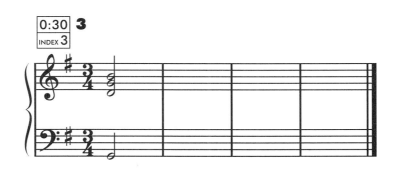

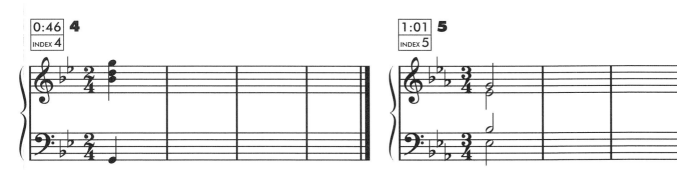

Scoring on Reverse ▶

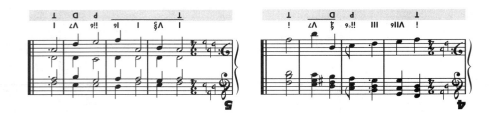

SCORING

183

− _____ Total x

Your Score:

- If your score is 165 or more, proceed to Lesson H.
- Otherwise, repeat Lesson G.

If you add together all the notes of the two preparatory chords IV and ii^6, you will have all the notes of another, more dissonant preparatory chord—ii$^6_5$, the strongest **P** studied thus far. Examples 1 and 2 show ii$^6_5$ (ii$^{\circ6}_5$ in the minor mode) used in this function. The figures 6 and 5 in the roman numeral identification tell you that there are two notes in the chord that are a step (or a 7th or a 9th) apart. Listen for that dissonance and its resolution. One of the notes of the resolution is the leading note that is an essential part of V or V^7. In examples 3 and 4, ii$^6_5$ is included in a dominant extension.

Play all the examples in the introduction once through. Then go back and play only ii$^6_5$–V or ii$^6_5$–V^7.

For each one, do you hear a 2nd, 7th, or 9th? Listen also to the difference between ii$^6_5$ in the major mode and ii$^{\varnothing6}_5$ in the minor mode.

> ☞ **Tip:** This Lesson summarizes most of the topics of Section II. If there is any progression that you are not sure of, now is the time to turn to a previous Lesson and review that progression. A good way to practice any progression is to play it in all twelve keys.

0:00 **1**
INDEX 1

0:18 **2**
INDEX 2

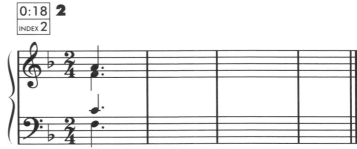

0:34 **3**
INDEX 3

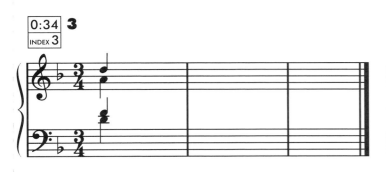

0:55 **4**
INDEX 4

1:17 **5**
INDEX 5

1:34 **6**
INDEX 6

Scoring on Reverse ➡

SCORING

214

− _____ Total x

Your Score:

- If your score is 193 or more, you have finished Section II.
- Otherwise, proceed to Lesson HH.

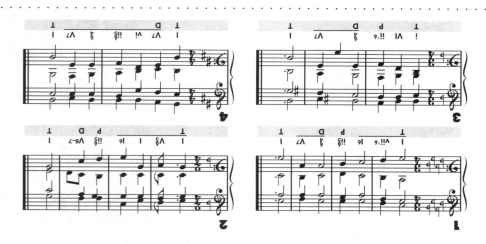

0:00 **1**
INDEX 1

0:15 **2**
INDEX 2

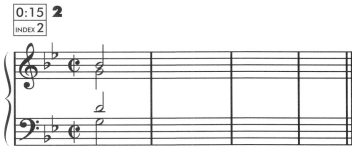

0:31 **3**
INDEX 3

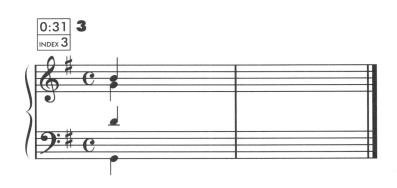

0:45 **4**
INDEX 4

1:00 **5**
INDEX 5

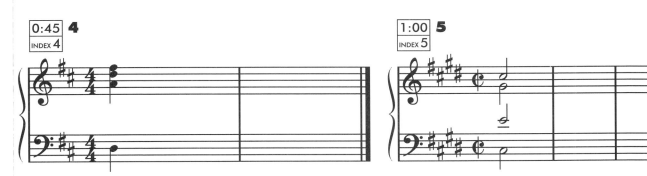

Scoring on Reverse ▶

SCORING

185

—_____ Total x

Your Score: _____

- If your score is 167 or more, congratulations!
  You have finished Section II.
- Otherwise, repeat Lesson H.

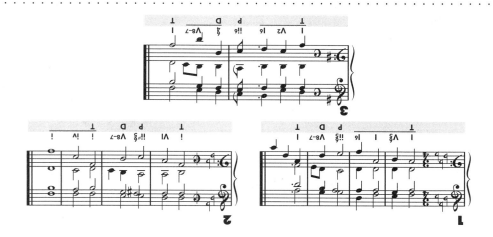

1

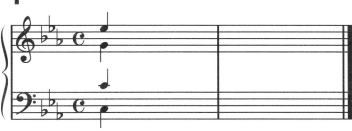

2

3

4

5

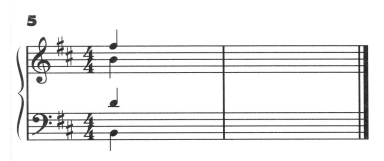

6

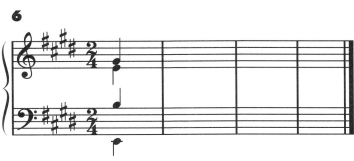

SCORING

223

– _____ (total x)

Your score:

Now convert your score to a letter grade:

A: 223–201   B: 200–178   C: 177–156   D: 155–134

Your Grade

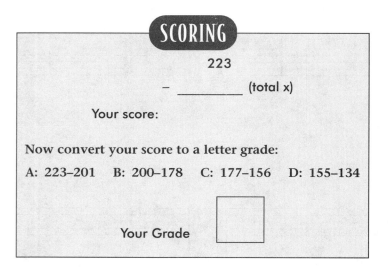

Name: _____

1
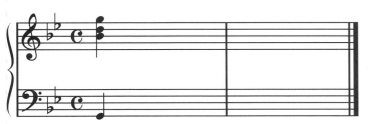

2
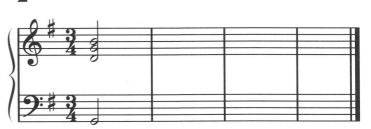

3

4

5
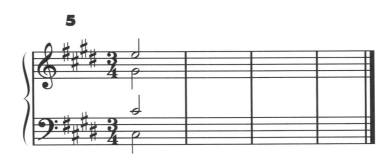

SCORING

189

− _____ (Total x)

Final Score: _____

Final Grade: _____

STUDENT RECORD SHEET

- Circle the Lesson you are to do next: (A)
- After completing that Lesson, draw a line through the circle (A) and circle the Lesson the instructions tell you to do next: (B)
- Keep this sheet up to date. It is intended solely for your guidance.

A	AA
B	BB
C	CC
D	DD
E	EE
F	FF
G	GG
H	HH

Starting date _____

Completion date _____

Keep this page in this book.

HOW TO STUDY SECTION III

Secondary dominants are introduced throughout Section III, with secondary leading-note chords starting in Lesson F. These simply transpose the V–I (or vii°7–I) progression to other scale degrees. The entire process by which a secondary dominant leads to a secondary tonic is called tonicization. Since tonicization is an important feature in much tonal music, it is emphasized in this section.

The chromatic notes within secondary dominants are mostly leading notes, whose resolution a half step up is a clue to the nature of the progression. You are not asked to give specific roman numerals for secondary dominants and secondary leading-note chords in this program; rather, indicate such chords with an arrow (→).

The last two Lessons present phrases that begin in one key and modulate to a closely related key, in both major and minor. You will be asked to identify the pivot chords in those modulations.

More mode mixture enters the program in Section III. In particular, ♭$\hat{6}$, taken from the minor mode, is heard in the ii°, iv, and vii°7 chords in major-mode progressions. This adds to the color and variety of the harmony.

You will hear a gradual increase in passing motion, mainly in the outer voices but occasionally in the inner voices.

The meter $\frac{6}{8}$ is introduced in Lesson A, quarter-note upbeats in Lesson D.

In the first three Lessons the only note you will find on the Worksheets is the first bass note. Be sure to score the upper voices of this first chord. From Lesson D on, exercises may start with I or V6. You will hear the prep chord, which is always the tonic. As soon as the exercise begins, decide on the opening chord and determine whether it is an upbeat or a downbeat as quickly as you can.

LESSON A | INTRODUCTION

The bass pattern $\hat{8}$–$\hat{6}$–$\hat{4}$–$\hat{2}$ in the major mode is introduced in this Lesson. In Example 1, it is presented as a chain of descending 3rds. In Example 2, those 3rds are divided into steps by passing tones. The ii chord at the end of the chain is usually the **P** chord. The chords between I and ii simply fill the space of a 7th and therefore do not require any function symbol.

A new extension of tonic harmony, covered in this Lesson, moves from I through vi to I⁶ in the major mode, i–VI–i⁶ in the minor mode, as illustrated in Examples 3–5. In Example 3, the initial 3rd descent in the bass is elaborated with a passing note; in Example 4, it is preceded by sounding the tonic an octave lower. In Example 5, the 3rd descent is replaced by its inversion, the rise of a 6th.

A new melodic elaboration of the cadence consists of $\hat{3}$–$\hat{2}$ over the dominant seventh chord, as found in Examples 3 and 5. In these examples, $\hat{3}$ is generated by the preceding $^6_4$ chord and is heard either as an incomplete neighbor or suspension. Note the direction of the stems

on the eighth notes that show the $\hat{3}$–$\hat{2}$ motion. In piano texture, when one voice on the treble clef staff moves faster than the other two, its notes are indicated with their own stems. In the cadence of Example 3, as in those in many previous exercises, you hear the leading note in the alto resolve to the tonic in the soprano.

Observe that Example 7 consists entirely of a tonic extension.

From this point on, only the first note in the bass appears on the Worksheet. The preparatory chord still is sounded before the exercise begins. If you can write the notes of the first chord on hearing the preparatory sound, you will have a head start in doing the exercise. Write quickly.

> ☞ **Tip:** Before playing the first illustration, play the first note in the bass only. Then silently play the entire example in your imagination. Then play the entire example and see how closely you have approximated it.

More on Reverse ➡

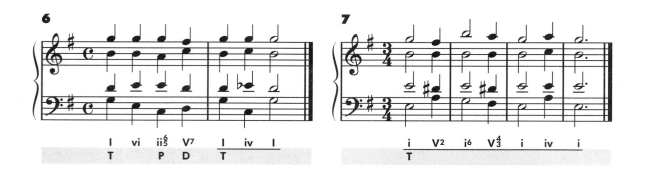

CD 4/TRACK 1 Name: _____

0:00 **1**
INDEX 1

0:15 **2**
INDEX 2

0:40 **3**
INDEX 3

0:56 **4**
INDEX 4

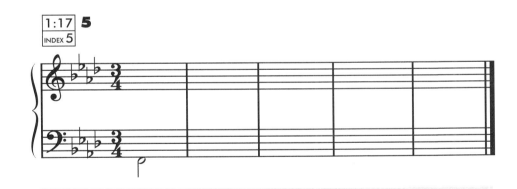

1:17 **5**
INDEX 5

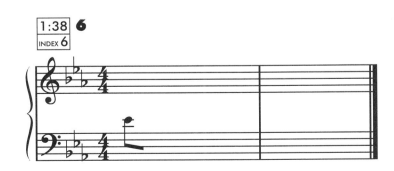

1:38 **6**
INDEX 6

Scoring on Reverse ➡

Name: _____

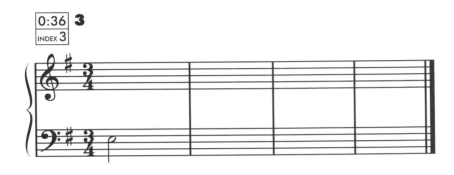

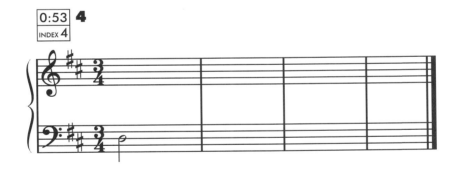

SCORING

202

— _____ Total x

Your Score:

- If your score is 182 or more, proceed to Lesson B.
- Otherwise, repeat Lesson A.

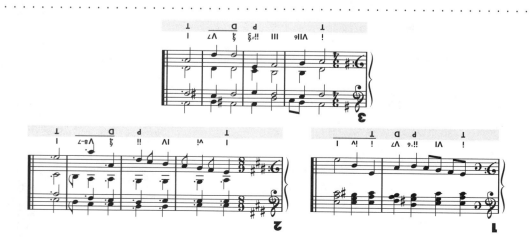

A strong dominant preparation is V of V or V⁷ of V. In this Lesson, one of its inversions, V⁶ of V, is introduced. In Examples 1 and 2 this chord is supported by ♯4̂, the leading note of the dominant. The bass ascent from 1̂ to 5̂ includes the chromatic ♯4̂.

Any secondary dominant, including the dominant of the dominant, is abbreviated with an arrow in this program. Use an arrow (→) to indicate any secondary dominant, no matter what its inversion.

An important chromatic note, ♭6̂, is introduced in the major mode. It is taken from the minor mode, another example of mode mixture. In this Lesson, ♭6̂

forms the interval of a minor 3rd over the bass in a iv, ii°⁶, or ii°⁶₅ chord. For that reason, minor-mode chord identifications are used in major-mode progressions, as in Examples 3, 4, and 5. These chromatic chords function the same way as their diatonic counterparts.

> **Tip:** Which exercise begins with an exchange of notes between the bass and one of the upper voices? Sing that upper voice while playing the bass and listen carefully to the intervals that are formed.

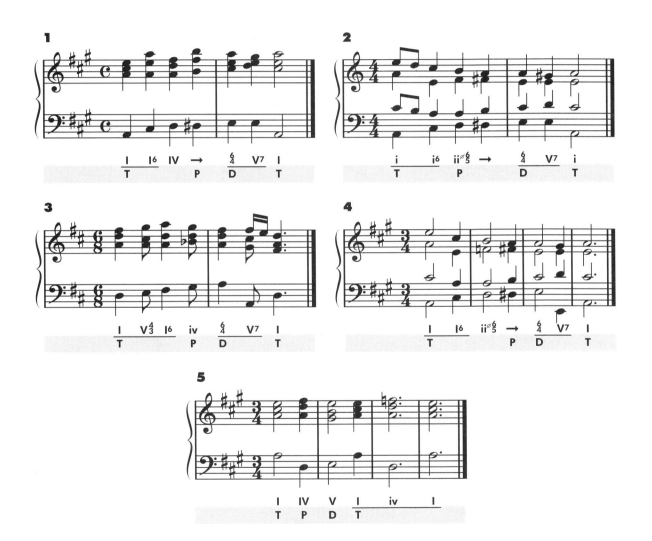

Name: _____

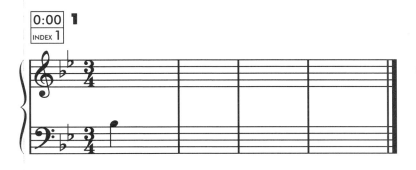

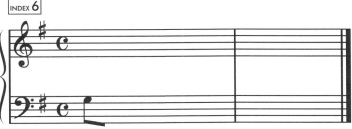

Scoring on Reverse ➡

SCORING

253

– _____ Total x

Your Score: _____

- If your score is 228 or more, proceed to Lesson C.
- Otherwise, proceed to Lesson BB.

0:00 1
INDEX 1

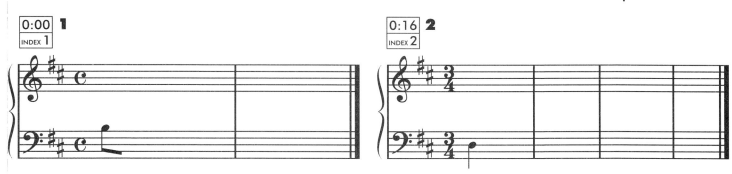

0:16 2
INDEX 2

0:33 3
INDEX 3

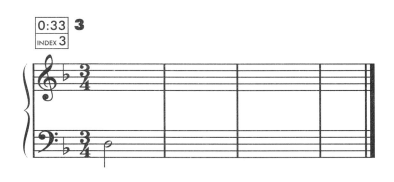

0:49 4
INDEX 4

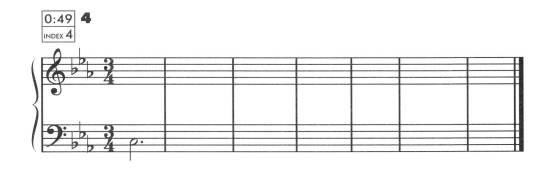

1:10 5
INDEX 5

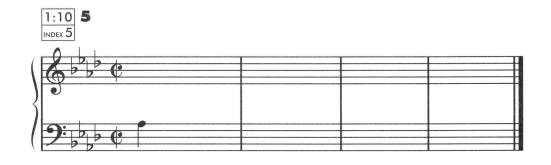

Scoring on Reverse ➡

SCORING

204

− _____ Total x

Your Score: _____

- If your score is 184 or more, proceed to Lesson C.
- Otherwise, repeat Lesson B.

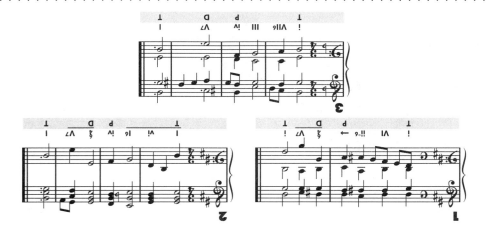

This Lesson presents two new secondary dominants. In the major mode, you will hear the dominant of ii. In Example 1, the leading note of ii is in the soprano. Also, the ii leads to a preparatory chord, which in Example 1 is V⁷ of V, a new **P**. In Example 2, the leading note of ii is in the bass. The ii chord need not appear in root position, as you can see in Example 3. You will not hear the dominant of ii in the minor mode because ii is a diminished triad.

In the minor mode, III (the relative major) plays an important role. You have already heard the dominant

of III, which is simply VII. From this point, instead of VII, VII⁶, or VII⁷, write an arrow (→) to indicate that VII functions as a secondary dominant, as in Examples 4 through 6. In Example 6, the dominant of III is in ⁶₃ position.

> ☛ **Tip:** Find all the exercises in which one of the inner voices moves from 8̂ to 7̂ to 5̂ in the final cadence.

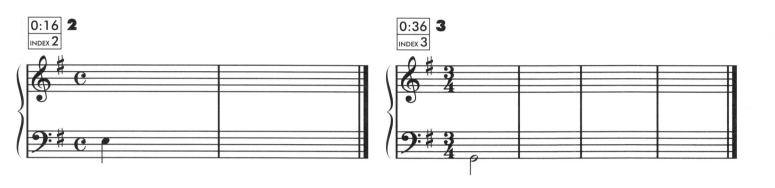

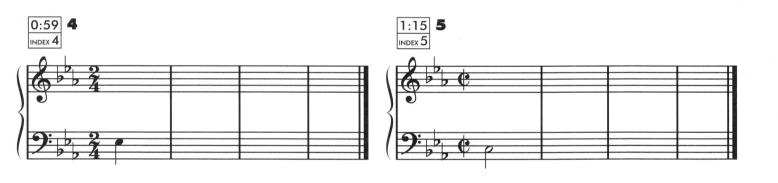

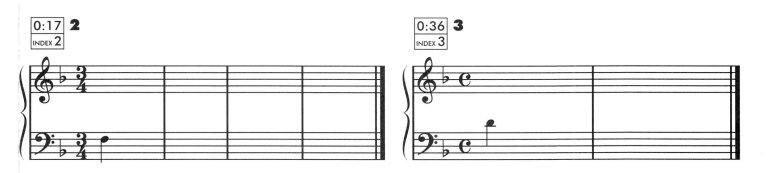

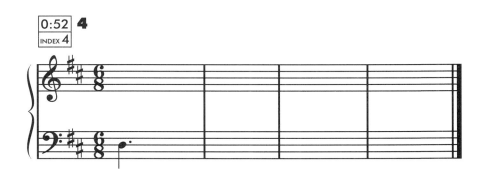

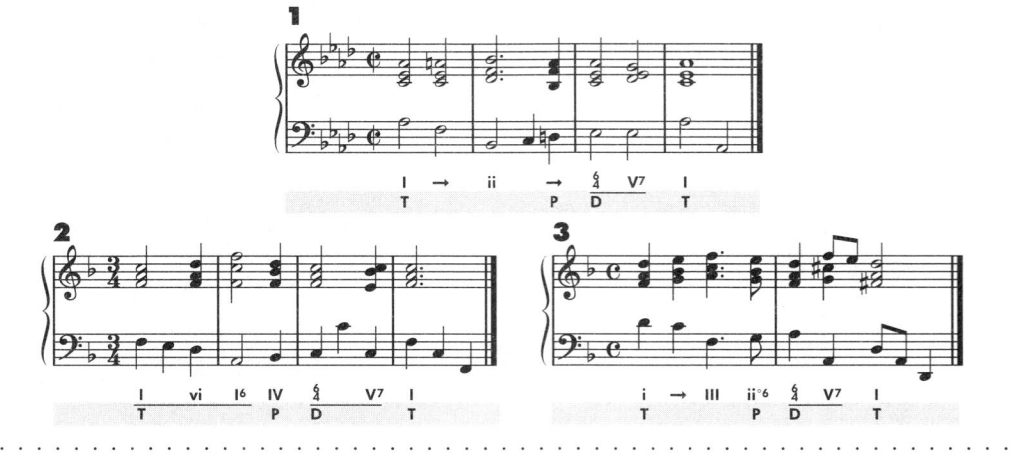

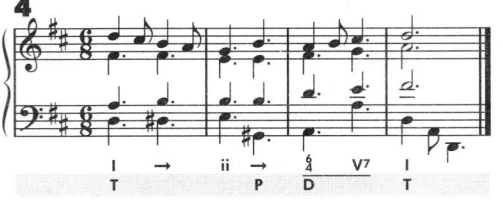

The dominant of IV is introduced in Example 1. Find the other examples of the dominant of IV in this Introduction. IV (or iv) may be in either $\frac{5}{3}$ or $\frac{6}{3}$ position. Since the dominant of IV has the seventh in the bass in Examples 3 and 4, the chord to which it leads is IV⁶.

Notice that Example 5 begins with an upbeat chord, V⁶. When exercises begin with upbeat chords other than the tonic, the preparatory sound will still be the first tonic triad in the exercise. The chord pair of the upbeat plus the downbeat tonic is considered as tonic harmony in this program.

Observe that in Example 7 V$\frac{6}{5}$ of V is part of the dominant extension.

The bass note no longer appears on the Worksheet. The key signature will tell you that the exercise is in one of two keys, one major and one minor. Decide on the mode when you hear the prep chord, which is always the tonic, and then listen closely to determine whether the first chord in the exercise is V⁶ or I (i).

☛ **Tip:** Try to memorize the soprano and bass of an exercise on one hearing and write that down quickly.

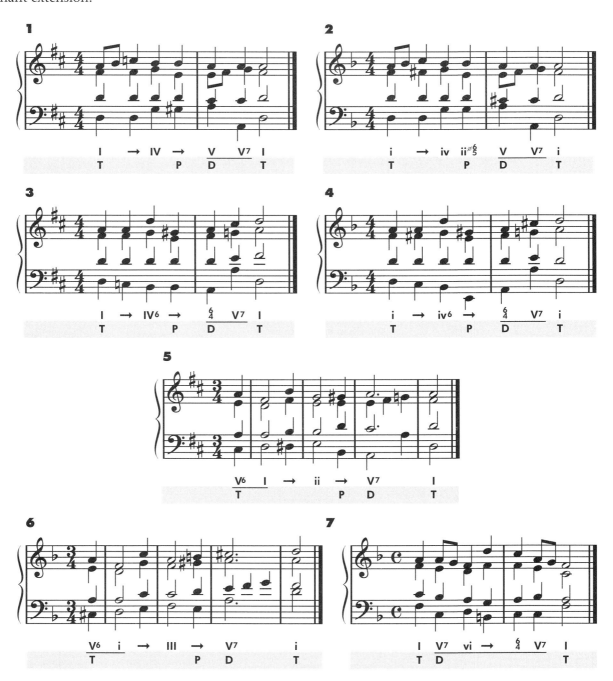

Name: _____

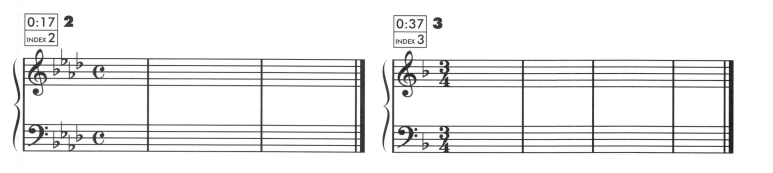

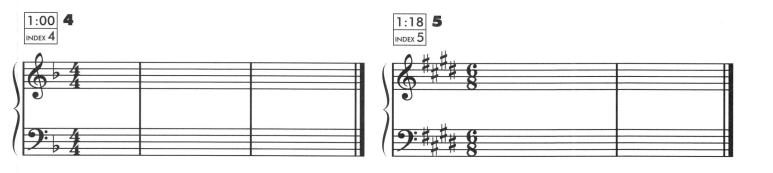

SCORING

250

−　_____　Total x

Your Score:

- If your score is 225 or more, proceed to Lesson E.
- Otherwise, proceed to Lesson DD.

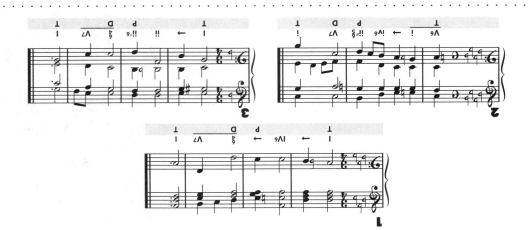

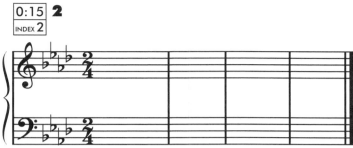

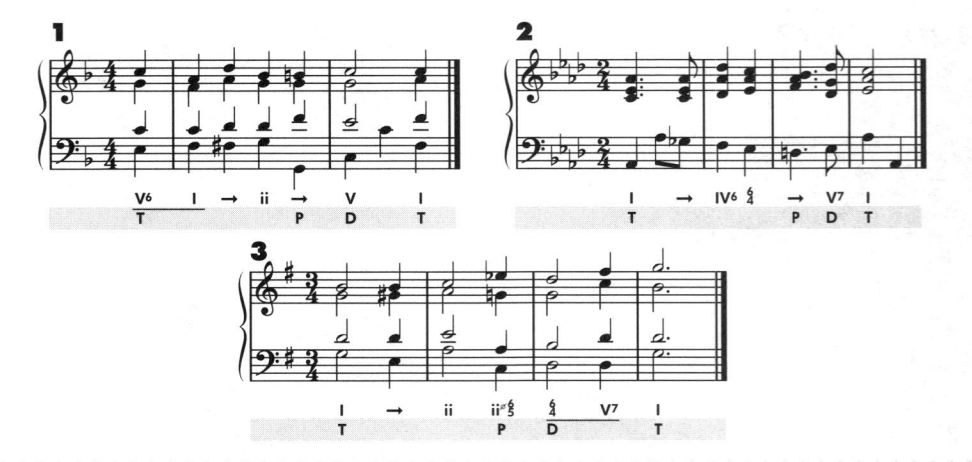

1. V⁶ / T — I → ii → V / D — I / T

2. I / T → IV⁶ ⁶₄ / P → V⁷ / D — I / T

3. I / T → ii → ii°⁶₅ / P — ⁶₄ / D — V⁷ — I / T

SCORING

207

——— − ——— Total x

Your Score: ———

- If your score is 186 or more, proceed to Lesson E.
- Otherwise, repeat Lesson D.

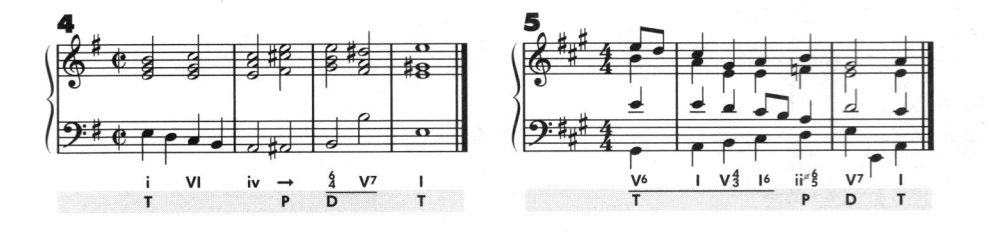

4. i / T — VI — iv → ⁶₄ / P — V⁷ / D — I / T

5. V⁶ / T — I — V⁴₃ — I⁶ — ii°⁶₅ / P — V⁷ / D — I / T

In the minor mode, a chromatic neighbor chord, vii°⁷, is heard between two statements of the tonic, extending the tonic function over three or more chords. Try to hear those three chords as a single entity. Example 1 shows the minor-mode origin of the chord. The same chord may be imported into the major mode, as in Example 2, yet another example of mode mixture.

Starting in this Lesson, the upbeat chord may be I or i, as in Examples 3 and 4. In addition, you will find more passing motion in the upper voices in this and subsequent Lessons.

> ☛ **Tip:** From this point, you may find any inversion of secondary dominants. Indicate them all with the arrow (→).

0:00 **1**
INDEX 1

0:20 **2**
INDEX 2

0:37 **3**
INDEX 3

0:54 **4**
INDEX 4

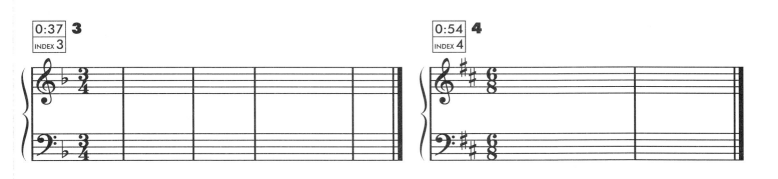

1:13 **5**
INDEX 5

1:33 **6**
INDEX 6

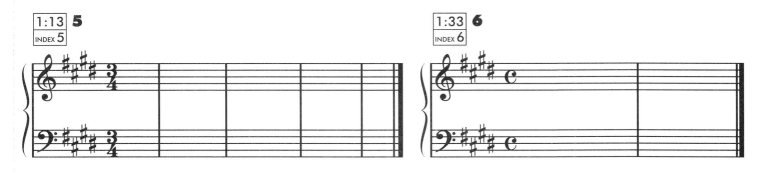

Scoring on Reverse ➡

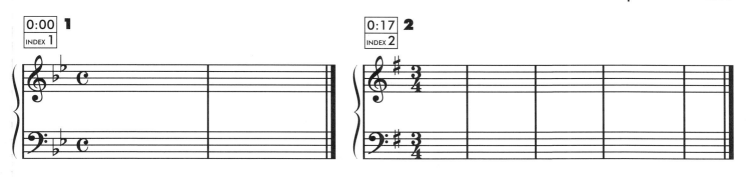

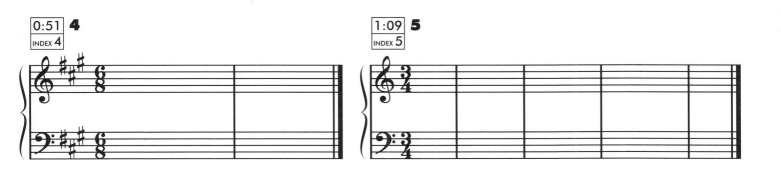

SCORING

222

− _____ Total x

Your Score: _____

- If your score is 200 or more, proceed to Lesson F.
- Otherwise, repeat Lesson E.

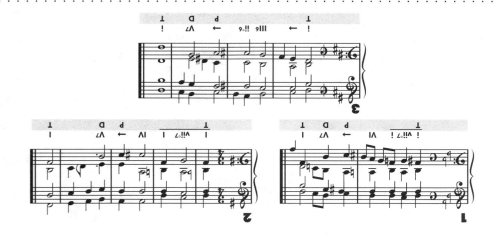

Another strong preparatory chord is vii°7 of V in the minor mode, indicated with an arrow (→). Again, this is very effective with ♯4̂ in the bass, as in Example 1. The leading note of the dominant has a very strong impulse to move to 5̂, and if you learn to hear ♯4̂–5̂ it can help focus your listening.

In the major mode, vii⌀7 of V is sometimes used, as in Example 2. Listen to the difference between the two forms of vii7 of V. There is only a half-step difference, as you can see by comparing the two chord identifications: ° versus ⌀. But the difference in sound is unmistakable.

Example 3 shows the vii°7 in the major mode, another example of mode mixture. Example 4 spells the seventh of the vii°7 chord F♯ becuase of the voice leading. In this program, enharmonic spellings in vii°7 chords are considered correct.

The vi (VI) chord may be preceded by its own dominant. Listen for the leading note of 6̂. In Examples 4 and 5, in the major mode, the leading note of 6̂ is in the soprano. It is a chromatic note. In Example 6, in the minor mode, the leading note of 6̂ is diatonic, but the seventh of V7 of VI is chromatic.

☛ **Tip:** Remember the precautionary accidentals!

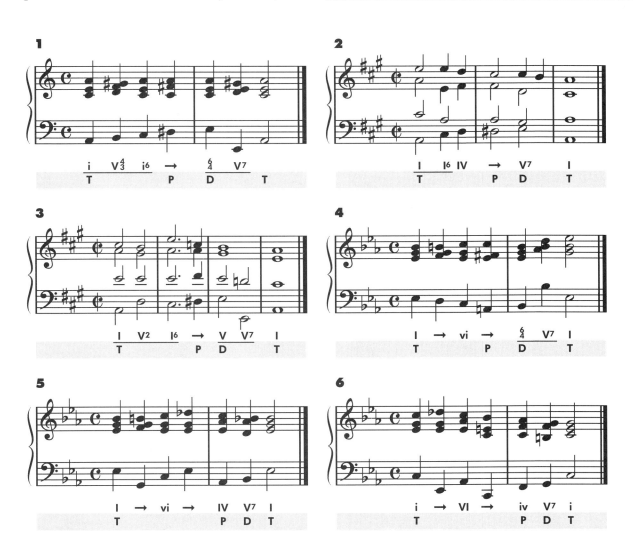

0:00 1
INDEX 1

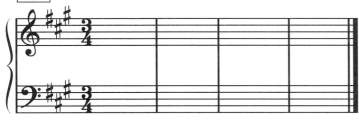

0:21 2
INDEX 2

0:36 3
INDEX 3

0:57 4
INDEX 4

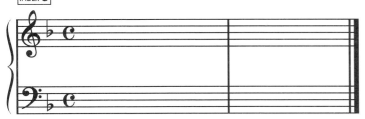

1:16 5
INDEX 5

1:32 6
INDEX 6

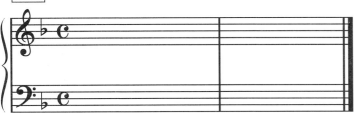

Scoring on Reverse ➡

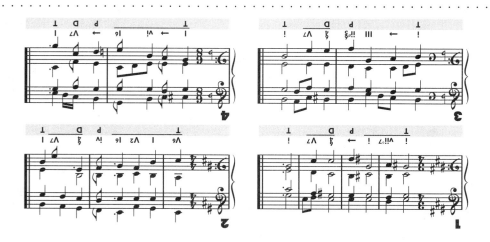

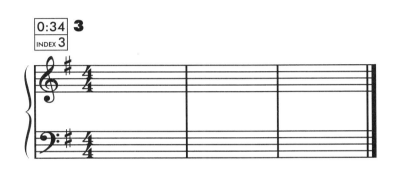

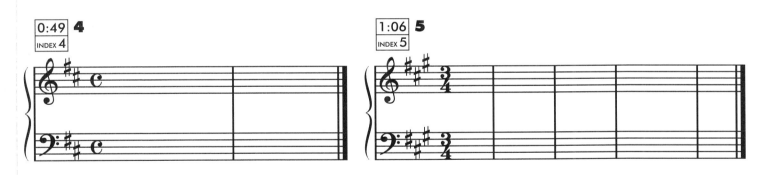

Scoring on Reverse ➡

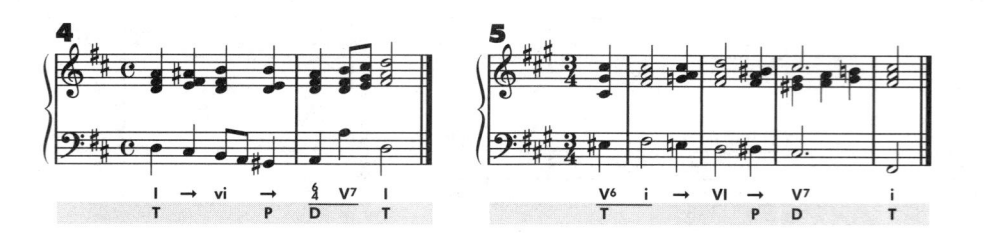

LESSON G | INTRODUCTION

Lesson G introduces exercises that modulate to a cadence in the dominant. In the major mode, two pivot chords are illustrated. The most common is vi becomes ii, as in Examples 1 and 2. The other, I becomes IV, as in Example 3, is also found in the minor mode as i becomes iv (Example 6). A second pivot chord in the minor mode constitutes III becomes VI, as in Example 5. Notice, in Examples 3 and 6, that the fourth chord serves two purposes: it ends the tonic extension and serves as the pivot chord.

To make the modulation perfectly clear, write the names of the first and second keys with the chord identifications. Start the new key with the pivot chord, and write the new chord symbol directly under that for the old key. Do not score the key names. Do score, however, both parts of the pivot chord identification. Observe that the **T** is in the first key, whereas **P**, **D**, and the second **T** are in the goal key.

This Lesson also introduces the ii^7 chord in the major mode, and ii$^{\varnothing 7}$ in the minor mode, in $\frac{5}{3}$ position. Modal mixture is evident when ii$^{\varnothing 7}$ occurs in the major mode, as in Example 1.

> ☛ **Tip:** Decide on first hearing whether the exercise ends in the same key with which it began.

Name: _____

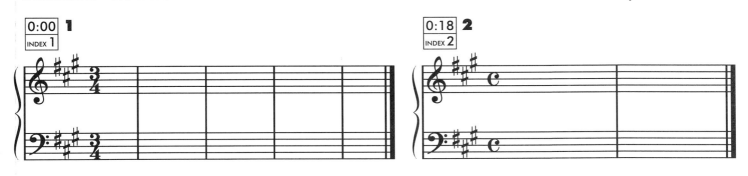

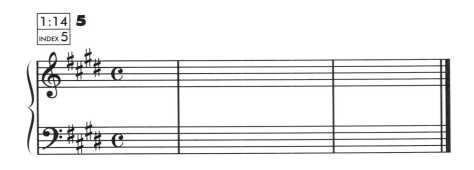

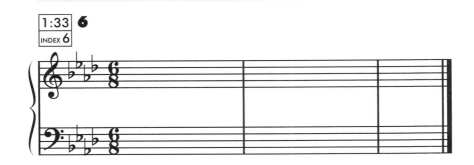

Scoring on Reverse ➡

SCORING

281

− _____ Total x

Your Score:

- If your score is 253 or more, proceed to Lesson H.
- Otherwise, proceed to Lesson GG.

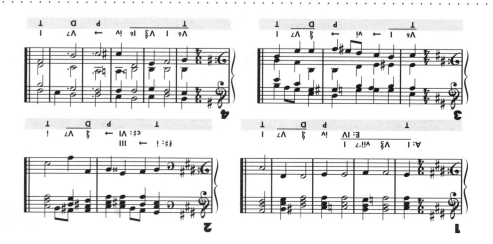

1 `0:00` `INDEX 1`

2 `0:18` `INDEX 2`

3 `0:34` `INDEX 3`

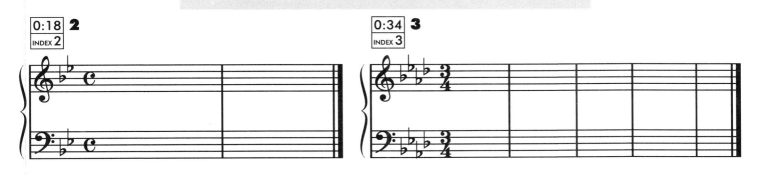

4 `0:52` `INDEX 4`

5 `1:11` `INDEX 5`

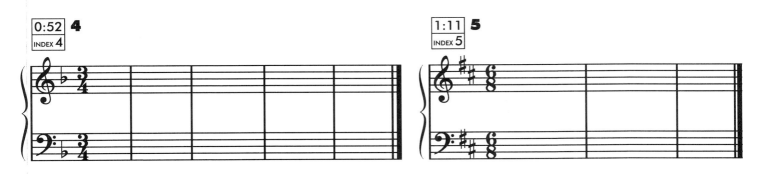

Scoring on Reverse ➡

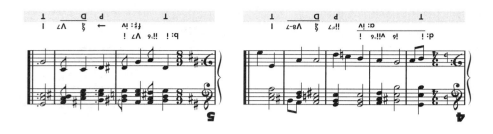

SCORING

235

_____ − _____ Total x

Your Score: _____

- If your score is 212 or more, proceed to Lesson H.
- Otherwise, repeat Lesson G.

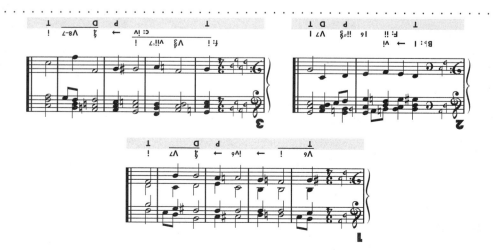

The relatively simple modulation from a minor key to its relative major may use one of two pivot chords: i becomes vi may sound familiar because it is the same route followed in tonicizing III. But whereas III has been a stepping stone on the way to **P** up to this point, it now becomes the goal of motion. In Example 1, note that the pivot chord is also the **P**. The second pivot chord is VI becomes IV.

Lesson H contains several exercises that show these modulations, but also many that review the progressions studied earlier in this section.

> ☞ **Tip:** Pivot chords cannot be heard. You can figure them out after the music has settled into the new key.

Scoring on Reverse ➡

1 b: i V$^4_3$ i → VI | D: IV $^6_4$ V^7 I
T P D T

2 d: i iv i → VI | F: IV ii°^{7} V^7 I
T P D T

3 I V^7 vi → V^7 I iv I
T D T

293

Total x _____ − _____

Your Score: _____

- If your score is 264 or more, you have finished Section III.
- Otherwise, proceed to Lesson HH.

SCORING

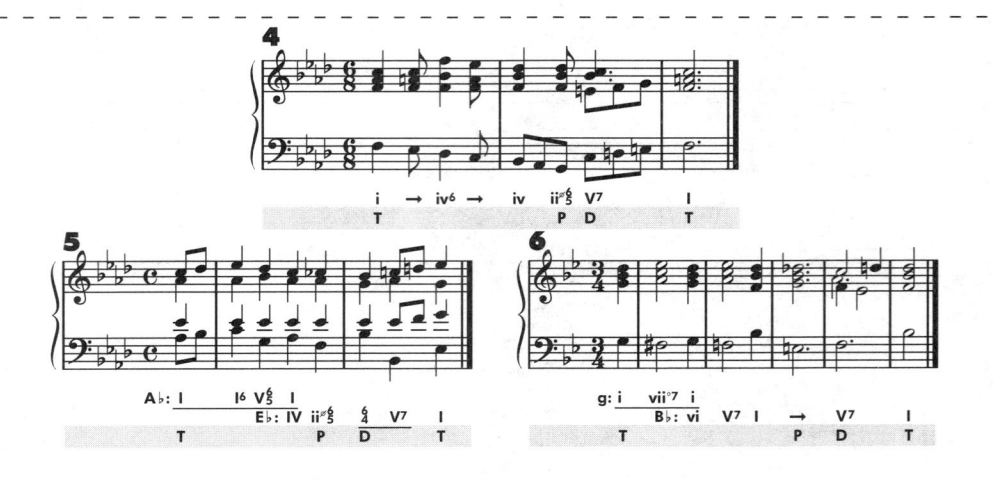

4 i → iv^6 → iv ii°$^6_5$ V^7 I
T P D T

5 A♭: I I^6 V$^6_5$ I | E♭: IV ii°$^6_5$ $^6_4$ V^7 I
T P D T

6 g: i vii°^{7} i | B♭: vi V^7 I → V^7 I
T P D T

0:00 **1**
INDEX 1

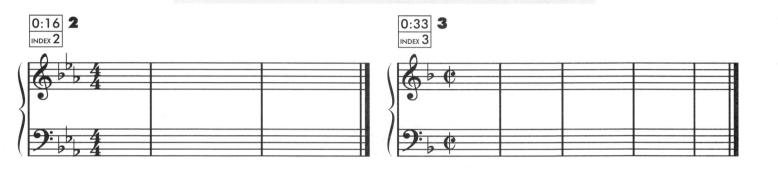

0:16 **2**
INDEX 2

0:33 **3**
INDEX 3

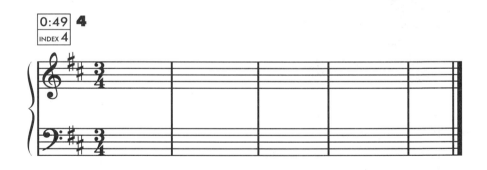

0:49 **4**
INDEX 4

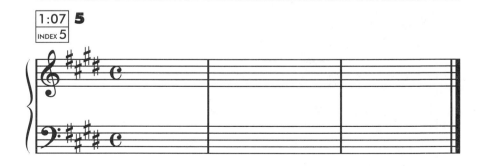

1:07 **5**
INDEX 5

Scoring on Reverse ➡

SCORING

249

     – _____ Total x

Your Score:

- If your score is 224 or more, congratulations! You have finished Section III.
- Otherwise, repeat Lesson H.

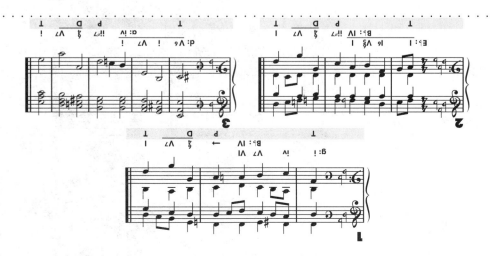

Name: _____

1

2

3

4

5

6

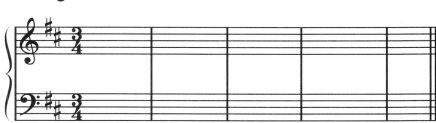

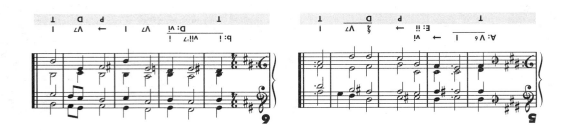

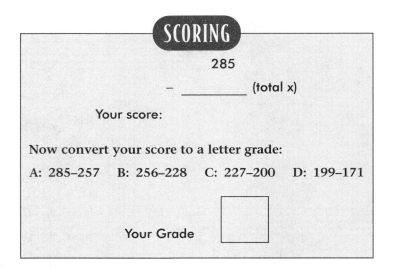

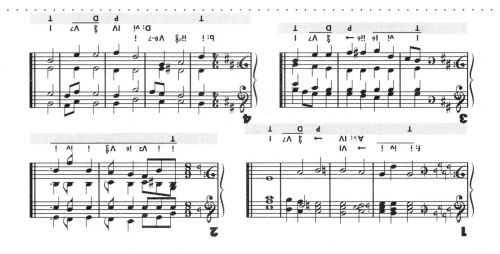

1

2

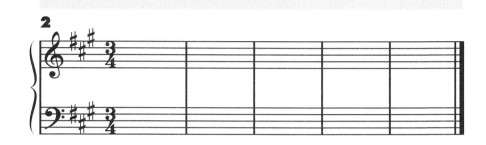

3   **4**

5

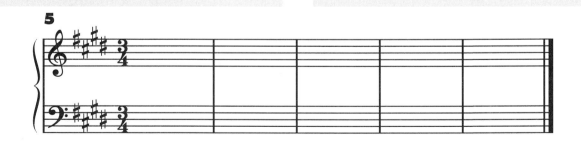

SCORING

243

− _____ (Total x)

Final Score: _____

Final Grade: [   ]

SECTION IV

STUDENT RECORD SHEET

- Circle the Lesson you are to do next: (A)
- After completing that Lesson, draw a line through the circle ~~(A)~~ and circle the Lesson the instructions tell you to do next: (B)
- Keep this sheet up to date. It is intended solely for your guidance.

A	AA
B	BB
C	CC
D	DD
E	EE
F	FF
G	GG
H	HH

Starting date ____________________

Completion date ________________

Keep this page in this book.

HOW TO STUDY SECTION IV

Section IV continues the study of secondary dominants and leading-note chords, with intensified chromaticism. The technique of elision, which makes it possible to have two secondary dominants in succession, is introduced in Lesson F. Elision often engenders chromatic soprano and bass lines, which you will hear in this section.

Mode mixture plays an important part in the chromaticism of Section IV. Other chromatic chords introduced here include the augmented sixth and ♭II. In addition, the augmented 5th plays a role in creating a chromatic form of dominant harmony. These chromatic chords have a very distinctive sound, which you can recognize readily. The augmented sixth chord usually progresses to a $^6_4$ chord. The triad built on the flatted supertonic is often used as a preparatory chord.

Lesson B introduces a basic chord progression, which travels through the circle of 5ths and includes all diatonic chords. This progression is heard quite often in Baroque music.

Up to this point, all cadences in Chapter Two have been authentic. You will now hear deceptive cadences as well, starting in Lesson A.

It's important to listen carefully to the prep chord, which tells you not only the mode of the exercise but also the spacing of the chord. Pay particular attention to the top voice, which may be the root, the third, or the fifth of the triad.

Some of the exercises in this Lesson end with the deceptive cadence: V7–vi in major and V7–VI in minor. It will be easy for you to distinguish that cadence from the authentic cadence, heard in all previous Lessons. Since the last chord is not the tonic, do not put a function symbol in the gray band.

Notice that in Example 1, in piano texture, one of the upper voices moves independently of the others. The stems indicate this.

In addition to emphasizing secondary dominants, this Lesson introduces a new form of dominant harmony, V9, as in Examples 3 and 6. Listen for the resolution of the 9th. Just as in V7, the fifth of the V9 is often omitted; in popular music, the third is occasionally omitted, as can be seen in Example 7.

> ☞ **Tip:** Observe that the bass line is becoming increasingly chromatic, both ascending and descending.

0:00 **1**
INDEX 1

0:18 **2**
INDEX 2

0:35 **3**
INDEX 3

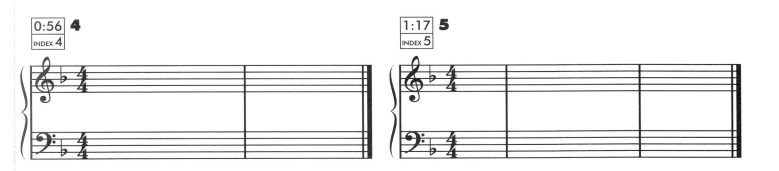

0:56 **4**
INDEX 4

1:17 **5**
INDEX 5

1:38 **6**
INDEX 6

Scoring on Reverse ➡

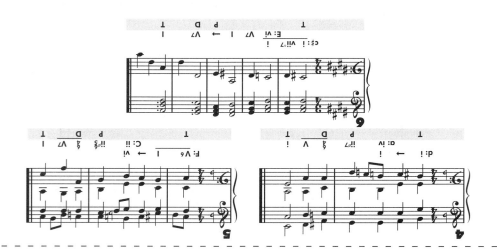

SCORING

283

—＿＿＿＿＿ Total x

Your Score: ＿＿＿＿＿

- If your score is 255 or more, proceed to Lesson B.
- Otherwise, proceed to Lesson AA.

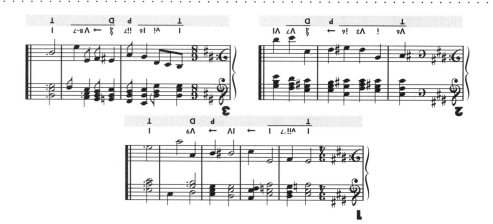

1 0:00 INDEX 1

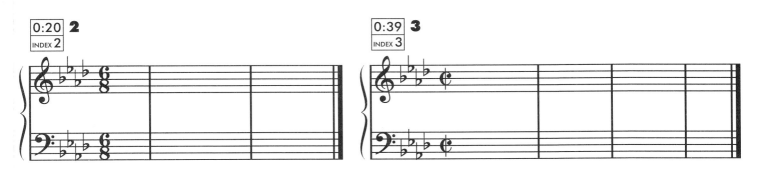

2 0:20 INDEX 2

3 0:39 INDEX 3

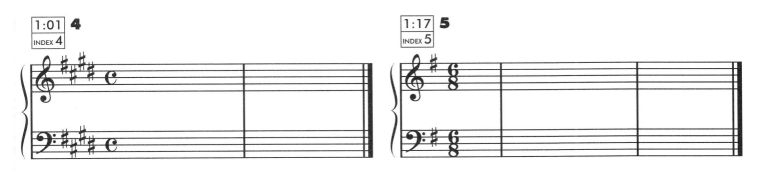

4 1:01 INDEX 4

5 1:17 INDEX 5

SCORING

240

−   _____   Total x

Your Score:

- If your score is 216 or more, proceed to Lesson B.
- Otherwise, repeat Lesson A.

Lesson B | INTRODUCTION

The bass progression in descending 5ths is a basic pattern in tonal music. You will hear it more frequently in the minor mode than in the major. Since the bass cannot descend indefinitely, the descending 5ths usually alternate with ascending 4ths, as in Example 1. You can hear that each note in the bass supports a triad in root ($\frac{5}{3}$) position. The ii°6 chord breaks the pattern and prepares the dominant.

In the major mode, ii in root position is part of the descending 5ths progression but still prepares the dominant (Example 2). This progression may also alternate $\frac{5}{3}$ and $\frac{6}{3}$ positions, as in Example 3.

You will hear longer extensions of tonic and dominant harmony in this Lesson: Example 4 is built entirely on a tonic extension. As you will find in this Lesson, extensions of dominant harmony may include V9.

Passing and neighbor motion in all voices increases in this Lesson; you will also hear suspensions in all voices. The ii2 chord results from neighbor-note motion in the upper voices and a suspension in the bass (Example 5). In this example in five voices, from Book I of Johann Sebastian Bach's *Well-tempered Clavier*, the four chords form a tonic extension.

> ☞ **Tip:** Study the descending 5ths progressions by singing either the soprano or bass and playing the other outer voice, paying particular attention to the contrary motion at every point.

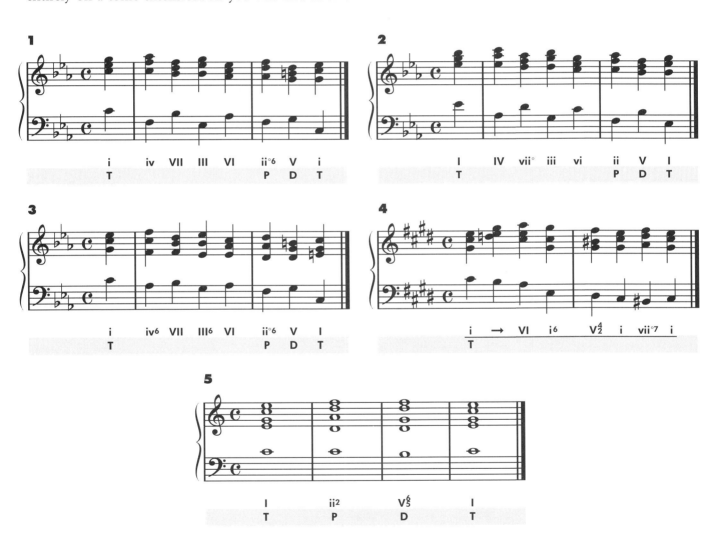

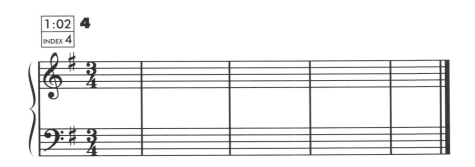

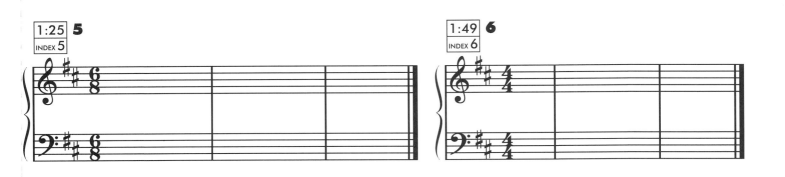

SCORING

284

284 − _____ Total x

Your Score: _____

- **If your score is 256 or more, proceed to Lesson C.**
- **Otherwise, proceed to Lesson BB.**

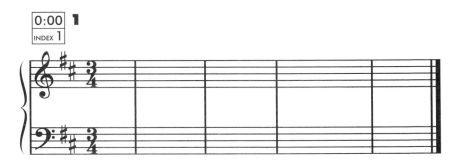

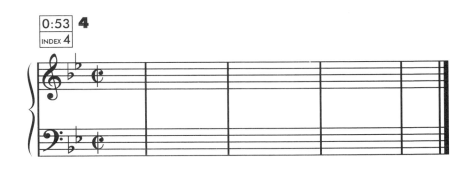

Leading-note seventh chords of all consonant triads are heard in this Lesson. The use of more than one such chord in a progression may produce a chromatic bass, as in Example 1. In Example 2, the bass, starting from the fourth note, has the appearance of a dominant extension, but that G (fourth note) is part of vii°7/VI. Example 3 shows two → in succession. The first marks V7/IV, the second vii°⁶₅/ii. These are voice-leading chords; the best way to hear them is by following the stepwise motion in the voices. Listen for the difference between the incomplete triad that ends Example 3 and the complete triads that end other examples.

In Example 4, the leading note of $\hat{2}$ in the bass is a passing note, but the leading note of $\hat{5}$ is approached by a skip.

Starting in this Lesson the **P** chord may be extended with its own dominant, as in Example 7.

In this program, enharmonic spellings are considered correct.

> ☞ **Tip:** Mode mixture figures more prominently in this Lesson. Observe that mode mixture may involve triads and seventh chords of many types.

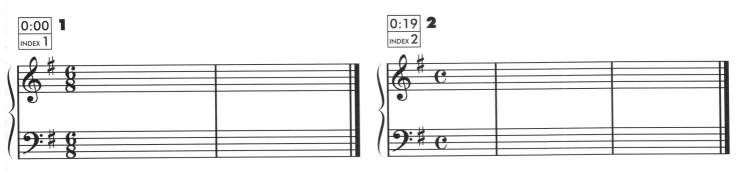

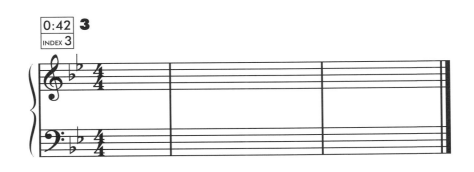

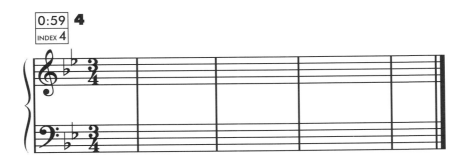

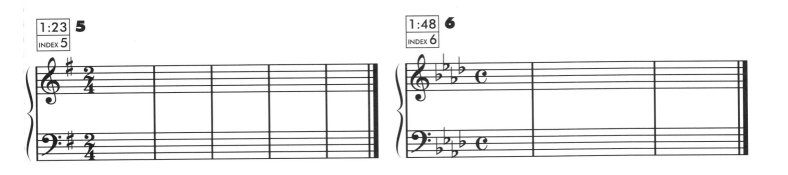

SCORING

296

－ _____ **Total x**

Your Score:

- **If your score is 266 or more, proceed to Lesson D.**
- **Otherwise, proceed to Lesson CC.**

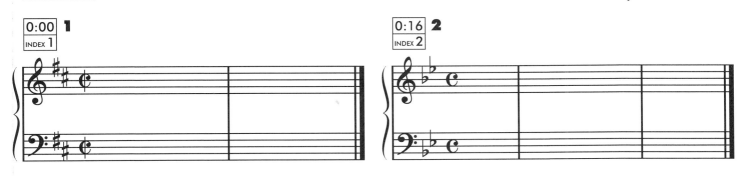

0:00 **1** / INDEX 1

0:16 **2** / INDEX 2

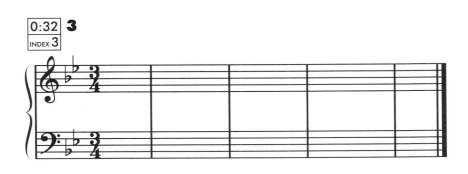

0:32 **3** / INDEX 3

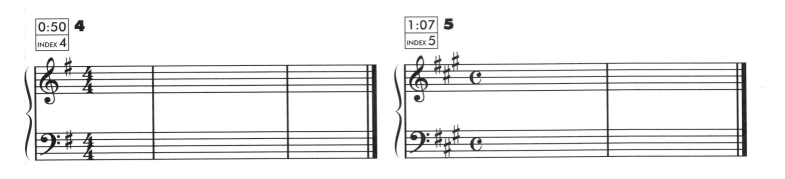

0:50 **4** / INDEX 4

1:07 **5** / INDEX 5

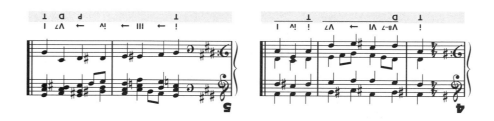

SCORING

229

−　_____　Total x

Your Score:

- If your score is 206 or more, proceed to Lesson D.
- Otherwise, repeat Lesson C.

LESSON D | INTRODUCTION

Play the outer voices in Example 1. Listen to the way they pull apart from each other through the fourth chord. The interval between bass and soprano at that point is an augmented 6th. That interval has a strong impulse to resolve to an octave. The two G's in the next chord stress the dominant, which is why we call the augmented 6th chord a dominant preparation. The augmented 6th chord most often leads to a $\frac{6}{4}$ chord, as in Example 1, but it may also go directly to V or V7.

Two ways to identify the augmented sixth chord are through the interval of the augmented 6th itself, which often results from contrary motion, and by the special sound that augmented sixth chords have. In this Lesson, we stress the so-called German augmented sixth chord, labeled "Ger6" in the examples.

The augmented sixth chord can play an important role in the extension of dominant harmony, as in Examples 2 (minor mode) and 3 (major mode). This chord can also come between the $\frac{6}{4}$ and the V7. In the major mode, the augmented sixth chord is associated with mode mixture.

In Example 4, the fifth of the augmented sixth chord is spelled with an E♭; it can also be enharmonically spelled with a D♯. Both spellings are considered correct in this program.

Review the suspensions in Example 5.

> ☞ **Tip:** Since the augmented sixth chord often results from contrary motion, pay close attention to the bass and the upper voice that moves against it.

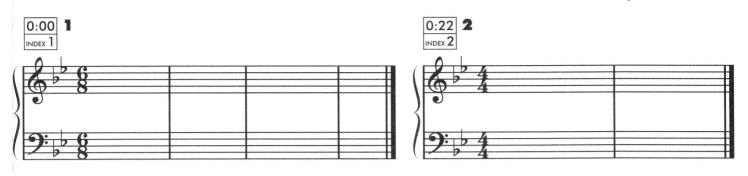

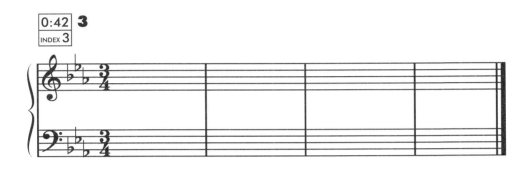

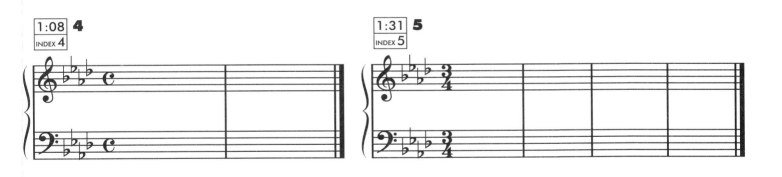

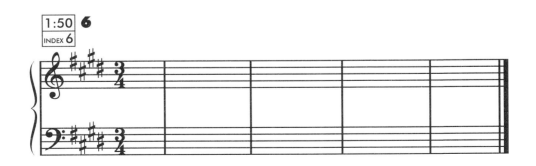

SCORING

297

– _____ Total x

Your Score: _____

● **If your score is 267 or more, proceed to Lesson E.**
● **Otherwise, proceed to Lesson DD.**

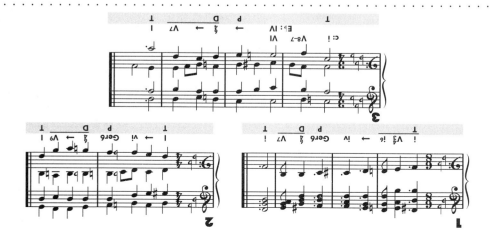

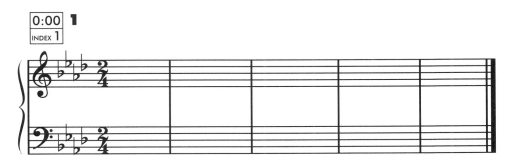

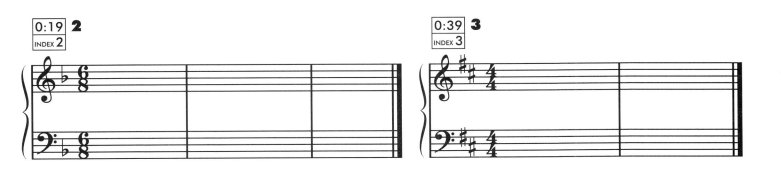

SCORING

252

− _____ Total x

Your Score:

- If your score is 227 or more, proceed to Lesson E.
- Otherwise, repeat Lesson D.

LESSON E | INTRODUCTION

This Lesson introduces two new chromatic chords, the ♭II⁶ and the augmented triad. The ♭II⁶ is most often used as a preparatory chord, the augmented triad as a secondary dominant or as the main dominant.

In the minor mode, a simple approach to the ♭II chord is through iv, which has two notes in common with it. Example 1 illustrates this. Another approach to ♭II is through its dominant (Example 2), which is VI in the minor and ♭VI in the major mode. As in these two examples, the ♭II chord usually appears in ⁶₃ position.

In Example 5 you hear two augmented triads, the first as a secondary dominant and the second as the main dominant. When used as a secondary dominant, the augmented triad is indicated in the same way as other secondary dominants and secondary leading-

note chords: →. When used as the main dominant, indicate the augmented triad with V+. Use the V+ chord identification as well when this chord is heard in a tonic extension, as in Example 6. In this program, all augmented triads resolve to major triads.

The augmented triad may play a role in another type of tonic extension that moves from I to I⁶. Here, it serves as a dominant of IV, as in Example 7.

This Lesson also introduces another type of augmented sixth chord, the so-called French augmented sixth, as in Examples 3 and 4. Label this chord "Fr6."

> ☛ **Tip:** Pay close attention to the enharmonic spellings as well as the suspensions in these introductory examples.

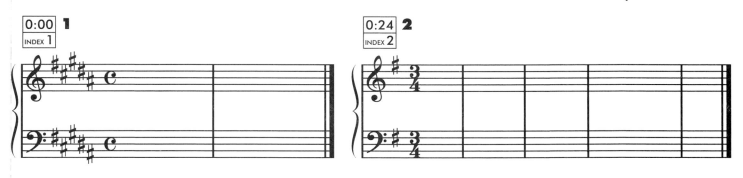

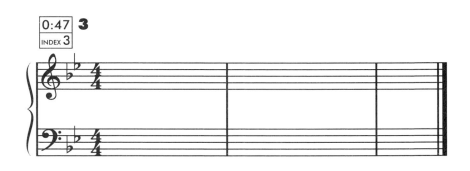

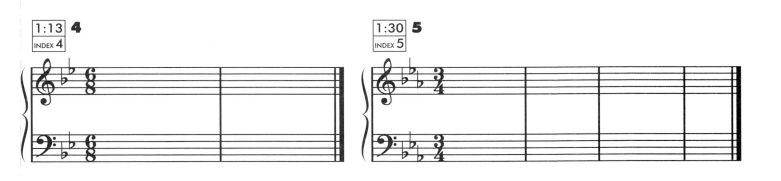

1. I → IV I⁶ ♭II⁶ → V⁷ I
T   P   D   T

2. V⁶ i → III Fr6 $^6_4$ V⁸⁻⁷ i
T   P   D   T

3. g: i vii°⁷ i
B♭: vi → IV → $^6_4$ V⁹ I
T   P   D   T

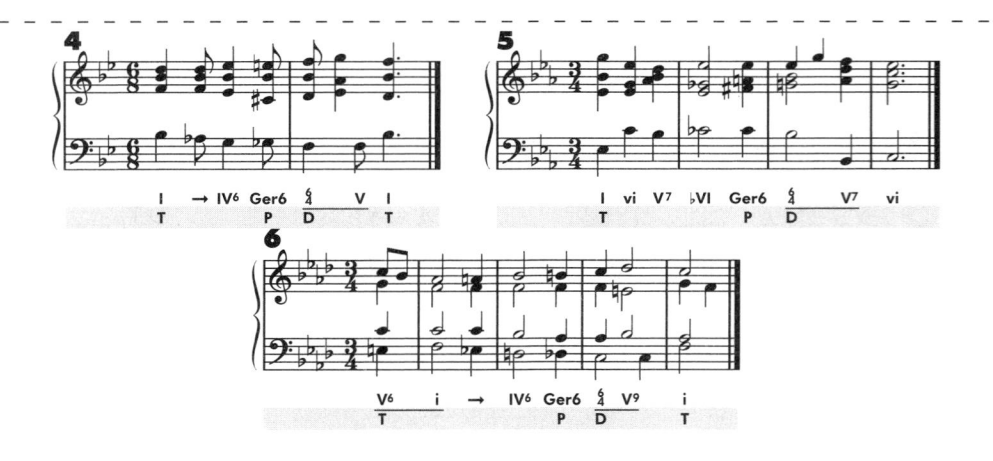

4. I → IV⁶ Ger6 $^6_4$ V I
T   P   D   T

5. I vi V⁷ ♭VI Ger6 $^6_4$ V⁷ vi
T   P   D   T

6. V⁶ i → IV⁶ Ger6 $^6_4$ V⁹ i
T   P   D   T

Name: _____

0:00 **1**
INDEX 1

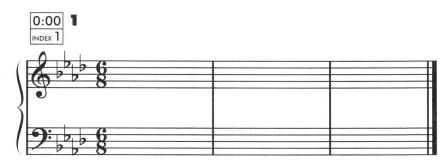

0:18 **2**
INDEX 2

0:36 **3**
INDEX 3

0:54 **4**
INDEX 4

1:13 **5**
INDEX 5

Scoring on Reverse ➡

SCORING

SCORING

247

− _____ Total x

Your Score:

- If your score is 222 or more, proceed to Lesson F.
- Otherwise, repeat Lesson E.

LESSON F | INTRODUCTION

The chromatic soprano and bass lines in Examples 1 and 2 are the result of elisions, in which one dominant chord resolves to another. In Example 1, the V$\frac{4}{3}$ chord goes directly to V$\frac{6}{5}$/IV. Notice that in the fifth chord of this example, the interval of an augmented 6th has been inverted to form a diminished 3rd, or rather a diminished 10th. But the impulse of that interval to converge on $\hat{5}$ is something that you can hear quite clearly. Now play the outer voices of Examples 1 and 2, focusing your attention on the contrary motion between soprano and bass. In Example 2 the contrary motion goes in the opposite direction from that heard in Example 1.

The progression built over the bass motion in descending 5ths is elaborated with suspensions in Example 3. This results in a series of seventh chords, with a distinctive sound of its own.

In this Lesson you will also find chords made of three neighbors in the upper voices over a stationary bass, as in Examples 4 and 5. Some of the neighbors are chromatic. Since these chords are generated entirely by neighbor-note motion, simply label them "N" and draw a line to show the extension. The chord being extended may or may not have a primary harmonic function. Score the line showing the extension as you score other such lines, marking an x if its length is not correct.

☛ **Tip:** If any of these progressions seems unfamiliar to you, memorize it quickly and transpose it to another key.

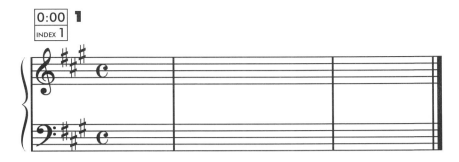

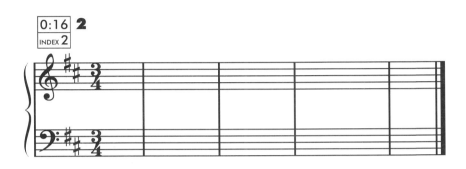

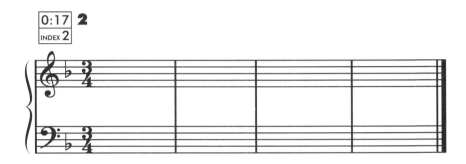

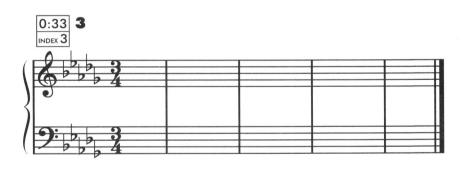

Scoring on Reverse ➡

SCORING

238

− _____ Total x

Your Score: _____

- If your score is 214 or more, proceed to Lesson G.
- Otherwise, repeat Lesson F.

Lesson G continues the progressions studied previously, with an increasing level of chromaticism that approaches what is found in some late nineteenth-century compositions. Voice leading also appears more complex due to octave shift and increased use of suspensions. However, all the progressions are firmly rooted in tonality, aided by the long extensions of tonic and dominant harmonies.

An additional form of dominant harmony introduced in this Lesson is the dominant seventh chord with a raised (augmented) 5th. This occurs only in the major mode. When this chord is used as the main dominant or as a tonic extension (both are heard in Example 6), use the chord identification V+7. When it

is used as a secondary dominant, as in Example 1, chord 2, use the →, as you do for all other secondary dominants.

In Example 4, notice the doubled D in the deceptive resolution of V7/vi to IV.

Like the vii°7 chord, the augmented sixth chord may be used as part of an extension of tonic harmony, as in Example 5.

> ☛ **Tip:** As you play the bass line, sing, from bottom to top, the notes of the chord above each bass note.

Name: _____

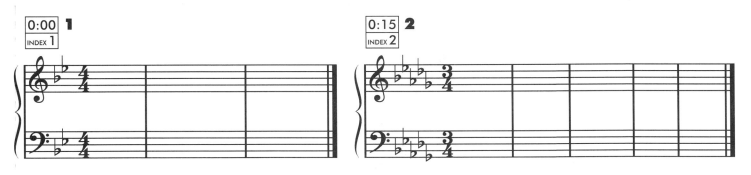

0:00 1 INDEX 1

0:15 2 INDEX 2

0:41 3 INDEX 3

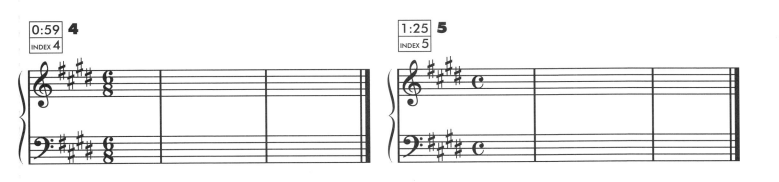

0:59 4 INDEX 4

1:25 5 INDEX 5

1:48 6 INDEX 6

Scoring on Reverse ➡

SCORING

285

−

_____ Total x

Your Score:

- If your score is 257 or more, proceed to Lesson H.
- Otherwise, proceed to Lesson GG.

Name: _____

0:00 **1**
INDEX 1

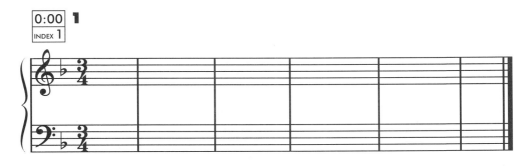

0:20 **2**
INDEX 2

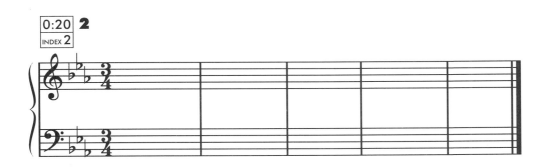

0:39 **3**
INDEX 3

0:55 **4**
INDEX 4

1:12 **5**
INDEX 5

Scoring on Reverse ➡

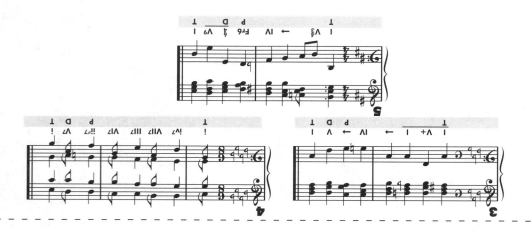

SCORING

231

— _____ Total x

Your Score:

- If your score is 208 or more, proceed to Lesson H.
- Otherwise, repeat Lesson G.

0:00 **1**
INDEX 1

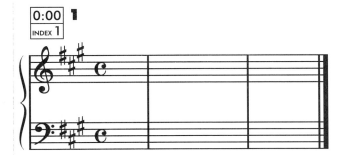

0:18 **2**
INDEX 2

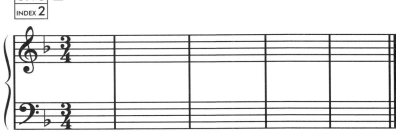

0:44 **3**
INDEX 3

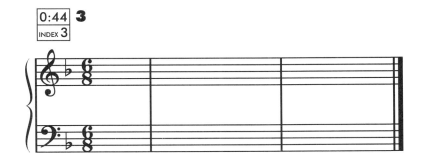

1:06 **4**
INDEX 4

1:25 **5**
INDEX 5

1:48 **6**
INDEX 6

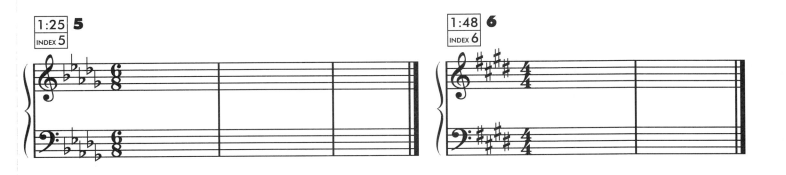

Scoring on Reverse ➡

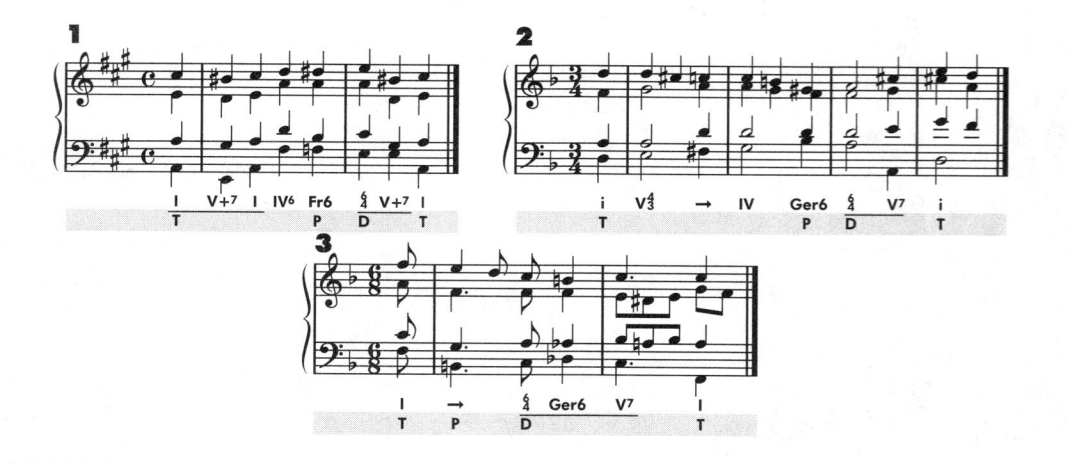

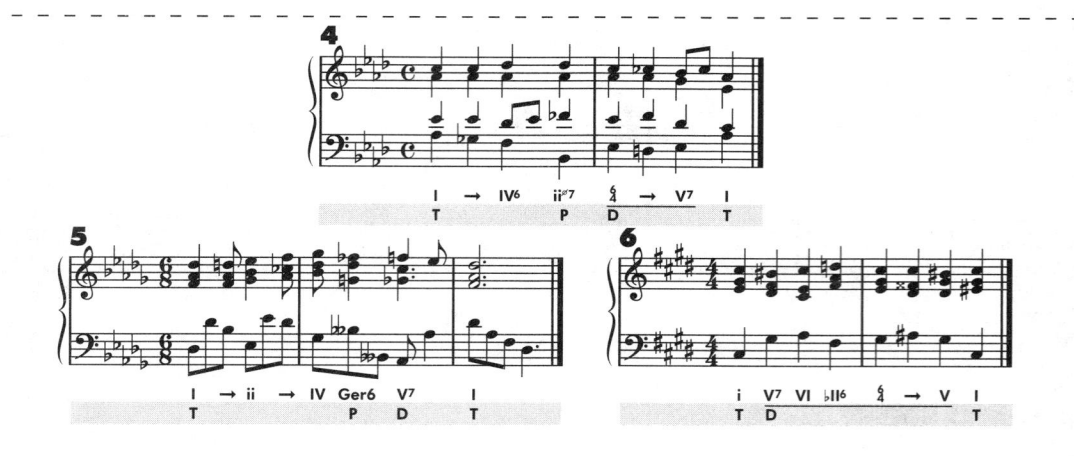

SCORING

281

Total x _____ = _____

Your Score: _____

- If your score is 253 or more, you have finished Section IV.
- Otherwise, proceed to Lesson HH.

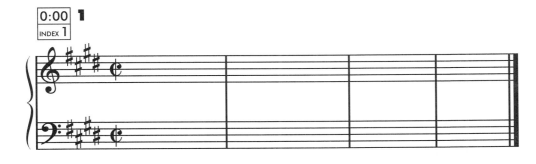

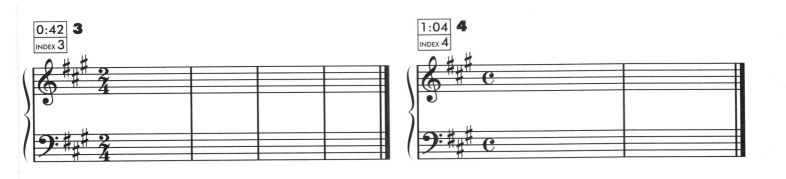

SCORING

237

− _____ Total x

Your Score:

- If your score is 213 or more, congratulations! You have finished Section IV.
- Otherwise, repeat Lesson H.

Name: _____

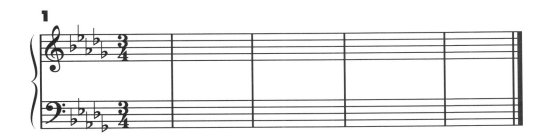

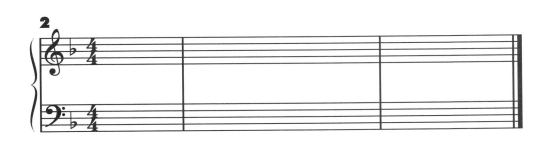

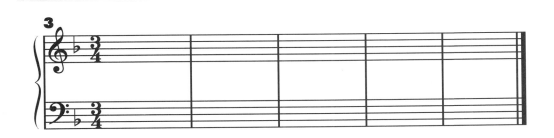

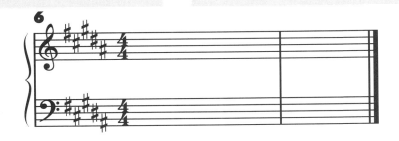

Scoring on Reverse ▶

1
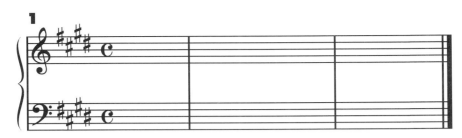

2
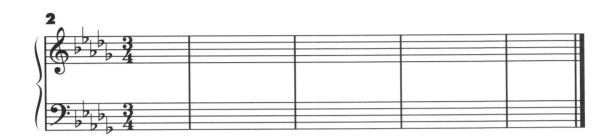

3   **4**

5
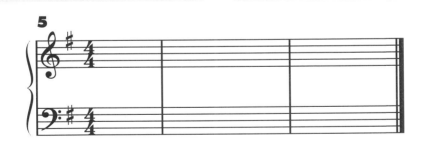

SCORING

231

– _____ (Total x)

Final Score: _____   Final Grade: [   ]

Sources of the Melodies in Chapter One

SECTION I

Lesson C
5. Mozart, Requiem in D minor, K.626, "Tuba mirum"

Lesson E
5. Brahms, Symphony No. 2 in D major, Op. 73, first movement

SECTION II

Lesson A
Demonstration melody: Schubert, Symphony in C major ("Great"), first movement

Lesson D
4. Mozart, Minuet, K.2

SECTION III

Lesson A
1. Bach, Passacaglia in C minor, BWV 582
2. Mozart, Symphony No. 39 in E♭ major, K.543, third movement
4. Vivaldi, Concerto for strings in F major, first movement
6. Brahms, Violin Concerto in D major, Op. 77, first movement

Lesson AA
4. Mozart, Symphony No. 25 in G minor, K.183, fourth movement
6. Bach, *The Well-tempered Clavier*, Book 1, No. 15, Fugue

Lesson B
Demonstration melody: Brahms, Symphony No. 1 in C minor, Op. 68, fourth movement
3. Bizet, *Carmen*, Act II
5. Beethoven, Symphony No. 6 in F major ("Pastoral"), Op. 68, third movement
6. Mozart, Piano Concerto in A major, K.488, first movement

Lesson BB

1. Haydn, *The Creation*, No. 3
3. Haydn, Symphony No. 104 ("London"), fourth movement
5. Mozart, String Quartet in B♭ major, K.589, first movement

Lesson C

Demonstration melody: Schubert, Moment Musical, Op. 94, No. 6
4. Haydn, String Quartet, Op. 76, No. 3, third movement
5. Schumann, *Papillons*, Op. 2, No. 3
7. Purcell, Harpsichord Suite in D major

Lesson CC

2. Beethoven, Piano Sonata in G major, Op. 79, third movement
5. Schubert, Symphony No. 5 in B♭ major, third movement

Lesson D

3. Haydn, String Quartet in E major, Op. 54, No. 3, fourth movement
4. Schubert, *Winterreise*, Op. 89, "Wasserflut"
5. Beethoven, Rondo a capriccio in G major ("Rage Over a Lost Penny"), Op. 129
6. German Folk Song, "Wie komm' ich denn zur Tür herein?"

Lesson DD

1. Beethoven, Piano Trio in E♭ major, Op. 70, No. 2, third movement
4. Brahms, "Am Sonntag Morgen," Op. 49, No. 1

Lesson E

1. Dvořák, Symphony No. 9 in E minor ("From the New World"), first movement
2. Mendelssohn, *Midsummer Night's Dream*, Scherzo, Op. 61, No. 1
4. Ragué, Symphony, Op. 10, No. 1, first movement
5. Brahms, String Quartet in A minor, Op. 51, No. 2, third movement
6. Bizet, *Carmen*, Trumpet Call from Act I

Lesson EE

1. Bellini, *Norma*
3. Bach, Suite No. 2 in B minor for flute and strings, first movement
5. Pergolesi(?), Concertino for strings in G major

Lesson F

1. Mozart, Symphony No. 28 in C major, K.200, first movement
2. Mozart, Symphony No. 29 in A major, K.201, first movement
3. Haydn, Symphony No. 92 in G major ("Oxford"), first movement
5. Donizetti, *L'Elisir d'amore*

Lesson FF

1. Beethoven, Violin Sonata in E♭ major, Op. 12, No. 3, third movement
2. Haydn, String Quartet in F minor, Op. 20, No. 5, third movement
4. Mozart, Piano Concerto in B♭ major, K.595, first movement

Lesson G

2. Handel, Concerto No. 6 in B♭ major for organ and orchestra, Op. 4, No. 6, third movement
4. Smetana, *The Bartered Bride*

Lesson GG

2. Schubert, German Dance in D major for piano

Lesson H

2. Mozart, Quartet in D major for flute and strings, K.285, third movement
3. Handel, Concerto No. 10 in D minor for organ and orchestra, Op. 7, No. 4, third movement
5. Donizetti, *L'Elisir d'amore*

Lesson E

Demonstration melody: Beethoven, Symphony No. 6 in F major ("Pastoral"), Op. 68, fifth movement
1. Chopin, Mazurka, Op. 67, No. 3
2. Schubert, String Quartet No. 14 in D minor ("Der Tod und das Mädchen"), first movement
5. Mozart, Sonata in E minor for violin and piano, K.304, first movement
6. Beethoven, Symphony No. 2 in D major, Op. 36, second movement

Lesson EE

3. Haydn, String Quartet in D major, Op. 76, No. 5, first movement

Lesson F

Demonstration melody: Mozart, Requiem in D minor, K.626, "Domine Jesu"
1. Haydn, Symphony No. 78 in C minor, first movement
2. Handel, Concerto grosso in E minor, Op. 6, No. 3, third movement
3. Chopin, Mazurka, Op. 59, No. 1
5. Schubert, *Winterreise*, Op. 89, "Erstarrung"

Lesson FF

3. Dvořák, *Gypsy Song*, Op. 55, No. 7
5. Bizet, *Carmen*, Act III

Lesson G

1. Bizet, *Carmen*, Habanera from Act I
2. Chopin, Mazurka, Op. 17, No. 2
3. Handel, Concerto grosso in G minor, Op. 6, No. 6, second movement
4. Wagner, *Tristan und Isolde*, Introduction to Act II
5. Bach, *The Well-tempered Clavier*, Book 2, No. 7, Fugue
6. Paganini, *Caprice*, Op. 1, No. 24

Lesson GG

5. Dvořák, *Poetic Tone Pictures*, Op. 85, No. 7

Lesson H

Demonstration melody: Chopin, Mazurka, Op. 33. No. 3
1. Beethoven, Violin Sonata No. 9 in A major ("Kreutzer"), Op. 47, second movement
3. Mozart, Symphony No. 40 in G minor, K.550, fourth movement
4. Bizet, *Carmen*, Gypsy Song from Act II

Short Drill 16

1. Handel, *Messiah*, "Rejoice greatly, O daughter of Zion"
2. Schumann, *Album for the Young*, Op. 68, "The Wild Horseman"
3. Mozart, Symphony No. 35 in D major ("Haffner"), K.385, fourth movement
4. Scarlatti, Sonata in A minor

Review

1. Bach, Concerto for two violins in D minor, first movement
2. Beethoven, String Quartet in F major, Op. 18, No. 1, first movement
4. Bach, Suite No. 5 in G minor for violoncello
6. Mozart, *The Marriage of Figaro*, K.492, Overture

Test

1. Handel, *Water Music*, Trumpet Suite in D major
3. Wagner, *Tristan und Isolde*, Act II
4. Bach, *Musical Offering*
5. Cimarosa, *The Secret Marriage*, Overture